Democratizing China's Political Imaginaries

Rongxin Li

Democratizing China's Political Imaginaries

palgrave
macmillan

Rongxin Li
Lecturer at the School
of International Studies/Academy
of Overseas Chinese Studies
Jinan University
Guangzhou, China

ISBN 978-981-97-3669-0 ISBN 978-981-97-3670-6 (eBook)
https://doi.org/10.1007/978-981-97-3670-6

Cover illustration: Alex Linch/shutterstock.com

This Palgrave Macmillan imprint is published by the registered company Springer Nature Singapore Pte Ltd.
The registered company address is: 152 Beach Road, #21-01/04 Gateway East, Singapore 189721, Singapore

This book is dedicated to my days in Peking and Guangzhou, which made it all possible

Preface and Acknowledgements

The term "democracy" finds its origins in the discourse on "popular sovereignty" dating back to ancient Greece. Following World War II, democracy emerged triumphant over other ideological contenders, assuming a predominance in Western political institution and governance. Termed by Bernard Crick as "the most promiscuous" notion, its purported ascendancy seemed to herald the "end of human history," as discussed by Francis Fukuyama in the context of liberal democracy. However, does this assertion hold true?

The trajectory of democratization does not unfold as a linear progression, a reality underscored not only by Samuel Huntington's portrayal of the "third wave of democratization," characterized by the complexities of "democratic (re)consolidation," "democratic transition," and "democratic backsliding," but also by the ideological undercurrents that concealed within the "confusion of concepts" arising from the multifaceted interpretations of democracy. Furthermore, since the latter half of the twentieth century, deliberations on "state capacity" and "social order" have also entered the discourse, challenging the oversimplified classification of political regimes into "democratic" and "non-democratic" dichotomies.

Furthermore, Alexander Weiss's proposed "Comparative Democratic Theory" presents a fresh approach to the re-examination of democracy, distinct from conventional understandings of global or world democracy. Its primary emphasis lies in the critical reassessment and recurrent validation of democratic principles through the scrutiny of analogous democratic practices existing beyond the Western paradigm. This proposition significantly aligns with the imperative of indigenization prevalent among developing or post-colonial countries. The enduring pertinence of typological investigations into democracy emanates from our capacities to consistently explain and broaden the (re)conceptualization of democracy across various delineations—be they power—relational, structural geographical, or modalities of governance. In this sense, the demystification of democracy and the rectification of biased scholarship, particularly concerning mainstream Western liberal democratic paradigms and practices, assume paramount importance.

In last four decades, the scholarship pertaining to Chinese democracy has proliferated, presenting diverse lens. While employing the notion "Chinese democracy" in this monograph, I personally incline towards "democracy in China," as the latter more aptly encapsulates the interplay between the universality of democracy and China's uniqueness. Nonetheless, as we delve deeper into the paradigms, theories, and conceptual frameworks underpinning the study of Chinese democracy, the explanation of its core becomes increasingly intricate. Particularly amid contemporary ideological confrontations, disentangling political theory from the real politics proves challenging, wherein democracy and authoritarianism assume rhetoric that authors cannot readily discard. Consequently, this book adopts a distinct trajectory. Following a foundational understanding of democracy and "Chinese democracy," the focus shifts towards empirically comprehending Chinese democracy through a meticulous examination of its foremost democratic discourses and practices, particularly within the context of modern China.

This endeavor is focused on the examination of various key forms of democracy, namely "People's Democracy," "Intraparty Democracy," "Grassroots Democracy," "Whole-Process People's Democracy," "Consultative Democracy," and "Chinese Democracy,"[1] particularly in the post-reform era. These democratic forms have progressively materialized and gained prominence as fundamental components of "Chinese

[1] I juxtapose the concept of "Chinese democracy" with other concrete forms of democracy within China due to this term's inherent duality. It connotes not only a form of democracy akin to American, Indian, or French models within typological frameworks but also signifies the unique attributes of democracy as observed within the Chinese context. Hence, it bears semblance to the aforementioned democratic frameworks.

democracy." They do not represent abstract and ambiguous conceptualizations of Chinese democracy, as often depicted by both domestic and foreign scholars who portray it as "Confucian democracy," "authoritarian democracy," "paternalistic democracy," "patriarchal democracy," among other terms. Instead, these practices, along with the democratic forms and discourses constructed upon them, constitute indispensable avenue for comprehending Chinese democratic principles. Commonly, these democratic discourses are shaped by a multitude of factors, including Chinese traditional-cultural influences, the legacies of modern revolutions, and the developmental trajectory of the Chinese Communist Party in the modern era. Furthermore, the purported models of "Chinese democracy," whether tangible or conceptual, do not merely entail a simple amalgamation of these democratic discourses. Otherwise, such an approach would engender further paradoxes and perpetuate endless debates.

In a grand narrative, the advocacy, suppression, and marginalization of some forms of democracy, alongside their intricate interrelations, serve as reflections of China's ongoing political changes. For instance, the dynamic grassroots democracy exemplified by the village elections in the 1990s encountered substantial impediments in the twenty-first century, notably in the past decade, as grassroots autonomy steadily waned amid a recentralization. In Xi Jinping' era, the diminishing prominence of intra-party democracy within Party documents and propaganda is progressively supplanted by rhetoric accentuating the Whole-Process People's Democracy. Consultative democracy, after its thorough assimilation into China's political consultation framework and United Front strategy, gradually reconciles with China's democratic narrative and evolves into a manifestation of the purported superiority of Chinese democracy. In sum, rather than becoming ensnared in nebulous conceptions of Chinese democracy, a more fruitful endeavor lies in exploring its tangible practices in reality.

This monograph emanates from the reports I delivered during my postdoctoral tenure at Peking University. Of notable significance, its completion coincided with the onset of the pandemic. The myriad experiences engendered by the pandemic afforded me a very opportunity to reassess the significance of democracy within the context of China. Contemplation of this overarching theme frequently occupied my intellectual pursuits: should the populace demand democracy from their governing authorities? Alternatively, might its realization transpire solely through top-down, party-driven reforms or through incremental grassroots-driven democratic endeavors? Furthermore, could it manifest through forms of neo-authoritarianism, as conceptualized by some new leftists transitioning towards democracy? Albeit the conclusive answers to these inquiries remain elusive, manifestations and advocacies of democratic practices are indeed unfolding within the Chinese land, notwithstanding its inherent imperfections. In this vein, I extend my gratitude to esteemed professors specializing in democratic studies at Peking University, namely Keping Yu, Zengke He, Youxing Lang, Demin Duan, Changjiang Wang, and other esteemed colleagues. Additionally, I express appreciation to Yves Sintomer, my doctoral mentor, and all anonymous reviewers for their invaluable feedback, which have substantially shaped the contours of this monograph. While acknowledging that this monograph may not be devoid of imperfections, its contentious propositions are poised to stimulate robust discourse among scholars and practitioners engaged in the study of Chinese politics.

Guangzhou, China Rongxin Li

Introduction

Studying Chinese politics inevitably entails delving into the conception of "Chinese Democracy." Perceived as a paradox by empiricists, it encapsulates China's highly centralized authoritarian rule under the one-party dictatorship of the Chinese Communist Party on one hand, and the evolving concept of Chinese democracy depicted as distinct from Western liberal democracy, on the other. Amid the gradual divergence of these paradigms, the model of "Chinese democracy" struggles to attain credibility. Despite the CCP's incorporation of elements such as good governance, social order, and governmental responsiveness over the past four decades, the aspiration for democracy remains elusive. This study becomes increasingly enigmatic as democracy undergoes politicization, not only within China but also in the West. Disillusionment and disenchantment with democracy have fueled sustained waves of populism, racism, and anti-globalization. Western authors have expressed concerns over the crisis and decline of liberal democracy on numerous occasions, yet viable solutions remain elusive. In China, politicized democracy manifests through the Communist Party's pursuit of retaining authoritarian rule and seeking legitimacy by showcasing a governance model centered on good governance rather than electoral processes. In such a context, the concept of democracy becomes overly broad and loosely defined.

To avoid succumbing to the endless ambiguity inherent in conceptualization, while simultaneously guarding against the allure of triumphal indigenization and the pitfalls of complete Westernization, I adopt a contrarian stance in this monograph. Here, the focus is directed towards the "practices of democracy" unfolding across the Chinese landscape. While still engaging with the conceptual framework of democracy, this approach however seeks to minimize misunderstandings regarding democracy's theoretical and conceptual implications for further comprehending the actual state of democracy in China. These discursive discourses encompass the most core democratic narratives of contemporary China, including the People's Democracy, Whole-Process People's Democracy, Grassroots Democracy, Intraparty Democracy, Consultative Democracy, and Chinese Democracy. This constitutes a bottom-up process of comprehending Chinese democratic practices, while also striving to circumvent a methodological nationalism in the analysis. However, it is crucial to note that Chinese democracy cannot be simply reduced to a mere collection of these core democratic discourses; rather, they may manifest intricate interrelations—sometimes inclusive, overlapping, or substitutive. This raises an open question: How can we bridge the gap between the macro-narratives of understanding Chinese democracy and its real-world practices, alongside their interactions?

People's democracy is the core value and ideal utilized by the Communist Party to describe Chinese democracy. It represents not only a modern iteration of China's millennia-old *Minben* traditions, despite the myriad dilemmas accompanying this transition, but also serves as a rejoinder to the Western "electoralism." In essence, the Party portrays a democratic model that transcends mere reliance upon, or limitation to, election and vote, instead prioritizing the people and fostering their welfare. The term of "Whole-Process People's Democracy" was introduced by Xi Jinping in 2019 as a novel democratic paradigm aimed at transcending various pre-existing democratic discourses within China. The former relegates the latter under a comprehensive conceptual umbrella, thereby reconciling them procedurally and substantively. While seemingly iterative, it (re)consolidates the multifaceted conditions necessary for achieving people's democracy within a cohesive system of concepts and discourse. However, its inception is deeply entrenched in the contextual complexities of the time, emerging amid the rising national confidence and intensified discursive competition between China and the United States regarding the narrative surrounding democracy.

Intraparty democracy is a form of democracy spontaneously promoted by the Communist Party, embodying distinct characteristics of Chinese democracy, often considered as a counterpart to the Western interparty democracy. In Leninist-style party-states like China that with high centralization, the delegation of powers and decentralization are typically met with reluctance or at least caution, despite the existence of democratic pressures. Incremental attempts at democracy, from within and from top to bottom, constitute the original intention of intraparty democracy design, aiming to bridge the gap between intraparty democracy and people's democracy, with the former driving the latter. However, in practice, the harmony between the internal and external systems remains elusive, at least for short runs, with blurred boundaries existing in areas such as law, oversight, and administration. Worse still, in the era of Xi Jinping, the call for intraparty democracy has waned, giving way to a resurgence of centralization and an obsession with stability and security. Grassroots democracy is another controllable, gradual, and readily effective form of bottom-up democracy endorsed by the Communist Party. At the turn of the century, grassroots democracy, exemplified by village-level elections, experienced a robust resurgence, seemingly catalyzing democratization efforts in China organically and externally. In some regions, even the vote of party cadres expanded to encompass township level. Grassroots autonomy in China is deeply rooted, underscored by the maxim "the emperor's authority does not extend to the counties," which delineates the boundary between state and society. However, over the past two decades, the encroachment of state power has precipitated a crisis for grassroots democracy. It appears that the ambition to advance Chinese democratization through grassroots democracy has encountered significant obstacles.

In comparison with preceding democratic discourses, which have encountered challenges amid the contestation between authoritarianism and democracy in recent years, "consultative democracy" emerges as a formidable contender. Not only does it assume a primary role alongside electoral democracy in characterizing China's democratic image, but "consult the people" has also evolved into a pivotal instrument for good governance, thereby underscoring the efficacy of democracy in China. Traditional analyses of Chinese consultative democracy have often tethered it to Western models of deliberative democracy, viewing the latter as a divergent form of the former. Particularly evident is the authoritarian repression of such a democracy-promoting mechanism as consultation. However, this intertwined relationship is gradually disentangling within the Chinese political milieu, as consultation not only integrates with the fundamental institutionalizations of Chinese political consultation and the

United Front method but also increasingly emphasizes a distinctive mode of governance diverging from democratic and governance structures founded on consensus building achieved through systematic consultation fostering free participation. Here, empowerment and freedom are deemed necessary but insufficient conditions in Chinese consultations.

Chinese democracy, as explored in my monograph, represents both a typological manifestation of democracy, akin to American, French, Japanese, and Indian democracy, among many others, categorized by regional distinctions. Simultaneously, Chinese democracy encapsulates a form of democratic governance grounded in the distinctive characteristics of democracy as observed within China, thus differing little from the aforementioned concrete forms of democracy. Especially in contexts where the conception of Chinese democracy lacks clarity and justifiability, delineating its primary features becomes imperative for subsequent examination into a critical concept.

Such an analytical process would yield a more nuanced comprehension of democracy in China. Irrespective of one's optimism or pessimism regarding China's political trajectory, their analysis should be firmly rooted in the pragmatic considerations of reconciling the potential democratic principles with the development trajectory under the one-party authoritarian rule of the Chinese Communist Party. While theoretically conceptualizing a scenario that dismantles the Communist Party and restructuring Chinese political dynamics may not be entirely implausible, it remains practically unfeasible. Thus, an examination of democracy in China that sidesteps this fundamental reality inherently veers towards varying degrees of utopianism.

Within this context, contemplating the uncertain future of democracy in China transforms into a reexamination of concrete democratic discourses and their evolving relationships. Throughout this process, one must not only consider the very myriad standards and conditions for measuring the (re)consolidation and decline of democracy traditionally, but also refine these measurements based on the actual circumstances in China, without violating basic democratic values. Furthermore, it is essential to balance and integrate various factors concerning state capacity, social order and stability, and governance that have been addressed since the mid- to late twenty-first century, rather than focusing solely on democracy as a variable. Only by balancing and amalgamating these factors into a toolkit could the relations between popular sovereignty and people's livelihoods be reconciled once again. In China, democracy and democratization are closely interlinked with the rule of the Communist Party. Examining shifts towards democracy or authoritarianism in China serves as a crucial indicator for assessing the prospects of democracy, highlighting the disproportionate influence of political figures and parties in China where democratic institutions are absent and democratic values have yet to take root compared to the West, where democracy, despite facing crises, remains restrained by institutional constraints, therefore preventing it from spiraling out of control. However, social scientists have never been adept at predicting the future, all we can do is contribute our efforts to promote the advancement of democratization in China.

Contents

A Definition of Democracy

Democracy in Language

Concepts are initially instantiated through language, a proposition substantiated by the definitions provided by McKenna and Robinson (1990), and Orwell (2021) of their discourses on the interplay between politics and the English language. The linguistic portrayal of "democracy" as "the power of the people" primarily elucidates its very literal sense, encapsulating its descriptive meaning while neglecting the normative or prescriptive connotations associated with "democracy." Consequently, Sartori (2016) then further distinguishes between the normative facet (value) and the institutional dimension (is-ness) of democracy, thereby delineating the relationship between the tangible and the ideal aspects of democracy. Against this background, we could further engage in a more refined categorization of the concept of democracy, distinguishing normative democracy (representing the ideal of democracy), descriptive democracy (encompassing the prescription of democracy), and pragmatic democracy (pertaining to the practical or institutional framework of democracy).

In etymology, the term "semantic democracy" could be replaced with any other descriptors, such as "polyarchy," "oligarchy," "monarchy," and the like. However, the latter set of terms fails to transcend their specific paradigms in portraying an idealized conception of "democracy." The ideal or normative implication of democracy directs us towards a

R. Li, *Democratizing China's Political Imaginaries*,
https://doi.org/10.1007/978-981-97-3670-6_1

utopian dimension beyond the realm of reality. Within this ideal, the absolute sovereignty of the people is unconditionally safeguarded, while the framework of mechanisms employed to achieve this goal falls within the realm of factual descriptions of democracy. These descriptions encompass concepts like radical democracy, direct democracy, pluralist democracy, elite democracy, liberal democracy, republican democracy, consensual democracy, and so forth. Such diverse descriptions delineate various paths towards the realization of the democratic ideal.

Complex democratic practices and institutional arrangements, however, reevaluate the ideal and description of democracy at the practical level. Although ideal democracy and actual democracy are far from being identical, they interact in a dynamic relationship, with the former propelling the development of the latter and serving as a critical and exemplary model. Nevertheless, the semantic confusion and conceptual stretching of the term "democracy" often leave the field of democracy research in a state of disarray.[1] Therefore, it is imperative to reevaluate the very core elements of democracy that exist on the spectrum between abstract ideals and concrete reality. In other words, if "popular sovereignty" constitutes a fundamental element of the concept of democracy, we must delve into a comprehensive understanding of "the people," "sovereignty," and the intricate relation that exists between the two.

First and foremost, the notion of "the people" warrants a very meticulous exploration. Tracing its etymological lineage from the venerable Greek *demos*, through the intermediary Latin translation "populus" (a pivotal linguistic medium during the medieval epoch), and onward to the multifarious interpretations across subsequent linguistic manifestations, encompassing, but not confined to, the Italian "popolo," the French "peuple," the German "Volk," and the prevailing contemporary English rendition "people" (inclusive of the Chinese "*Renmin* 人民"), it becomes patently evident that diverse linguistic incarnations carry distinct connotations. Hence, a facile assumption that "the people" embody a "sheer

[1] The semantics of democracy that from Sartori's "conceptual travailing" and "conceptual stretching" to Collier and Mahon's "family resemblance" and "conceptual Radial," these studies collectively illustrate the importance of adopting an approach that takes into account the interplay of language, context, concept, theory, and paradigm in comparative analysis to elucidate the applicability of democracy and authoritarianism in various contexts. See Sartori (1970) and Collier and Mahon (1993).

majority's absolute dominion" inherently misconstrues the essence of democracy.

The semantic ambivalence inherent in *demos* that renders it equally amenable to denoting both the "collective citizenry" and, in isolation, the "commoners" (comprising the underprivileged strata of society). Aristotle, grounding his seminal exposition upon normative categorization, opines thus: "...the numerical composition of those in power, whether it be the minority of an oligarchic polity or the majority of a democratic one, does not constitute an intrinsic attribute of the polity. For, indeed, the affluent consistently constitute the minority, while the indigent perpetually constitute the majority... In any realm governed by the affluent, regardless of whether they are comprised a majority or a minority, it remains an oligarchic polity; whereas, in domains presided over by the indigent, a democratic polity prevails."[2] In a democratic polity, the preeminent segment of "the people"—as aptly elucidated by Sartori (1989)—remains the majority, which may, in turn, oscillate into the minority, and the minority may likewise metamorphose into the majority, thus affirming the imperativeness of the principle of the "limited majority" rule as the sole tenable bedrock within democratic governance.[3]

(Re)interpreting democracy as the "principle of limited majority" or the principle of constraining majority rule with minority principles introduces an additional etymological paradox. This paradox lies in the fact that a minority, relying solely on the so-called will of the people, cannot restrain the authority of those duly elected to govern. It is crucial to note that the term "people" or "the people" does not simply pertain to individual persons but rather symbolizes a society comprising individual persons, in contrast to the traditional concept of a community, known as "Gemeinschaft" or "community." The former is conceived as a rather objective, non-personal external mode of coexistence, while the latter often denotes the most profound form of coexistence attained through mutual interpenetration among individuals.[4] The abstract distinction between the "people" and "society" is however predicated on factors like the scale of human development, complexity, and estrangement.

[2] Aristotle (1932). Trans. H. Rackhamp. pp. 33–34.

[3] Sartori (1987, p. 25).

[4] Tonnies and Loomis (2002) and Friedrich (1959).

Authors like Ortega y Gasset, Karl Mannheim, Karl Jaspers, Hannah Arendt, Arthur Kornhauser, and others have elucidated the idea of social man, often referred to as "the masses," as a collective attribute.[5] These highly abstract definitions and analyses underscore the importance of establishing the foundation of studies on democracy based on the concept of the people, encompassing aspects like consensus, representation, and so forth.

Secondly, what is "power"? A pivotal inquiry that pertains to the power dynamics (transference) between "the people" and "the sovereign." Despite Jean Rousseau's vehement opposition to the relinquishment of individual sovereignty in practices,[6] the inexorable nature of "representation" is palpable in contemporary political landscapes. Therefore, it is imperative to initially comprehend the etymological nuances of power before forging technological connections between power and the populace. Power, in essence, embodies the force and capacity to govern others, encompassing the "authority to direct their destinies and subject them to the caprice of mortality."[7] Within this framework, power assumes a political character rather than an ethical one. From classical political theory to modern political science, the fundamental definition of power centers on the governance *by* the people. Therefore, in scenarios where the direct exercise of "power by the people (direct democracy)" is pragmatically unattainable in reality (or only applicable in some exceedingly specific circumstances), the query arises: How should the people harness power to govern the state? This necessitates an exploration of institutional configurations of modern democracy—representation.

The actualization of representation holds three layers of significance: firstly, the methodology for generating representatives; secondly, how representatives authentically embody the interests of the people; and finally, the substantive purpose of representation. Logically, principles

[5] A more pivotal discourse that concerning the intricate interplay between individuals and society is found in Emile Durkheim's examination of the "social division of labor." Durkheim challenges Adam Smith's depiction of individuals as "atomized," propelled solely by self-interest and self-love. He synthesizes the concepts of the "social division of labor" and "morality" to reconcile the individual personality with societal cohesion. This discourse encapsulates a longstanding, classical divergence between liberalism and republicanism. See Durkheim (2018) and Smith (1776).

[6] Rousseau (2018).

[7] Further explications on the concept of power see also Weber (2016) and Locke (1947).

such as freedom, competition, fairness, and periodic elections safeguard the legitimization of the transference of popular sovereignty to representatives.[8] But elections do not inherently confer representativeness upon representatives, thereby underscoring the very need for accountability to the electorate. This accountability could be partially attained via mechanisms like re-election, entailing the replacement and censure of the representatives. Nevertheless, the exigencies of the modern politics dictate that representatives must possess diverse qualities, including responsiveness, therefore, to fortify the nexus between power transference and representativeness.

To resolve the paradox arising from the representation of the people in a system of representative democracy, wherein the power subject is the people, yet the objects of power exercise remain the people, it is imperative to delineate democracy into two distinct scenarios. Firstly, "conceptual democracy," which revolves around the "popular sovereignty," is employed to counterbalance and differentiate itself from dictatorial powers. Secondly, post-dictatorship, the substantive principles of people's power (nominal power) find realization through various democratic concepts.[9]

If we etymologically understand the "will" of the people as the "consensus" of the people, and if the democratic system is structured based on the principle of a "limited majority," the conceptual facets of democracy in language can progressively metamorphose into institutional arrangements in reality. The dual challenge of the people exercising power collectively—both as a majority and a minority, and the incapacity to collectively wield power—will gradually diminish. In essence, the institutional design of democracy must be in accord with the principle of a limited majority while safeguarding the interests of minority groups. Should the criterion for the majority shift towards absolute rule, the peril of a "tyranny of the majority" becomes imminent. Democracy necessitates affording political expression to minority groups while ensuring their safety, as "suppressing minorities is suppressing popular sovereignty."[10]

[8] Gierke (1900, p. 64).

[9] Marx's "dictatorship of the proletariat" undoubtedly encapsulates some analogous sentiments, portraying proletarian dictatorship as a transitory moment leading to a world devoid of classes, state, and ultimately characterized by universal freedom for all. See also Kautsky and Stenning (1964).

[10] Sartori (1987, p. 12).

In the realm of linguistic representation, democracy, epitomizing popular sovereignty, intricately intertwines the twin pillars of the people and sovereignty. The conceptualization that endows power to the populace not only furnishes a foundational elucidation for the legitimacy and legality of authority within the democratic paradigm but also seamlessly aligns with the loftiest ideals inherent in the democratic ethos. However, the trajectory of discourse experiences an abrupt termination at this juncture. Western democratic theories extensively expound upon the mechanisms through which individuals wield power, and asserting that "...it implies that authentic power emanates exclusively from delegated authority, reflecting the volition of the people, and grounded in a discernible foundational consensus... Our aspirations and imperatives for democratic framework necessitate the prioritization of society over the state, with 'people' superseding 'sovereignty'... Only when the government subsists for the people, as opposed to the inverse, can a democratic system manifest."[11]

Nevertheless, these explications intricately tether themselves to the rather milieu of contemporary Western liberal democracy and constitute the predominant narrative that shapes our contemporary comprehension of democracy. It is imperative to underscore that as democracy metamorphoses into a "political correctness" ubiquitously espoused by nations worldwide, this phenomenon is precisely rooted in the diverse array of perspectives proffered by democratic scholarship, which furnishes us with multifaceted insights for apprehending the complexities inherent in democratic governance.

The semantic perplexity inherent in the term "democracy" lies implicitly in its intimate association with commendation for systems or societies founded upon it. From the intellectual realms of Plato to Aristotle, and spanning the epochs from classical democratic theorists such as Lipset Seymour Martin and Morris W. H. Jones to more contemporary luminaries like Schumpeter Joseph, Popper Karl, Berlin Isaiah, Mosca Gaetano, and Pareto Vilfredo, democracy, or its ideal manifestation, has perennially evaded its categorical endorsement as the paramount choice among diverse political frameworks. Despite the widespread embrace of democracy by nearly all nations in the post-World War II epoch, whether substantively or formally, the characterization of "modern democracy"

[11] Ibid., p. 67.

diverges significantly from its "ancient" counterpart.[12] Notably, the former increasingly venerates the "elite democracy," instrumentalizes democratic mechanisms, and veers away from the idealistic underpinnings and values intrinsic to democracy, opting instead to underscore the operational modalities and efficiency of the political system. In stark contradistinction, myriad ancient political theorists and modern proponents of democratic principles, typified by Moses Finley, steadfastly advocate for the normative examination of democracy, construing it as a moral pinnacle and ultimate aspiration.

The contention enveloping these debates and the unequivocal exaltation of democracy undeniably heighten the semantic confusion surrounding this conception. This, in turn, renders many political institutions or governmental structures no longer analogous to democracy. Simultaneously, the semantic portrayal of democracy—across many linguistic dimensions—is undergoing constriction, diverging significantly from the moral, idealistic, civic education, and enlightenment purposes inherent in classical democracy during the Ancient Greek period. Modern elite politics, particularly, confines the interpretation of democracy to bureaucratic, governance, technological dimensions, among others.

Furthermore, the very relationship and delineations between democracy and liberal democracy are progressively becoming obscured. Fukuyama once prophesied that liberal democracy marked the end of human history. Although he later reflected on this assertion, it underscores the perceived arrogance within the realm of liberal democracy.[13] Hence, there exists an exigent imperative to scrutinize the semantic essence of democracy as a prerequisite, including its ambiguous and confused expressions. This scrutiny encompasses disparities in the meanings of democracy in ancient and modern contexts, the interplay between democracy and other forms such as republics and monarchies, and the disjunction between democratic ideals and realities. Such an examination is paramount for a nuanced comprehension of the values pursuit and institutional arrangements integral to democracy.

[12] Finley (1985).

[13] See Fukuyama (1995, 2015).

Democracy in Value

Does there exist a transcendent and value-neutral (Wertfreiheit) conceptualization of democracy? Given the protracted debates enveloping democracy throughout various epochs, cultures, and geographical domains, does the endeavor to formulate an entirely value-neutral and universally applicable democratic conceptual framework prove tenable? To note, the theory of value neutrality assumes three discernible manifestations: the dichotomy between evaluative and descriptive value neutrality; the extremity of a value vacuum that within neutrality; and the stratagem of evading or transforming values within the ambit of neutrality. In practice, preponderance of value judgments and descriptions tends to gravitate towards the third category, wherein one veils their inherent value orientation to align with prevailing societal values.

The accentuation of democratic values assumes paramount significance as the conceptualization and theorization of democracy undergo a perceptible transition from an excessively descriptive posture to an unwarranted advocacy of values. This proclivity towards specific democratic values, in turn, undermines the foundational precepts of mainstream democratic theory. In grappling with the quandary of democratic values, it becomes imperative to navigate the intricate interplay that between the "empirical theory (non-normative)" and "non-empirical theory (normative)." While democracy theory assumes a macroscopic orientation, democratic praxis, usually, operates on a microscopic scale. Consequently, the predicament of "modern democracy" resides in the inversion of intended evaluations of factual occurrences and practices through experiential lenses. The efficacy of such an inversion, and its concordance with theoretical logic, transmogrifies into a micro-level undertaking that serves as a litmus test for macroscopic theory. Furthermore, the erosion of the neutral values intrinsic to democratic theory is exacerbated by the emergence of negative and extreme evidence. This deleterious influence permeates the very fabric of democratic ideals, contributing to a palpable corrosion of their neutrality.

The value of democracy commonly pertains to the "ideal" of democracy, with its principles that delineated and comprehended from a normative standpoint that transcends factual considerations. In contemplating the value of democracy, one must navigate through diverse philosophical lens. From Plato's conception of the ideal form (eidos) embodied in the "philosopher king" to Marx's vision of the "philosopher of revolution," and from Thomas More's Utopia (later transmuted by Mannheim into a mere amalgamation of utopia, tinged with ideology),[14] then, to Macpherson's elucidation of myth—wherein "myth relinquishes any connection to the dichotomy of true and false, encapsulating the entirety of human values and ideas."[15] These philosophical paradigms offer some intricate explanations for the inherent contradictions that manifest between the theoretical underpinnings and practical manifestations of democratic principle. Sartori, for instance, interprets this disjunction as a "practical contradiction," denoting a conflict intricately woven into the fabric of action. The assertion is that the contradiction is inherently tied to the process of engagement. One cannot *simultaneously* partake in the consumption of the proverbial cake and retain possession of it, as the pursuit of both objectives results in an unconditional impossibility.

The comprehension of this paradox is not inherently challenging; it can be delineated along two dimensions. Firstly, on the factual plane, among the core tenets of numerous democracies, equality undeniably stands out as one of the most pivotal. Jefferson's assertion, that "all men are created equal,"[16] appears to have evolved into a self-evident truth in terms of values. However, in reality, the proposition "all men are born unequal" is equally self-evident. Secondly, on the practical plane, democracy implies individual autonomy, with Marxist communist theory envisioning "true human autonomy arising from the demise of the state… and the union of free individuals." Does such autonomy possess practical feasibility? It is nearly insurmountable. Complete autonomy can only be confined to individual persons and cannot extend to groups, collectives, societies, and nations. Moreover, complete autonomy may exist in a fleeting moment but cannot endure permanently, as exemplified by the Paris Commune.[17] This validates Sartori's argument that concerning the inverse relationship between the potential intensity of autonomy and the requisite breadth

[14] Mannheim (2013).

[15] MacIver (1965).

[16] See The Declaration of Independence of the United States, June 4, 1776.

[17] This should not be construed as a denigration of the pioneering ethos that inherent in the "proletarian dictatorship" manifested by the Paris Commune. Indeed, the subsequent socialist revolutions in Russia and the embracement of the socialism in China are merely constituent elements within the rather procedural affirmation of applied Marxism. The configuration of tangible systems can optimize the augmentation of autonomy, yet it is precluded from achieving absolute autonomy.

and continuity of autonomy, specifically addressing the formula involving the value of freedom and the factual realities.

So, what is the significance of delving into the values of democracy? Discussions concerning the values of democracy should not become entangled in the question of whether it could be fully realized or to what extent and significance it could be maximized.[18] The value of democracy lies firstly in establishing an ideal set of standards and metrics for practical reference. Secondly, the values of democracy provide a paradigm for critiquing reality. If we accept the assertion that there is an irreconcilable contradiction that lies between democratic values and facts, the realization of democratic values transforms into the institutional design of the actual democratic practices, rather than a self-determination with reality for the extreme reinforcement of values. Otherwise, it would lead to the dilemma of individuals possessing power in terms of values but being unable to exercise power in reality, known as the "danger of the opposite."[19]

In an interpretative analysis of democracy from the perspectives of semantics and values, a more profound comprehension of its intrinsic and normative characteristics can be gleaned. Unraveling the connotations of democracy along a progressive trajectory first requires a clarification of its essence and what distinguishes it. Subsequently, this involves an exploration of how democratic political systems could be optimized through practical institutional design. The determination of what constitutes democracy or deviates from it necessitates a categorical assessment, while the refinement of democratic institutions falls within the realm of degree. The sequential arrangement of these considerations is crucial; only by initially addressing the qualitative distinctions between democracy and its antitheses can a meaningful discourse on the democratization of various political entities and systems transpire.

[18] In the domain of democratic inquiry, classical philosophical discourse, political science, and empirical investigations coalesce in the endeavor to optimize the realization of democratic values. The radical conceptualization of "democracy" frequently engenders an extreme instantiation of "non-democracy." For instance, authoritarianism and the absolute freedom and unmitigated autonomy emerge as consequential extremes emanating from an excessively reverential treatment of democracy. Hence, it becomes imperative to introduce qualifying considerations antecedent to the pursuit of liberal values, contemplating the optimization and equilibrium of the disjunction between democratic ideals and their pragmatic instantiation.

[19] Herz (1919, 1981).

Schmitter, Philippe C., and Karl Terry Lynn, in their article "What Democracy is… What It is Not…," encapsulate the fundamental traits of democracy, independent of the specific institutional designs and arrangements. These traits encompass elements like a regime or system of governance, the public realm, citizens, competition, elections, majority rule, cooperation, and representatives. These inherent qualities define the essential nature of democracy.[20] Any deviation from these traits situates a political entity outside the democratic spectrum, designating it as the non-democratic or hybrid—examples being tyranny, dictatorship, authoritarianism, and totalitarianism.

Simultaneously, democracy does not always invariably translate into efficiency in economic and administrative domains, nor does it unfailingly promote the social stability, order, and consensus. Authoritarianism, for instance, stands as the antithesis of democracy, primarily due to its exclusion of freedom. It is essential to distinguish between authority and authoritarianism. Authority, rooted in the Latin term "augere,"[21] originally referred to the charismatic influence wielded by those with authority to strengthen, consolidate, and endorse certain behaviors and thoughts, distinct from the power. It was not until Weber interpreted authority as "domination" that it became somewhat intertwined with power, representing a form of influential power. Authority describes a form of legitimate moral influence that does not rely on coercion.[22] Consequently, authority and democracy are closely intertwined, with democracy aiming to transform the coercive power (vis coactiva) into authority (deractiva) imbued with guidance and moral appeal, without rendering democratic power feeble.

However, the connotation of the "authoritarianism" (especially in its political sense) underwent a transformation in the early twentieth century. This change is evident in the conflation of authority with coercive, false, and non-democratic authority, resembling the deceptive authority of a thief. This form of authoritarianism no longer recognizes the individual freedom and rights. As Friedrich Carl Joachim remarked, "in a totalitarian society true authority is altogether destroyed."[23]

[20] Schmitter (1991).

[21] Arendt (1958) and De Grazia (1959).

[22] Bendix (1978).

[23] Friedrich (1954, p. 274).

In contemporary political discourse, totalitarianism, or absolute rule, constitutes another antithesis of democracy, both emanating from a manifestation of total and absolute power in governance. Totalitarianism has historical roots in examples such as Italian fascism, National Socialism (under Hitler), and Bolshevikism (under Stalin) in the twentieth century. It is not merely a conceptual spirit[24]; rather, it is more accurately described as a systemic design or political form emphasizing the ruler's comprehensive control over power. The term "absolute rule," as expounded by interpretations from Machiavelli, Guicciardini, and Bodin, denotes a mode of governance characterized by the unrestrained exercise of power without recourse to trial. Absolute rule not only inherits traits from traditional absolute monarchies but also embodies a modern incarnation of highly concentrated state governance, establishing a political structure unbounded by legal constraints and supervision. Consequently, it represents an inherently undemocratic political system and institution.[25]

Of course, a multitude of non-democratic political systems could be enumerated. Therefore, the aforementioned analysis not only contributes to a more fundamental comprehension of the core concept of democracy and its antithesis but also facilitates the differentiation of democratic degrees among various political systems in real-world politics. This comprehensive evaluation proves instrumental in assessing the consolidation and decline of democracy. However, it inevitably gives rise to another contradiction. On the one hand, some non-Western countries vehemently advocate for "indigenization" to eradicate Western modernization hegemony and colonialism. On the other hand, they grapple with the challenge of overcoming the dichotomy between democracy and authoritarianism or dismissing democratic values, primarily exemplified by the West (liberalism). Most developing countries still find it challenging to extricate themselves from the democratic exportation of the West and struggle to chart their own path of "indigenized" democracy.

Nevertheless, this does not imply the failure of those non-Western case studies. Quite the contrary, diversity in democratic or democratic research is precisely exemplified in the examination of cases within different contexts, cultures, politics, economies, societies, and so forth. Among

[24] Carr (1947) and Baechler (1985).

[25] A regime distinguished by the absolute rule of an individual or a group; however, should the populace overthrow the tyrant and assume full control, it is prone to metamorphose into another extreme: the absolute rule of the people.

them, the Chinese experience[26] undoubtedly provides a quintessential case for the analysis of democracy in comparative political studies. This book will also concentrate on the macro-historical background of Chinese democracy and its discourse within the distinctive political context in China, with the aim of exploring the world through the lens of China and establishing a global understanding of the country.

Democracy in China

Many authors within Western and Chinese academia utilize the notion of "Chinese democracy" to explain a typology of democracy, particularly prevalent among Chinese domestic scholars. They juxtapose the concept of Chinese democracy with Western liberal democracy, situating both within the encompassing umbrella of democracy. Nevertheless, these analyses are vulnerable to stretching the conceptual boundaries of democracy. In essence, if everything is labeled as democracy, then democracy is nothing. Since the Opium War, democracy (*Minzhu*) in China has been manifested an exceptionally diverse array of theories and practices. In contemporary discourse, the very term "Chinese democracy" has become prevalent in elucidating the distinctive features of democracy in China, thereby distinguishing it from other democratic models, particularly those of Western origin. Over the relatively brief span of democratic exploration, spanning just over a century, the nexus between China and the West, the dynamics of indigenization and universalization, and the interplay of specificity and generality have consistently constituted focal points of debate.

Entrenched in factors like Chinese tradition, culture, the trajectory of democratic practices, and the political parties, Chinese democracy inherently embodies a discernible of the "Chineseness" or "Chinese Characteristics." Nevertheless, all these questions persist as to whether these distinctive features suffice to underpin the discourse self-construction of Chinese democracy. Consequently, a thorough reexamination of the key concepts and characteristics of Chinese democracy, viewed through the lenses of historical evolution and Sino-Western comparisons, particularly within the realm of Western studies on China, contributes to a more

[26] Chinese uniqueness is commonly being summerized as "China experience," "China mode," "China road." See, for example, Bell (2016), Zhao (2010), Chan et al. (2008), Maxwell (2014), Fangjun (2009), Tsai (1986), and Rawski (1995).

comprehensive understanding of the theory and practice of democracy in the Chinese context.

Democratic Pursuit in Modern China

The proverbial adage, "The freezing of three feet of ice is not formed in a single day," serves as an apt metaphor for the gradual dismantling of China's millennia-old feudal autocratic tradition.[27] The eradication of this ingrained system demands more than a brief democratic enlightenment; it necessitates a protracted and nuanced approach. Similarly, the (re)construction of a discourse on contemporary Chinese democracy cannot be achieved through a simplistic emulation of the West or a closed indigenized strategy. This endeavor is bound to be a protracted and contentious pursuit. Despite China's rich civilization spanning thousands of years, its formal engagement with the wave of modernization commenced in the mid-nineteenth century, whether by choice or coercion. During this period, China began to shed the feudal dogma of "tributes from all directions, nations coming to pay homage (八方进贡 万国来朝 *Bafang Jingong, Wanguo Laichao*)," and "the proud son of heaven, unique and supreme (天之骄子 唯我独尊 *Tianzhi Jiaozi, Weiwo Duzun*)." This marked a critical juncture in China's introspection on its feudal autocratic system, signifying an earnest attempt to chart a path towards modern political development.

However, this transformative process was far from seamless. From the mid-nineteenth century until the prelude to the Reform and Opening Up era in 1978, democratic exploration laid the groundwork for subsequent development. Democratic ideologies and practices alternated, providing invaluable insights for the evolution of modern Chinese democracy. In the

[27] In his seminal work, "Political Systems of Empires," S. N. Eisenstadt posits the Chinese Empire as the "largest and most enduring empire," asserting that the pivotal dynastic transitions in Chinese history did not yield substantive transformations in the foundational symbols and essential institutions of the political framework. Eisenstadt contends that "rebellions and dynastic cycles failed to engender significant alterations to the fundamental structure of the political order—the core dynamics governing the socio-political system's interplay with other pivotal institutional domains within society." Even amid China's compelled modernization during the late nineteenth century, influenced by Western paradigms leading to a shift from empire to nation-state, Chinese culture remarkably preserved its inherent imperial characteristics, demonstrating a remarkable degree of stability. For an in-depth exploration of these concepts. Eisenstadt (2017, pp. 487–488).

mid-nineteenth century, trailblazers such as Wei Yuan (魏源), Xu Jieshe (徐继畬), and Liang Tingnan (梁廷楠), alongside their seminal works "Illustrated Gazetteer of Maritime Kingdoms (海国图志 *Haiguo Tuzhi*)," "A Brief Chronicle of the Vast Realm (瀛环志略 *Yinghuan Zhilüe*)," and "A Treatise on the Unification of Provinces and Nations (合省国说 *Hesheng Guoshuo*)," introduced the Western political systems and democratic ideals, particularly those from Western Europe and America, as China's gates were forcibly opened. However, this descriptive exposition did not elicit a comprehensive critique of China's monarchic autocracy amid the populace. The Taiping Heavenly Kingdom movement and the Second Opium War further laid bare the corruption and incompetence of the Qing Dynasty. Feng Guifen (冯桂芬), in his lamentation in "The Protest of Xiaolu and Ban (校庐邠抗议 *Jiaolu Bin Kangyi*)," asserted, "people without abandoning talent are inferior to the barbarians, land without residual benefits is inferior to the barbarians, military and civilians not separated are inferior to the barbarians, and the reality must match the reputation is inferior to the barbarians."[28] The realization of "knowing shame and then courage" prompted a cohort of progressive intellectuals to re-scrutinize the root causes of China's vulnerability by drawing comparisons between Western and Chinese political systems.

However, reforms such as "no separation between ruler and subject (君臣不隔 *Junchen Buge*)," "public dismissal and appointment (公黜陟 *Gongchubu*)," and "returning to hometown positions (复乡职 *Fuxiangzhi*)" merely constituted superficial modification to Chinese bureaucratic system, devoid of any democratic essence. The principle of emulating the West with "Chinese essence as the foundation and Western methods as auxiliary (以中为本、以西为辅 *Yizhong Weiben, Yixi Weifu*)" subsequently became the core of the Self-Strengthening Movement—"Chinese in form, Western in use (中体西用 *Zhongti Xiyong*)"—borrowing from the Western institutions while preserving the essence of Chinese traditions. Regrettably, these endeavors faced insolvency in the crucible of the late nineteenth-century Sino-Japanese War.

The enlightened bureaucrats and benevolent scholars of the late Qing Dynasty have all provided counsel and proposals for the nation's salvation. However, most were unable to break free from the deep-seated

[28] "Zhiyang Qiyi [In the Discourse on Western-Style Weaponry]." In *Wuxu Bianfa [Reform Movement of 1898]*. Shanghai Renmin Chubanshe, Shanghai People's Press, 1957. pp. 29–30.

constraints of China's feudal monarchic authoritarian ideology. Zheng Guanying's (郑观应) "The Discourse (议言 *Yiyan*)" advocates China should emulate the Western "parliament," an early manifestation of the "shared governance between the monarch and the people" ideology. Similarly, Wang Tao's (王焘) "Concern for the People (重民 *Zhongmin*)" also supports emulating the Western "constitutional monarchy," with both Zheng and Wang incorporating the concept of "civil rights" into their ideas.[29]

Enlightened bureaucrats within the Qing court, such as Guo Songtao (郭嵩涛), the Fujian censor, praised the British model of "shared governance between the monarch and the people" in his work "On Matters of Coastal Defense (条议海防事宜 *Tiaoyi Haifang Shiyi*)." He emphasized that "to strengthen the country, one must begin by learning the Western politics, not merely imitating their material culture."[30] Cui Guoyin (崔国因), the Imperial Readers, Zhang Shusheng (张树声), the Governor-General of Guangdong and Guangxi, and Peng Yulin (彭玉麟), the Minister of War, all petitioned the Qing court to establish a "parliament" for self-strengthening. In the half-century following the Opium War, early democratic enlightenment unfolded amid calls for "saving the nation (救亡图存 *Jiuwang Tucun*)" and "self-strengthening (自强 *Ziqiang*)." However, the era's limitations confined the development of "democracy" in this historical period to the realms of material or institution rather than ideology, as people were aware of the result but not the underlying reasons.

The Wuxu Reform, advocated by Kang Youwei (康有为) and Liang Qichao (梁启超), propelled China's democratic enlightenment into another stage, focusing on "human rights." In the first draft of "The Complete Book of Public Law (实理公法全书 *Shili Gongfa Quanshu*)," Kang Youwei highly praised the Western concept of "inalienable human rights" using the analogy of "geometric axioms." This progress was not merely a simple study of systems but an elevation of ideology. Many of

[29] In the late 1880s, in addition to Zheng and Wang, many intellectuals also embraced the study of Western institutions and contemplated China's autocracy. Prominent figures in this intellectual movement included Tang Zhen (汤震), Shao Zuozhou (邵作舟), Chen Chi (陈炽), Song Shu (宋恕), He Qi (何启), Hu Lihuan (胡礼桓), and others.

[30] *Guo Songtao Riji [The Diary of Guo Songtao]*. Yuelu Chubanshe, Yuelu Publishing House, 1983. p. 84.

Yan Fu's (严复) articles attributed the West's strength to the concept of "having freedom as its essence and democracy as its application."[31]

The reformists' critique of autocracy was more radical, negating not only traditional autocratic rule and feudal doctrines but also advocating for the "emperor change (易其人 *Yi Qizhu*)" and "joint abolition (共废之 *Gong Fei Zhi*)." They argued that China's poverty and weakness stemmed from the cruel monarch.[32] To alter the current situation, they believed in the necessity of "Reform and Renewal." Despite embracing Western ideas of freedom and human rights, the reformists viewed democracy as a tool for reforming the country within the context of traditional concepts such as "harmony between the family and the state (家国同构 *Jiaguo Tonggou*)," "unity of the family and the country (家国一体 *Jiaguo Yiti*)," "民族危机 national crisis (*Minzu Weiji*)," and "国家社稷 state and ancestral shrines (*Guojia Sheji*)."

The Boxer Rebellion and the invasion of China by the Eight-Nation Alliance in 1900 marked the commencement of political upheavals in twentieth-century China. The early political reforms at the turn of the century were a collaborative effort between the official government and the intellectual elite. Following the signing of the Boxer Protocol in 1901 and the conclusion of the Russo-Japanese War in 1904, constitutional reforms became the mainstream discourse, compelling the Qing government to consider political restructuring that to readdress both domestic and foreign pressures for reform. The official implementation of the "New Policy Reforms (新政改革 *Xinzheng Gaige*)" initially had significant impacts on industries, social structures, and ideological currents of the time. Government officials, such as Zhang Qian (张謇 in Japan), Sun Baoqi (孙宝琦 in France), Yuan Shikai (袁世凯), Zhang Zhidong (张之洞), Zhou Fu (周馥), Zai Ze (载泽), Dai Hongci (戴鸿慈), among others, were all ardent advocates for constitutional reforms.

However, the official understanding of "constitutionalism" differed significantly from that of the intellectual and gentry. In 1906, the Qing government's "preparatory constitutionalism" continued the traditional practice of "centralizing authority in the Qing court, while making the public affairs known to the public (大权统于清廷, 庶政公诸舆论 *Daquan*

[31] Yuanqiang [Yuanqiang]. In *Yan Fu Ji [The Collected Works of Yan Fu]*, Vol. 1. Xhonghua Shuju, Zhonghua Book Company, 1986. p. 12.

[32] Pihan [Disapproving of Han]. In *Yan Fu Ji [The Collected Works of Yan Fu]*. Xhonghua Shuju, Zhonghua Book Company, 1986. p. 56.

Tongyu Qingting, Shuzheng Gongzhu Yulun)." The Central Advisory Council and the Local Councils established during constitutional reforms were still trapped in the shackles of aristocracy and hierarchical platitude. They showed no sign of incorporating the gentry into political participation, a stark contrast to the emphasis on "constitutional governance" by external elite gentry, such as Kang and Liang, who stressed the substantive functions that beyond safeguarding "civil rights." This discord led to the later petition movement for the "convocation of a national assembly," but these grassroots reform movements were soon suppressed, shattering the fantasy of the late Qing gentry seeking "democracy from the emperor."

The Xinhai Revolution in 1911 overturned China's millennia-old feudal autocracy, establishing the Republic of China and initiating the exploration of Chinese "republican deliberative" politics. Amid the chaotic period, various factions, including (radical) constitutionalists, revolutionaries, republicans, conservatives, and reformists, vied for power both within and outside the government. The compromise result was the establishment of a "republican representative system" in China, formalized by the Provisional Constitution of the Republic of China. However, the "Responsibility Cabinet System" under Yuan Shikai's (袁世凱) dictatorial rule differed significantly from Western cabinet systems in terms of core principles such as power checks and judicial independence. Party politics on this basis fell into internal strife due to a lack of popular support and foundation, as noted by Liang. Whether under a monarchy or a republic, constitutional governance in China all proved unattainable, leading only to despotism, exemplified by Yuan Shikai's attempted restoration of the imperial system.[33] The political and democratic reforms in the early Republic of China were experimental results of various Western political ideologies and system designs after the overthrow of the feudal autocracy of the Qing court. The exploration of democracy under the "enlightened despotism" inevitably failed, and the substantive authoritarian system continued to prevail in China, disguised behind terms such as "republic," "representative," and "constitutional monarchy."

The "Protect the Nation and Uphold the Law Movement (护国护法运动 *Huguo Hufa Yundong*)" initiated by Sun Yat-sen (孙中山) marked the inception of a novel concept of modern democratic systems. His democratic ideas were constructed upon a critical examination of Western

[33] *Yinbingshi Heji [Collected Works of the Yin Bingshi]*, Vol. 33. Zhonghua Shuju, Zhonghua Book Company, 1989.

models and the republican system that established in the early years of the Republic of China. Sun's vision challenged the conventional notion of "representative democracy" while advocating for principles such as "direct popular sovereignty," "county autonomy," and "division of powers."[34] However, these ideas and designs were notably rudimentary, characterized by many vague conceptions that posed challenges in their implementation. Intellectuals responded with more sharp critiques, such as Huang Yuanyong's (黄远庸) examination of "vague generalization (笼统主义 *Longtong Zhuyi*)," readdressing the erosion of individuality across Chinese society, culture, politics, and systems. Lan Gongwu's (蓝公武) theory of "servility (奴性 *Nuxing*)" rebuked traditional Confucian ethics for constraining the individual freedom. Simultaneously, Chen Duxiu's (陈独秀) establishment of the magazine "New Youth (新青年 *Xin Qingnian*)" during the May Fourth New Culture Movement advocated for human liberation, emphasizing individual value and freedom. This movement also reflected on the shortcomings of the bourgeois political revolution in the European Renaissance. World War I, the October Revolution in Russia, and the May Fourth Movement against imperialism and patriotism gradually gave rise to early socialist democratic thought, transcending individual values and emphasizing collective and organizational strength. This intellectual trend was spearheaded by proponents of the materialist viewpoints of history and the tenets of scientific socialism, particularly the early Marxists.

However, the democratic views of early Marxists like Li Dazhao (李大钊), Tan Pingshan (谭平山), and Chen Duxiu were not grounded in a comprehensive and accurate understanding of Marxist scientific socialist theory.[35] Instead, their ideas appeared as a fusion of democratic perspectives and socialism derived from Western modern social and political theories. Their aim was to surpass the West on the foundation of bourgeois democracy, employing "democracy" as a strategic instrument to

[34] "Separation of the Five Powers" refers to the checks and balances as well as the division among legislative power, executive power, judicial power, control power, and electoral power. See *Zai Zhongguo Fuomindang Benbu Teshe Zhuyue Banshichu de Yanshuo [On Establishing a Special Office in Guangdong at the Headquarters of the Kuomintang]*, Vol. 5. In Sun Yat-sen Quanji, The Complete Works of Sun Yat-sen.

[35] See, for example, *Li Dazhao Wenji [Collected Works of Li Dazhao]*. Renmin Chubanshe, People's Publishing House, 1984; *Tan Pingshan Wenji [Collected Works of Tan Pingshan]*. Renmin Chubanshe, People's Publishing House, 1986; *Chen Duxiu Wenji [Selected Writings of Chen Duxiu]*. Renmin Chubanshe, People's Publishing House, 1986.

eradicate the private property ownership and class inequality. Notably, they avoided delving into the establishment of a socialist state with "proletarian dictatorship," as observed in the statement: "They originally moved from democracy towards socialism, but when they became revolutionary socialists, 'democracy' faded in their thoughts."[36] This elucidates the early Marxists' fervor for engaging in revolution.

Beyond the intellectual elite, bureaucratic politicians and capitalists also sought viable avenues for Chinese democracy. Figures like the military warlord Wu Peifu (吴佩孚) proposed the "National Assembly," while various warlords from the Beiyang clique, including Cao Kun (曹锟) and Zhang Zuolin (张作霖), advocated for initiatives like "abolishing governors, disbanding troops," as well as subsequent measures such as the "constitutionalism for the nation" and "provincial autonomy." However, all these democratic endeavors, despite echoing democratic slogans, lacked a profound understanding of democracy and the Chinese situation, thus failed with weak popular support. The early democratic thought of the CCP, though directly rooted in Marxist ideology and the political practices of the Soviet Union, differs in its interpretation of "people's sovereignty." The notion of "people" specifically refers to the proletariat with an exclusively advanced and correct nature, in direct contrast to the concept of the "enemy," particularly the bourgeoisie, targeted for dictatorship.

The First National Congress of the CPC, acknowledging the premises of the "Soviet administrative system" and "proletarian dictatorship," chose the rather democratic Kuomintang as a collaborative partner while uniting with democratic parties against warlords.[37] During the Second, Third, and Fourth National Congresses, there were principled discussions on democracy and the ideal form of the state in the process of uniting with the Kuomintang. Following the Fifth Congress and the "August 7th Conference," the CCP-Kuomintang confrontation led to criticisms of Chen Duxiu's patriarchalism.[38] However, under the early "democratic

[36] Wang (1989, p. 347).

[37] *Zhonggong Zhongyang Wenjian Xuanji [Selected Documents of the Central Committee of the Communist Party of China]*. Ed. Central State Archives, Vol. 1, Zhonggong Zhongyang Dangxiao Chubanshe, Party School of the Central Committee of the CPC, 1989. p. 5.

[38] Guan (2005). In 1927, during the Fifth National Congress of the Chinese Communist Party, the "Party Construction" chapter was added to the "Resolution on the Third

centralism," there was an emphasis on the "unconditional obedience and execution by individuals to the organization, and by lower levels to higher levels." Additionally, after the Reform and Opening Up, the "collective leadership" within the CCP tended to emphasize centralization while downplaying or even neglecting democracy.

The Sixth National Congress of the CPC established "People's Sovereignty" in institutionalized form through the establishment of the Workers' and Peasants' Soviet regime with the principle of the "unity of representation and administration (议行合一 *Yixing Heyi*)." During the period of the land revolution (1927–1937), Mao, while implementing the Comintern (Moscow) line, explored a revolutionary path distinct from the Soviet model, emphasizing "armed independence and rural encirclement of cities." The First National Congress of the Chinese Soviet Republic passed the *Outline of the Constitution of the Chinese Soviet Republic*, emphasizing the class nature, broad nature, and institutional "unity of representation and administration: of "people's sovereignty" in China.[39]

During the Yan'an period, Mao described "people's sovereignty" as "constitutional governance,"[40] presenting a pathway that distinct from capitalism and socialism, known as "New Democracy (新民主 *Xin Minzhu*)." This was manifested through the establishment of the "Anti-Japanese National United Front" to resist Japan and oppose Chiang Kai-shek (蒋介石). That said, China would be a new nation built under the democratic centralism of "united dictatorship of various revolutionary classes." Institutional explorations by the Shaanxi-Gansu-Ningxia

Amendment to the Constitution of the CCP," wherein "democratic centralism" was established as a guiding principle for the CCP. Later in 1928, during the Sixth National Congress of the CCP, "democratic centralism" was officially incorporated into the party constitution.

[39] In the nascent phases of the establishment of the CCP, the promotion of a "genuinely democratic republic" transitioned briefly to the concept of the "Chinese Soviet Republic." Despite its fleeting duration and repression under the authority of the Nanjing central government, this ideological shift yielded profound insights into the fundamental facets of the Chinese revolution and the establishment of political authority. These intellectual forays, which delved into issues encompassing agrarian concerns and the trajectory of revolution, served as the bedrock for the subsequent ascension to power by the CCP and the enactment of democratic political processes, notwithstanding their ephemeral nature and suppression by the Nanjing central government.

[40] Li (1986, p. 499).

Border Region government, the "Three-Three System (三三制 *Sansan Zhi*),"[41] for example, was a representative institutional exploration of the constitutional democracy that time.

After the conclusion of the War of Resistance Against Japan, the CCP and the Kuomintang found themselves in a constitutional and executive opposition.[42] The CCP, asserting its position through the establishment of the "New Democratic Constitution"—the "Principles of the Shaanxi-Gansu-Ningxia Border Region Constitution," reiterated the "principle of people's democracy" as the foundation of state power. While Mao, in his discourse,[43] considered constitutionalism subordinate to democracy, the continuity of democratic discourse in China since the May Fourth Movement is evident. Throughout the 1940s, the New Democracy coexisted with the People's Democratic Dictatorship, with the former indicating a transitional intermediate form towards the socialism, and the latter specifically pointing to a democratic form and the nature of political power. Mao's concept of People's Democratic Dictatorship redefined the relationship between "the people" and "the enemy," as well as between "democracy" and "dictatorship (autocracy)." This redefinition found confirmation in the *Common Program of the Chinese People's Political Consultative Conference* until the "May Fourth Constitution (五四宪法 *Wusi Xianfa*)," when People's Democratic Dictatorship was replaced by the dictatorship of the proletariat.[44]

[41] The "Three-Three System" embodies the unified political strategy of the CCP during the Anti-Japanese War era. According to this policy, the distribution of personnel in the anti-Japanese democratic regime is broadly categorized into three equal segments: around one-third comprises Communist Party members, another one-third consists of left-wing progressive individuals, and the remaining one-third is composed of centrist and other elements. See *Deng Xiaoping Wenxuan [Selected Works of Deng Xiaoping]*, Vol. 1. Renmin Chubanshe, People's Publishing House, 1994. p. 349.

[42] Zhang et al. (2002, p. 220).

[43] For more definition of "people's democratic dictatorship").

[44] Mao Zedong's conceptualization of the "people's democratic dictatorship" sought to transcend Lenin's notion of "dictatorship" as a manifestation of class privilege. Rather than viewing the concept through the lens of class struggle, Mao positioned the "Chinese people" as a cohesive entity, constituting the collective subject of revolution. However, during the 1950s, Mao Zedong, alongside some other top leaders like Liu Shaoqi, concurrently employed both terms until the official reinstatement of "people's democratic dictatorship" in the preamble of the Constitution in 1982. Relevant sources, such as *Liu Shaoqi Wenxuan [Selected Works of Liu Shaoqi]*, Vol. 2. Renmin Chubanshe, People's Publishing House, 1985. p. 243; *Pengzhen Wenxuan [Selected Works of Peng*

The late 1950s and the political movements of the 1960s–1970s narrowly interpreted the "people's sovereignty" and "People's Democratic Dictatorship" as the "class struggle" and "direct (mass) democracy," causing a significant setback in Chinese democratic politics. This chaotic situation persisted until the late 1970s when the Reform and Opening Up policies recorrected the course, allowing China to re-establish connections with the outside world, and Chinese democracy began to rejuvenate. In today's era of expanding historical materials, the domestic academic community is replete with studies on the Chinese democracy. These diverse analyses, although with distinct emphases, overlap in various aspects, involving the sociology, political science, history, economics, philosophy, law, and other multidisciplinary fields. Their understandings of democracy are always linked to ideology, consciousness, values, culture, tradition, concepts, practices, and institutional design.

Studies include, but are not limited to, works such as Xiong Yuezhi's (熊月之) *A History of Modern Chinese Democratic Thought* and Chen Jue Xuan's (陈觉玄 Zhong Fan 钟凡) *A History of the Development of Chinese Democratic Thought*, which focus on the democratic thoughts of the historical figures and present arguments through a relay of their thoughts. Zhang Yufa's (张玉法) *A History of Modern Chinese Democratic Political Development* and Geng Yunzhi's (耿云志) *Western Democracy in Modern China* primarily emphasize the changes in democratic institutions and constitutional movements. Xu Zongmian's (徐宗勉) *The Pursuit of Democracy in Modern China* discusses Western-inspired democracy spreading to China from the lens of changing times. Jin Guantao (金观涛) and Liu Qingfeng's (刘青峰) *Research on the History of Ideas: The Formation of Key Political Terms in Modern China* and Xu Jilin's (许纪霖) edited work *Core Concepts of Modern Chinese Thought* specifically interpret the evolution of Chinese democracy through the transformation of political thoughts and terms in modern China. Li Tieying's (李铁映) *On Democracy* covers a wide range, from ancient Chinese people-oriented thinking to Marxist democratic theory, presenting a chronological narrative of the exploration of democratic theory and practice by the CCP after its founding. Liu Jie (刘杰) and others' *Chinese-style Democracy* unfolds a

Zhen]. Renmin Chubanshe, People's Publishing House, 1991. p. 440; *Deng Xiaoping Nianpu [Chronology of Deng Xiaoping]*, Vol. 2. Ed. Central Literature Research Office, Central Literature Publishing House, 2004. p. 1363.

narrative on Chinese democracy in terms of ideology, history, system, and institution in a structural manner. Yang Guangbin (杨光斌) and others' *Chinese-style Democracy: Trajectory and Trends (1978–2020)* analyzes the change of China's democratic discourse and practice from the perspective of realistic politics after the Reform and Opening Up.

Western Views on China: Biprism of Chinese Democracy

Western studies on China have historically unfolded within a dual narrative framework of time and paradigm. During the early 1950s, amid the Cold War, China, owing to its close association with the Soviet Union, was commonly categorized as a Stalinist-type totalitarian regime (MacFarquhar, 1958; Schwartz, 1960). Ideological clash and confrontation constituted the principal challenge in distinguishing between democratic and non-democratic regimes during this period, aligning with the conventional concept of "oriental despotism" (Wittfogel, 1969) prevalent in Western studies on China. In the post-World War II era, Oriental (Asian) studies in the West that progressively extended beyond language, arts, history, and philosophy to encompass political, economic, and legal dimensions. Hindered by the absence of diplomatic ties with most Western countries and China's self-imposed isolation, some Western authors, predominantly from Europe and America, frequently sought insights into Chinese political dynamics and development through alternative channels such as Taiwan, Japan, Hong Kong, and Macau. Contrary to emerging as an autonomous discipline, China studies in the West existed more as a subsidiary of the Asian (geopolitical) studies, closely intertwined with Soviet studies.

In the first decade following the establishment of the People's Republic of China, Western research on "Chinese democracy" exhibited three fundamental characteristics within this global context. Firstly, the prevailing paradigm was that of "totalitarianism." Scholars like Ebenstein (1958) drew comparisons between the features of early totalitarianism in Germany, Japan, Russia, and China. Cassinelli (1960) analyzed the correlation between the ideology and propaganda of early totalitarian states. Treadgold (1957) and Johnson (1965) delved into reflections on the limitations of the Western paradigm in studying Chinese totalitarianism and its affiliation with the Soviet Union. Secondly, there occurred a paradigmatic transformation in China studies. Skinner and Winckler's (1969) "compliance cycles" theory elucidated the extent and effectiveness of Communist Party rule and mobilization. In the realm of ideological studies, Schwartz (1949) demonstrated, through an analysis of the global socialist movement, how the Marxist-Leninist Chinese regime interacted among the Party, state, and society. Schram (1969) additionally conducted a comparative analysis examining the distinctions and ideological connotations inherent in Maoism and Marxist-Leninism, with the aim of identifying indigenized pathways within Chinese political discourse.

Lastly, specific political and policy research on the early days of the People's Republic of China encompassed studies on the bureaucratic system. Barnett (1957) and Schurmann (1959) provided a systematic analysis of the organizational structure of Chinese communism based on the "mass line," exploring how the Communist Party mobilized society and conducting a detailed analysis of government operations. Elite system studies, with a particular focus on the analysis of prominent figures, included Schram's (1967) reexamination of Mao Zedong's life, thought, ideology, and military strategies. Early sinologists featured Schurmann, Schwartz, Skinner, Winckler, Barnett, and Schram.

In the 1960s, the prevalent conflicts in the Western Europe and the United States, particularly the Vietnam War, along with various glaring social chaos, spurred a significant contingent of students to ponder and scrutinize the entrenched Western liberal democracy (Shang, 2008). Instead, they gravitated towards embracing Mao's Thought and its "mass democracy." Against this background, second-generation Western experts in Chinese studies initiated more intricate case studies on the Cultural Revolution, which commenced in the 1960s. Scholars like Blecher and Thompson (1976), White (1993), and Béja (1987) conducted studies, concentrating on the informal political behaviors of both the elites and the masses. This transformation from the overarching narrative of the initial generation of Chinese political studies, which centered on subjects such as the CCP and its regime, to more concrete narratives like the intra-party struggle (Nathan, 1973), political mobilization, and movements (Townsend, 1967; Vogel, 1969), enriched the agenda of Western studies on Chinese politics. From the 1950s to the mid-1980s, influenced by Western political science paradigms such as "behaviorism" and "rational choice," Western studies on China defaulted to and adopted this paradigmatic turn, especially in analyzing Chinese politics and institutional development.

The period from the conclusion of the Cultural Revolution to the late 1970s marked a pivotal juncture for the third generation of Western scholars observing China. Studies conducted by Tsou (1983), Walder (1981), Manion (1985), among others, in the late 1970s indicated that the political changes had led some Western China experts to believe the "potential" for China to undergo a democratic transition positively, based on economic development (Nathan, 1986). This perception was particularly pronounced when Francis Fukuyama asserted in 1979, through his work *The End of History*, that liberal democracy would be the culmination of human history. Western scholars and even some Chinese liberals tended to endorse the "democratic transition theory." Defiance on democratic values emerged, compelling both the Western and Chinese authors to pragmatically reassess Chinese democracy and its transition. The relatively permissive sphere for Sino-Western academic exchange, fostered by the Reform and Opening Up, naturally facilitated this scholarly shift.

The late 1970s to the early 1990s witnessed diverse aspects of Chinese political research, including: (1) more comprehensive studies on the bureaucratic system; (2) research on elite politics and policy formulation; (3) studies on interest groups and political participation; (4) research on state-society relations; (5) studies on central-local relationships; and (6) research on economic reform and policy changes (recited, Xu, 2013). The research paradigms of the 1980s were principally reshaped by the New Institutionalism, placing significant emphasis on the examination of both formal institutions and the influence of the informal behaviors and organizations on the individual political conduct. Scholars, notably Theda Skocpol, reintegrated the state into politics and political science, catalyzing the emergence of the Party-State-Society paradigm (Skocpol, 1979, see also Womack, 1987; Leng, 1977, 1993; Unger, 1989). Third-generation China experts amalgamated institutionalism with state theory, employing a "dialectical approach" (Harding, 1994) to re-scrutinize the intricate relations and interactions among the Party, State, Society, and individuals, and how the latter is molded by the former.

Simultaneously, there was a transformation in the very research paradigm from the pre-reform "revolutionary paradigm" to the "reformationary paradigm" in the 1980s, encompassing macro and micro lens of democratic political reforms. This era witnessed investigations into democratic initiatives during Deng Xiaoping's reforms, exemplified by Goldman's examination (1994), and Burns' (1989) exploration of governance reforms in the decade following the implementation of the open-door policy (Goldman, 1994). The focus also encompassed character-based analyses of the relationship between the CCP and Chinese democracy, delving into the democratic ideologies and reforms of figures like Deng Xiaoping, Hu Yaobang, and Zhao Ziyang (Sullivan, 1988; Goldman, 1995; Nathan, 2008). In summary, the evolution of research during this historical period, as succinctly encapsulated by Tsou (1994), involves a transformation from emphasizing macro-historical aspects to incorporating micro-level actions in scholarly inquiries.

In the 1990s, Western perceptions of China subtly shifted due to the significant improvements in China's economic condition since the Reform and Opening Up, particularly after Deng Xiaoping's Southern Tour in 1992. Huntington's (1993) prediction of the third wave of democratization faced more "recession" than a "transition" in the Third World. Contrary to Western expectations, the collapse of the CCP or the Chinese regime did not materialize. Nathan's (2003) analysis of the "resilience of authoritarianism" partly elucidated the relationship between the authoritarian system, economic development, social stability, and the national capabilities, suggesting that this resilience might pave the way for a smooth democratic transition in China.

During this period, China was depicted as a "threat," with widespread discussions that centering on collapse and threat theories of the CCP. In summary, Western studies on China in the 1990s primarily revolved around the theme of "political/democratic transition." Noteworthy research included Guo (1995) and Dittmer's (2001a, 2001b) analysis of China's shift from totalitarianism to authoritarianism, Baum's (1996) examination of Deng Xiaoping's politics in the post-Mao era, Shirk's (1993) institutionalist analysis of China's economic policies and reforms, and Sun's (1995) studies of changing societal ideologies in China from 1976 to the post-reform era. Particularly pivotal were studies on the prospects of Chinese democracy after the Reform and Opening Up by Andrew J. Nathan, Bruce Gilley, Cheng Li, and Owen Harries.

The research at hand frequently involves comparative analyses of democracy and some specific institutions. For instance, Winkler's (1999) examination delves into the departmental, hierarchical, and mechanistic aspects of the CCP's transition towards a Leninist model. Guo (2017) conducts a comparative study on China's democratic transition in relation to the Eastern European and South American models. Meanwhile, Dickson's (1998) work involves a comparative analysis between the CCP and Taiwan's Leninist party transformation. Simultaneously, in-depth research during this historical stage that focuses on concepts within democracy, citizenship (Solinger, 1999; Goldman, 2005), civil society (White et al.,

1996; Tang, 2005), accountability (Tsai, 2007), and grassroots elections (O'Brien, 2001), and the intricate relationship between the market, economy, and democracy (Yang, 2004; Pekkanen & Tsai, 2011). Traditional Chinese political studies in this stage, encompassing party policies (Hamrin & Zhao, 1995), elite politics (Brødsgaard & Zheng, 2006; Walder, 2006), political culture (Dirlik, 1996; Ogden, 2007), and so on, also constitute significant areas of concentration in Western China studies. In the late twentieth century and early 90s, Western study on Chinese politics (democracy) explored a myriad of topics, methodologies, and dimensions.

As the twenty-first century unfolded, China encountered changes in both the international and domestic environments. Frequent Western terrorism incidents, notably the 9.11 attacks, prompted political scientists to reassess liberal democracy (Fukuyama, 1995; Axtmann, 1996; Brown, 2003; Bell, 2009). Internally, following the "China Threat/Collapse Theory" of the 1990s, Western hostility, sanction, the Taiwan Strait crisis, and the rapid development of the market economy in post-Reform and Opening Up, debates emerged on the relation between democracy and economic order. Western China studies shifted their focus towards analyzing Chinese government governance (Shambaugh, 2016), the resilience and continuum of the authoritarianism in China (Nathan, 2001, 2009; Gilley, 2003; Gilley & Nathan, 2003), China's rise and economic development (Lin & Liu, 2006), and the study of the (early) "Chinese model" (Chan et al., 2008; Jacques, 2009; Zhao, 2010; Huang & Wang, 2011).

In the first decade of the twenty-first century, Western research on Chinese politics primarily revolved around the leadership collectives of Jiang Zemin and Hu Jintao that spanning political, military, economic, and diplomatic domains. Lam's (2007) series of works systematically expounded on the political reforms in Hu-Wen era China (Gilley, 1998; Tien & Chu, 2000), highlighting differences with the third-generation leadership collective of the CCP in military, political, economic, and diplomatic spheres. During this period, the national and diplomatic strategies of "keeping a low profile (韬光养晦 *Taoguang Yanghui*)" led to the gradual formation of a democratic model featured by "performance" in China (Berghuis, 2006). "Performance" not only included traditional analyses of economy (Sachs & Woo, 2001) but also emphasized the importance of "good governance" (Li & Naughton, 2007; Hasmath & Hsu, 2008), specifically encompassing economic reforms and policies benefiting the people in the Hu-Wen era (Naughton, 2003, 2004; Heilmann & Shih, 2013). The "performance" also became a major resource of legitimacy for the CCP (Zhu, 2011). However, whether it be the rapid economic development, significant improvement in livelihoods, or the expansion of political participation channels due to the rapid development of technology (network technology), the outdated political arrangements and ideologies that can no longer provide sufficient guarantees for individuals' rights. The transformation faced by China in the new century cannot be simply explained by post-communist theories, classic authoritarianism, developmental state theories, or general theories of political regime transition and democratization (Chen, 2005, see also Perry, 2007).[45]

In contrast to the extensive discourse surrounding China's democratic transition in the early years of this century, contemporary Western studies on China, following the 18th Party Congress, have predominantly embraced China's characterization as an "authoritarian" state. These studies have redirected their focus towards scrutinizing the intricacies of politics under authoritarianism (Wright, 2010). This encompasses the exploration of the interplay between capitalism and authoritarianism (Tsai, 2018), the dynamics that involving the middle class and authoritarianism (Chen, 2013), the phenomenon of authoritarian deliberation (Fishkin, et al., 2010; He & Thøgersen, 2010; He and Warren, 2011; Teets, 2013; Rory, 2017),[46] and the conduct of grassroots elections (O'brien & Han, 2014). There is a specific emphasis on the reconsolidation of central authority, particularly during the era of Xi Jinping (Fewsmith, 2013; Friedman, 2016; He, 2016). Throughout this epoch, analyses and inquiries into Chinese democracy frequently incorporate a broader contextual framework, involving themes such as the "Chinese Dream" (Gow, 2017), the "Belt and Road Initiative," (Callahan, 2016; Miller, 2019) and "Chinese-style modernization" (Landsberger, 2020).

[45] Perry persistently characterizes the political landscape of China post the turn of the new century as "revolutionary authoritarianism."

[46] The concept of authoritarian deliberation emphasis on deliberative influence, and, in certain instances, deliberative empowerment, coexisting with central authoritarianism. It constitutes a prominent strand within the realm of Sino-Western deliberative democracy studies.

Western research on China furnishes a valuable comparative vantage point for delving into the intricacies of Chinese democracy, notwithstanding its entanglement with divergent viewpoints, ideologies, political cultures, and conflicts. Notably, Western standpoint often categorizes China as an authoritarian or even totalitarian state since its inception, positioning liberal democracy as the *end* of history. Nevertheless, the West, as a trailblazer in democratic theory and practice, retains the capacity to impart rich experiences and lessons to a rather plethora of developing countries. In summation, a thorough comprehension of the progression and metamorphosis of democracy in China, along with critical considerations like disparities between Western and Chinese democratic paradigms, and the global positioning of Chinese democracy, could only be re-attained through a nuanced exploration encompassing historical (both past and present) and comparative (Sino-Western) perspectives.

References

"Zhiyang Qiyi [In the Discourse on Western-Style Weaponry]", in *Wuxu Bianfa [Reform Movement of 1898]*, Shanghai Renmin Chubanshe, Shanghai People's Press, 1957. pp. 29–30.

Arendt, Hannah. "What Was Authority?" *NOMOS: Am. Soc'y Pol. Legal Phil* 1 (1958): 81.

Aristotle. *The Politics*, translated by H. Rackham. Harvard University Press, 1932.

Axtmann, Roland. *Liberal Democracy into the Twenty-First Century: Globalization, Integration and the Nation-State.* Manchester University Press, 1996.

Baechler, Jean. "Démocraties, Calmann-Lévy." *Précis de la démocratie* (1985): 337.

Barnett, A. Doak. "Political Power in Communist China." *Journal of International Affairs* (1957): 102–110.

Barnett, A. Doak. *Cadres, Bureaucracy, and Political Power in Communist China.* Columbia University Press, 1968.

Baum, Richard. *Burying Mao: Chinese Politics in the Age of Deng Xiaoping.* Princeton University Press, 1996.

Béja, Jean-Philippe. "Chine: Après les nouvelles Cent fleurs un nouveau mouvement antidroitier?" *Esprit (1940–)* 126.5 (1987): 40–54.

Bell, Daniel A. "War, Peace, and China's Soft Power: A Confucian Approach." *Diogenes* 56.1 (2009): 26–40.

Bell, Daniel A. *The China Model.* Princeton University Press, 2016.

Bendix, Reinhard. *Kings or People: Power and the Mandate to Rule.* University of California Press, 1978.

Berghuis, Thomas J. *Performance Art in China*. Timezone 8 Limited, 2006.
Blecher, T. E., and Mildred J. Thompson. "Comparison of uridine uptake at 24 hours with thymidine uptake at 72 hours in phytohaemagglutinin-stimulated cultures of pregnant and other subjects." *Journal of Clinical Pathology* 29.8 (1976): 727–731.
Blecher, Marc J., and Gordon White. *Micropolitics in Contemporary China: A Technical Unit During and After the Cultural Revolution*. Macmillan, 1980.
Brødsgaard, Kjeld Erik, and Zheng Yongnian, eds. *The Chinese Communist Party in Reform*. Routledge, 2006.
Brown, Wendy. "Neo-Liberalism and the End of Liberal Democracy." *Theory & Event* 7.1 (2003).
Burns, John P. "China's Governance: Political Reform in a Turbulent Environment." *The China Quarterly* 119 (1989): 481–518.
Callahan, William A. "China's 'Asia Dream' the Belt Road Initiative and the New Regional Order." *Asian Journal of Comparative Politics* 1.3 (2016): 226–243.
Carr, Edward Hallett. "The Soviet Impact on the Western World." *Science and Society* 11.3 (1947).
Cassinelli, C. W. "Totalitarianism, Ideology, and Propaganda." *The Journal of Politics* 22.1 (1960): 68–95.
Chan, Lai-Ha, Pak K. Lee, and Gerald Chan. "Rethinking Global Governance: A China Model in the Making?" *Contemporary Politics* 14.1 (2008): 3–19.
Chen Duxiu Wenji [Selected Writings of Chen Duxiu]. Renmin Chubanshe, People's Publishing House, 1986.
Chen, Cheng. "Institutional Legitimacy of an Authoritarian State: China in the Mirror of Eastern Europe." *Problems of Post-Communism* 52.4 (2005): 3–13.
Chen, Jie. *A Middle Class without Democracy: Economic Growth and the Prospects for Democratization in China*. Oxford University Press, 2013.
Collier, David, and James E. Mahon. Conceptual "Stretching" Revisited: Adapting Categories in Comparative Analysis. *American Political Science Review*, 87.4 (1993): 845–855.
De Grazia, Sebastian. "What Authority Is Not." *American Political Science Review* 53.2 (1959): 321–331.
Deng Xiaoping Nianpu [Chronology of Deng Xiaoping], Vol. 2. Ed. Central Literature Research Office, Central Literature Publishing House, 2004.
Deng Xiaoping Wenxuan [Selected Works of Deng Xiaoping], Vol. 1. Renmin Chubanshe, People's Publishing House, 1994.
Dickson, Bruce J. "China's Democratization and the Taiwan Experience." *Asian Survey* 38.4 (1998): 349–364.
Dirlik, Arif. "Chinese History and the Question of Orientalism." *History and Theory* (1996): 96–118.
Dittmer, Lowell. "The Changing Shape of Elite Power Politics." *The China Journal* 45 (2001a): 53–67.

Dittmer, Lowell. “The Sino-Russian Strategic Partnership.” *Journal of Contemporary China* 10.28 (2001b): 399–413.
Durkheim, Emile. “The Division of Labor in Society.” In *Social Stratification*. Routledge, 2018. pp. 217–222.
Ebenstein, William. “The Study of Totalitarianism.” *World Politics* 10.2 (1958): 274–288.
Eisenstadt, Shmuel N. *The Political Systems of Empires*. Routledge, 2017.
Fangjun, Cao. “Modernization Theory and China’s Road to Modernization.” *Chinese Studies in History* 43.1 (2009): 7–16.
Fewsmith, Joseph. *Elite Politics in Contemporary China*. Routledge, 2015.
Fewsmith, Joseph. *The Logic and Limits of Political Reform in China*. Cambridge University Press, 2013.
Finley, Moses I. *Democracy Ancient and Modern*. Rutgers University Press, 1985.
Fishkin, James S., et al. “Deliberative Democracy in an Unlikely Place: Deliberative Polling in China.” *British Journal of Political Science* 40.2 (2010): 435–448.
Friedman, Edward. *National Identity and Democratic Prospects in Socialist China*. Routledge, 2016.
Friedrich, Carl J. “The Concept of Community in the History of Political and Legal Philosophy.” *NOMOS: Am. Soc’y Pol. Legal Phil.* 2 (1959): 3.
Friedrich, Carl J., ed. *Totalitarianism: proceedings of a conference held at the American Academy of Arts and Sciences, March 1953*. Harvard University Press, 1954.
Fukuyama, Francis. “A New Soviet Strategy.” *Commentary* 68.4 (1979): 52.
Fukuyama, Francis. “Reflections on The End of History, Five Years Later.” *History and Theory* (1995): 27–43.
Fukuyama, Francis. “The end of history?.” *Conflict after the Cold War*. Routledge, 2015.
G., H. & Donald W. Treadgold. Soviet and Chinese Communism: Similarities and Differences. *Journal of the American Oriental Society* 88.2 (1968): 368.
Gierke, Otto Friedrich. *Political Theories of the Middle Age*. History of Economic Thought Books, 1900.
Gilley, Bruce, and Andrew Nathan. *China’s New Rulers: The Secret Files*. New York Review of Books, 2003.
Gilley, Bruce. “The Limits of Authoritarian Resilience.” *Journal of Democracy* 14 (2003): 18.
Gilley, Bruce. *China’s Democratic Future: How It Will Happen and Where It Will Lead*. Columbia University Press, 2004.
Gilley, Bruce. *Tiger on the Brink: Jiang Zemin and China’s New Elite*. University of California Press, 1998.
Goldman, Merle. “Is Democracy Possible? The May 15 Petition.” *Current History* 94.593 (1995): 259.

Goldman, Merle. *From Comrade to Citizen: The Struggle for Political Rights in China*. Harvard University Press, 2005.
Goldman, Merle. *Sowing the Seeds of Democracy in China: Political Reform in the Deng Xiaoping Era*. Harvard University Press, 1994.
Gow, Michael. "The Core Socialist Values of the Chinese Dream: Towards a Chinese Integral State." *Critical Asian Studies* 49.1 (2017): 92–116.
Guan Huailun. "Shilun Liening Jizhongzhi de Lilun Tixi he Zhidu Jiegou-Duiyu Buershiweike Banben de Minzhu Jizhongzhi Yuanshengtai de Lilun Kaocha [An Attempted Analysis of Lenin's Theoretical System and Institutional Structure of Centralism—An Theoretical Examination of the Bolshevik Version of Original Democratic Centralism]." *Makesi Zhuyi Yanjiu, Marxist Studies* 4 (2005): 46–52
Guo Songtao Riji [The Diary of Guo Songtao]. Yuelu Chubanshe, Yuelu Publishing House, 1983.
Guo, Sujian. "Totalitarianism: An Outdated Paradigm for Post-Mao China?" *Journal of Northeast Asian Studies* 14.2 (1995): 62–90.
Guo, Sujian. *The Political Economy of Asian Transition from Communism*. Routledge, 2017.
Hamrin, Carol Lee, and Suisheng Zhao, eds. *Decision-Making in Deng's China: Perspectives from Insiders*. ME Sharpe, 1995.
Harding, Harry. "The Comtemporary Study of Chinese Politics: An Introduction." *The China Quarterly* 139 (1994): 699–703.
Hasmath, Reza, and Jennifer Hsu. "NGOs in China: Issues of Good Governance and Accountability." *Asia Pacific Journal of Public Administration* 30.1 (2008): 29–39.
He, Baogang, and Mark E. Warren. "Authoritarian Deliberation: The Deliberative Turn in Chinese Political Development." *Perspectives on Politics* 9.2 (2011): 269–289.
He, Baogang, and Stig Thøgersen. "Giving the People a Voice? Experiments with Consultative Authoritarian Institutions in China." *Journal of Contemporary China* 19.66 (2010): 675–692.
He, Baogang. *The Democratic Implications of Civil Society in China*. Springer, 2016.
Heilmann, Sebastian, and Lea Shih. "The Rise of Industrial Policy in China, 1978–2012." *Harvard-Yenching Institute Working Paper Series* 17.7 (2013): 1–24.
Herz, John H. "Political Realism Revisited." *International Studies Quarterly* 25.2 (1981): 182–197.
Herz, John H. *Political Realism and Political Idealism: A Study in Theories and Realities*. Intranet, 1919.
Huang, Yiping, and Bijun Wang. "Chinese Outward Direct Investment: Is there a China Model?." *China & World Economy* 19.4 (2011): 1–21.

Huntington, Samuel P. *The Third Wave: Democratization in the Late Twentieth Century*, Vol. 4. University of Oklahoma Press, 1993.

Jacques, Martin. *When China Rules the World: The End of the Western World and the Birth of a New Global Order*. Penguin, 2009.

Jin Guantao and Liu Qingfeng. *Xingsheng yu Weiji: Lun Zhongguo Shehui de Chaowending Jiegou [Prosperity and Crisis—On the Hyper-Stable Structure of Chinese Society]*. Falv Chubanshe, Law Press 2010.

Johnson, Chalmers. "The Role of Social Science in China Scholarship." *World Politics* 17.2 (1965): 256–271.

Kautsky, Karl, and Henry James Stenning. *The dictatorship of the proletariat*. Ann Arbor: University of Michigan Press, 1964.

Lam, Willy Wo-Lap. "China's Petroleum Diplomacy: Hu Jintao's Biggest Challenge in Foreign and Security Policy." In *China Turns to Multilateralism*. Routledge, 2007. pp. 222–240.

Landsberger, Stefan. *Chinese Propaganda Posters: From Revolution to Modernization*. Routledge, 2020.

Leng, Shao-chuan, and Cheng-yi Lin. "Political Change on Taiwan: Transition to Democracy?." *The China Quarterly* 136 (1993): 805–839.

Leng, Shao Chuan, ed. *Chiang Ching-kuo's Leadership in the Development of the Republic of China on Taiwan*. Vol. 3. University Press of America, 1993.

Leng, Shao-Chuan. "The Role of Law in the People's Republic of China as Reflecting Mao Tse-Tung's Influence." *J. Crim. L. & Criminology* 68 (1977): 356.

Li Dazhao Wenji [Collected Works of Li Dazhao]. Renmin Chubanshe, People's Publishing House, 1984.

Li Weihan. *Huiyi yu Yanjiu [Memories and Research]*, Vol. 2. Zhonggong Dangshi Ziliao Chubanshe, Chinese Communist Party History Information Press, 1986.

Li, Cheng. "Intra-Party Democracy in China: Should We Take It Seriously?" *China Leadership Monitor* 30.3 (2009): 1–14.

Li, Larry, and Tony Naughton. "Going Public with Good Governance: Evidence from China." *Corporate Governance: An International Review* 15.6 (2007): 1190–1202.

Lin, Justin Yifu, and Peilin Liu. *Development Strategies and Regional Income Disparities in China. No. 2006/129*. WIDER Research Paper, 2006.

Liu Shaoqi Wenxuan [Selected Works of Liu Shaoqi], Vol. 2. Renmin Chubanshe, People's Publishing House, 1985.

Locke, John. *Two Treatises of Government: With a Supplement, Patriarcha, by Robert Filmer*. No. 2. Simon and Schuster, 1947.

MacFarquhar, Roderick. "The Case of Communist China." *Probs. Communism* 7 (1958): 1.

MacIver, Robert M. *Web of Government*. Macmillan Co, 1965.

Manion, Melanie. "The Cadre Management System, Post-Mao: The Appointment, Promotion, Transfer and Removal of Party and State Leaders." *The China Quarterly* 102 (1985): 203–233.

Mannheim, Karl. *Ideology and Utopia*. Routledge, 2013.

Mao Zedong. Guanyu Chongyin "Zuopai Youzhi Bing" Di Erzhang Qianyan [On Reprinting the Preface to Chapter 2 of "Left-wing Infantile Disease"]. In *Zhonggong Zhongyang Wenxian Xuanji, Selected Documents of the Central Committee of the Communist Party of China*, Vol. 14, ed. Central Archives. Zhonggong Zhongyang Dangxiao Chubanshe, Party School Press of the Central Committee of the Communist Party of China, 1989–1992.

Mao Zedong. Lun Renmin Minzhu Zhuanzheng [On the People's Democratic Dictatorship]. In *Mao Zedong Wenji, Vol. 4, Collected Works of Mao Zedong*. Renmin Chubanshe, People's Publishing House, 1991.

Maxwell, Neville, ed. *China's Road to Development*. Elsevier, 2014.

McKenna, Michael C., and Richard D. Robinson. "Content Literacy: A Definition and Implications." *Journal of Reading* 34.3 (1990): 184–186.

Miller, Tom. *China's Asian Dream: Empire Building along the New Silk Road*. Bloomsbury Publishing, 2019.

Nathan, Andrew J. "A Factionalism Model for CCP Politics." *The China Quarterly* 53 (1973): 34–66.

Nathan, Andrew J. "Authoritarian Resilience: Institutionalization and the Transition to China's Fourth Generation." *US-China Relations in the 21st Century* (2003): 13–25.

Nathan, Andrew J. "China since Tiananmen: Authoritarian Impermanence." *Journal of Democracy* 20.3 (2009): 37–40.

Nathan, Andrew J. "The Tiananmen Papers." Foreign Affairs (2001): 2–48.

Nathan, Andrew J. *Chinese Democracy*. University of California Press, 1986.

Nathan, Andrew J. "Zhao Ziyang's Vision of Chinese Democracy." *China Perspectives* 2008/3 (2008): 136–142.

Naughton, Barry J. *The Chinese Economy: Transitions and Growth. MIT Press, 2006; Gong, Gang. Contemporary Chinese Economy.* Routledge, 2012.

Naughton, Barry J. "Economic Policy After the 16th Party Congress." *China Leadership Monitor* 5 (2003): 30–42.

Naughton, Barry. "Hunkering Down: The Wen Jiabao Administration and Macroeconomic Recontrol." *China Leadership Monitor* 11 (2004): 1–11.

O'Brien, Kevin J. "Villagers, Elections, and Citizenship in Contemporary China." *Modern China* 27.4 (2001): 407–435.

O'Brien, Kevin J., and Laura M. Luehrmann. "Institutionalizing Chinese Legislatures: Trade-Offs between Autonomy and Capacity." *Legislative Studies Quarterly* (1998): 91–108.

O'brien, Kevin J., and Rongbin Han. "Path to Democracy? Assessing Village Elections in China." In *Grassroots Elections in China*. Routledge, 2014. pp. 1–20.

Ogden, Suzanne. "Don't Judge a Country by Its Cover: Governance in China." In *China in the Twenty-First Century: Challenges and Opportunities*. New York: Palgrave Macmillan US, 2007. pp. 49–85.

Orwell, George. *Politics and the English Language*, Vol. 2. Renard Press Ltd, 2021.

Pekkanen, Saadia M., and Kellee S. Tsai. "The Politics of Ambiguity in Asia's Sovereign Wealth Funds." *Business and Politics* 13.2 (2011): 1–44.

Pengzhen Wenxuan [Selected Works of Peng Zhen]. Renmin Chubanshe, People's Publishing House, 1991.

Perry, Elizabeth J. "State and Society in Contemporary China." *World Politics* 41.4 (1989): 579–591.

Perry, Elizabeth J. "Studying Chinese Politics: Farewell to Revolution?" *The China Journal* 57 (2007): 1–22.

Pihan [Disapproving of Han]. In *Yan Fu Ji [The Collected Works of Yan Fu]*. Xhonghua Shuju, Zhonghua Book Company, 1986.

Rawski, Thomas G. "Implications of China' Reform Experience." *The China Quarterly* 144 (1995): 1150–1173.

Rousseau, Jean-Jacques. *Rousseau: The Social Contract and Other Later Political Writings*. Cambridge University Press, 2018.

Sachs, Jeffrey D., and Wing Thye Woo. "Understanding China's Economic Performance." *The Journal of Policy Reform* 4.1 (2001): 1–50.

Sartori, Giovanni. Concept Misformation in Comparative Politics. *American Political Science Review*, 64.4 (1970): 1033–1053.

Sartori, Giovanni. *The Theory of Democracy Revisited: Part One: The Contemporary Debate*, Vol. 1. CQ Press. 1987.

Sartori, Giovanni. "Videopolitica." *Italian Political Science Review/Rivista Italiana di Scienza Politica*, 19.2 (1989): 185–198.

Sartori, Giovanni. *The Theory of Democracy Revisited. Democracy: A Reader*. Columbia University Press, (2016): 192–196.

Schmitter, Philippe C., and Terry Lynn Karl. "What Democracy Is... and Is Not." *Journal of Democracy* 2.3 (1991): 75–88.

Schmitter, Philippe C. "Change in regime type and progress in international relations." *Progress in postwar international relations* (1991): 89–127.

Schram, Stuart R. "The Party in Chinese Communist Ideology." *The China Quarterly* 38 (1969): 1–26.

Schram, Stuart R., and Richard Matz. *Mao Tse-tung*. Baltimore: Penguin Books, 1967.

Schurmann, Herbert Franz. "Organization and Response in Communist China." *The Annals of the American Academy of Political and Social Science* 321.1 (1959): 51–61.
Schwartz, Benjamin. "Marx and Lenin in China." *Far Eastern Survey* 18.15 (1949): 174–178.
Schwartz, Benjamin. "Totalitarian Consolidation and the Chinese Model." *The China Quarterly* 1 (1960): 18–21.
Shambaugh, David L. *American Studies of Contemporary China*. Routledge, 2016.
Shang, Qingfei. *Guowai Mao Zedong Yanjiu [Research on Mao Zedong Studies Abroad]*. Jiangsu Renmin Chubanshe, Jiangsu People's Publishing House, 2008.
Shi, Tianjian. "The Democratic Movement in China in 1989: Dynamics and Failure." *Asian Survey* 30.12 (1990): 1186–1205.
Shirk, Susan L. *The Political Logic of Economic Reform in China*, Vol. 24. University of California Press, 1993.
Skinner, G. William, and Edwin A. Winckler. "Compliance Succession in Rural Communist China: A Cyclical Theory." *A Sociological Reader on Complex Organizations* (1969): 410–348.
Skocpol, Theda. *States and Social Revolutions: A Comparative Analysis of France, Russia and China*. Cambridge University Press, 1979.
Smith, Adam. *The Wealth of Nations [1776]*, Vol. 11937. na, 1937.
Solinger, Dorothy J. "Citizenship Issues in China's Internal Migration: Comparisons with Germany and Japan." *Political Science Quarterly* 114.3 (1999): 455–478.
Sullivan, Lawrence R. "Assault on the Reforms: Conservative Criticism of Political and Economic Liberalization in China, 1985–86." *The China Quarterly* 114 (1988): 198–222.
Sun, Yan. *The Chinese Reassessment of Socialism, 1976–1992*. Princeton University Press, 1995.
Tan Pingshan Wenji [Collected Works of Tan Pingshan]. Renmin Chubanshe, People's Publishing House, 1986.
Tang, Wenfang. *Public Opinion and Political Change in China*. Stanford University Press, 2005.
Teets, Jessica C. "Let Many Civil Societies Bloom: The Rise of Consultative Authoritarianism in China." *The China Quarterly* 213 (2013): 19–38.
Tien, Hung-mao, and Yun-han Chu, eds. *China under Jiang Zemin*. Lynne Rienner Publishers, 2000.
Tonnies, Ferdinand, and Charles Price Loomis. *Community and Society*. Courier Corporation, 2002.
Townsend, James Roger. *Political Participation in Communist China*, Vol. 1. University of California Press, 1967.

Treadgold, Donald W. "The Troubled Conscience of the Foreign Parties." *Probs. Communism* 6 (1957): 3.

Truex, Rory. "Consultative Authoritarianism and Its Limits." *Comparative Political Studies* 50.3 (2017): 329–361.

Tsai, Kellee S. *Capitalism without Democracy: The Private Sector in Contemporary China*. Cornell University Press, 2018.

Tsai, Lily L. *Accountability without Democracy: Solidary Groups and Public Goods Provision in Rural China*. Cambridge University Press, 2007.

Tsai, Shih-Shan Henry. *The Chinese Experience in America*. Indiana University Press, 1986.

Tsou, Tang. *State and Society in Contemporary China*. Cornell University Press, 1983.

Tsou, Tang. *Twentieth Century Chinese Politics: Viewed from the Perspective of Macro History and Micro Actions*. Oxford University Press, 1994.

Unger, Jonathan. "State and Peasant in Post-Revolution China." *The Journal of Peasant Studies* 17.1 (1989): 114–136.

Vogel, Ezra. "Land Reform in Kwangtung 1951–1953: Central Control and Localism." *The China Quarterly* 38 (1969): 27–62.

Walder, Andrew G. "Participative Management and Worker Control in China." *Sociology of Work and Occupations* 8.2 (1981): 224–251.

Walder, Andrew G. "The Party Elite and China's Trajectory of Change." In *The Chinese Communist Party in Reform*. Routledge, 2006. pp. 25–42.

Wang, Huilin. "Wusi Shiqi de Minzhu Sixiang Yanbian [Evolution of Democratic Thought during the May Fourth Period]." In *Wusi Shiqi de Minzhu Sixiang Yanbian, May Fourth Movement and the Construction of Chinese Culture*, Vol 1. Shehui Kexue Wenxian Chubanshe, Social Sciences Literature Press, 1989.

Weber, Max. "Economy and Society." in *Democracy: A Reader*. Columbia University Press, 2016. pp. 247–251.

White, Gordon, Jude A. Howell, and Shang Xiaoyuan, In *Search of Civil Society: Market Reform and Social Change in Contemporary China*, Online edn. Oxford Academic, Oxford, 1996.

Winckler, Edwin A., ed. *Transition from Communism in China: Institutional and Comparative Analyses*. Lynne Rienner Publishers, 1999.

Wittfogel, Karl A. "Results and problems of the study of oriental despotism." *The journal of Asian studies* 28.2 (1969): 357–365.

Womack, Brantly. "The Party and the People: Revolutionary and Postrevolutionary Politics in China and Vietnam." *World Politics* 39.4 (1987): 479–507.

Wright, Teresa. *Accepting Authoritarianism: State-Society Relations in China's Reform Era*. Stanford University Press, 2010.

White, Gordon. "Prospects for civil society in China: A case study of Xiaoshan City." *The Australian Journal of Chinese Affairs* 29 (1993): 63–87.

Xu, Haoran. *Jiedu Zhongguo Minzhu: Xifang Zhongguo Xuejia de Shijiao [Interpreting Chinese Democracy: The Perspective of Western Chinese Scholars]*. Zhongguo Shehui Kexue Chubanshe, China Social Sciences Press, 2013.

Yang, Dali L. *Remaking the Chinese Leviathan: Market Transition and the Politics of Governance in China*. Stanford University Press, 2004.

Yinbingshi Heji [Collected Works of the Yin Bingshi], Vol. 33. Zhonghua Shuju, Zhonghua Book Company, 1989.

Yuanqiang [Yuanqiang]. In *Yan Fu Ji [The Collected Works of Yan Fu]*, Vol. 1. Xhonghua Shuju, Zhonghua Book Company, 1986. pp. 12–46.

Zai Zhongguo Fuomindang Benbu Teshe Zhuyue Banshichu de Yanshuo [On Establishing a Special Office in Guangdong at the Headquarters of the Kuomintang], Vol. 5. In Sun Yat-sen Quanji, The Complete Works of Sun Yat-sen.

Zhang, Xueren et al., eds. *Er'shi Shiji Zhongguo Xianzheng [China's Constitutional Government in the Twentieth Century]*. Wuhan Daxue Chubanshe, Wuhan University Press, 2002.

Zhao, Suisheng. "The China Model: Can It Replace the Western Model of Modernization?." *Journal of Contemporary China* 19.65 (2010): 419–436.

Zhonggong Zhongyang Wenjian Xuanji [Selected Documents of the Central Committee of the Communist Party of China], Vol. 1. Ed. Central State Archives Volume 1, Zhonggong Zhongyang Dangxiao Chubanshe, Party School of the Central Committee of the CPC, 1989.

Zhu, Yuchao. "'Performance Legitimacy' and China's Political Adaptation Strategy." *Journal of Chinese Political Science* 16 (2011): 123–140.

People's Democracy

Among the myriad discussions surrounding Chinese democracy, "people's democracy" stands out as the most crucial. This term, with its direct interpretation of democracy as "the people in charge," not only inherits but also perpetuates the traditional Chinese political culture rooted in "people-oriented" thinking, a philosophy that has endured for millennia. Simultaneously, it progressively aligns with some modern democratic principles, evolving into the central ideology that elucidates contemporary Chinese democratic practices. In the twenty-first era, the CCP has recontextualized people's democracy within the theoretical framework of Marxist *people's democratic centralism*, positioning it as the foundational political value and principle of Chinese democracy. This not only distinguishes it from the Western model of liberal democracy that centered around elections but also serves as the fundamental entry point for comprehending Chinese democracy.

People-Oriented Ideation and the Continuum of Chinese Tradition

The Opium War shattered China's self-contained dynastic cycles that had endured for millennia, thrusting China into an open global competitive system. Nearly all discourses and movements that emerged in modern

R. Li, *Democratizing China's Political Imaginaries*,
https://doi.org/10.1007/978-981-97-3670-6_2

times, challenging the West, such as "reform (改革 *Gaige*)," "revolution (革命 *Geming*)," "new culture (新文化 *Xinwenhua*)," "development (发展 *fazhan*)," and "Chinese essence with Western applications (中体西用 *Zhongti Xiyong*)," vacillate between the adherence to Chinese tradition and incorporation of Western ideas. In essence, despite occasional radical endeavors, such as the New Culture Movement's radical attempts to topple the Kong Family Shop (overthrow Confucianism) or the subsequent efforts to fully reinstate the Confucianism during the Reform and Opening Up era,[1] Chinese tradition and culture have consistently served as an indisputable arsenal for self-defense or response to Western influence. Whether one perceives Chinese tradition as an impediment or a trove of cultural wealth, the core political concept of the dynastic period—people-oriented thinking—has endured and metamorphosed into the primary resource reshaping Chinese democracy amid dynastic changes and modern revolutions.

Modern Chinese democracy traces its roots to "people-oriented" thinking, embodying principles such as "the people are paramount, the ruler is secondary (民贵君轻 *Mingui Junqing*)," "grounded in the people (以民为本 *Yimin Weiben*)," and "attuned to the people, seeing through their eyes (民视民听 *Minshi Minting*)." However, the original conceptualization of "people-oriented" thinking differed. Firstly, its origins can be traced to *Book of Lord Shang: Strategies* (商君书·画策 *Shangjunshu: Huace*), where it is associated with "people-oriented, which is law (民本 法也 *Minben Faye*)." The initial intent was to employ the law to "govern the people (制民 *Zhimin*)," carrying the connotation of regulating the populace rather than placing the people at the foundation of the state. Secondly, the true (re)conceptualization of democracy as an ideology—especially during the New Culture Movement—was imported from translations in Japan. Figures from the New Culture Movement, Chen Duxiu and Li Dazhao, for example, introduced the elucidation of "people-orientedism" by Yoshino (1947) to China. They utilized it both as the Chinese translation of Western democracy and integrated

[1] Especially in modern China, there are many attempts to leverage the rejection of tradition to promote Chinese reform or revolution, while simultaneously claiming intricate connections with tradition to underscore the "legitimacy" and "Chineseness" of the reform or revolution. These efforts are essentially endeavors to respond to and break free from the shackles of Western imperialism on one hand and to escape the constraints of traditional Chinese norms on the other. See Perry (2012) and Metzger (1977).

it with the traditional Chinese people-oriented thought.[2] The expansive nature and tension within the people-oriented concept provide a framework for almost any theory or practice describing Chinese democracy to find inspiration and a home within its ambit.[3]

The examination of the evolution of *Minben* in Chinese history reveals that, prior to the late Qing Dynasty, *Minben*, despite displaying a rich connotation to signify the position and role of the people in relation to the monarch and the state, remained confined within the framework of the Chinese imperial system. On the one hand, for various purposes such as "the stability originates from the foundation of the nation (本固邦宁 *Bengu Bangning*)" and "water can carry a boat, but it can also capsize it (水能载舟亦能覆舟 *Shui Neng Zaizhou yi Neng Fuzhou*)", the monarch regarded the people as the source of royal authority and the fundamental stability of the country. On the other hand, for the needs of maintaining the imperial system and royal authority, the term "min (民 people)" was often considered as a tool to reconsolidate royal power. During the Qin and Han dynasties, Confucianism gradually absorbed *Minben* as the official interpretation of the source of the royal authority, the relationship between the monarch, the empire, and the people in the imperial court's ideology.

[2] Certainly, the analysis that encapsulates pre-Qin political thought and expounds upon it using the terms "民本思想 (minben thought)" or "民本主义 (minben ideology)" in the Chinese language originated with Liang Qichao. See Liang (1896); Chen (1919); Society for Research on the History of Modern Japanese Thought edited. *Jindai Riben Sixiangshi [History of Modern Japanese Thought]*, Vol. 2, translated by Li Min et al., Shangwu Yinshu Guan, The Commercial Press (1991): 162, 168, 169. By the 1940s, "民本 *Minben*" was no longer simply considered a translation of "democracy" in Chinese; instead, it evolved into a conceptual framework specific to China, serving as the counterpart to Western democracy. See Lu (2018).

[3] The theory of people-oriented encompasses nine propositions, which include the notions of "placing the people as the foundation (君以民为本说 *Min Yi Junben Shuo*)," "valuing the people and lightening the ruler (民贵君轻说 *Mingui Junqing*)," "establishing the ruler for the people (立君为民说 *Lijun Weimin*)," "the ruler nourishing the people, and the people supporting the ruler (君养民、民养君说 *Jun Yang Min, Min Yang Jun Shuo*)," "the ruler should not compete with the people for profit (君不可与民争利说 *Jun Buke yu Min Zhengli Shuo*)," "enriching the people is sufficient for the ruler (富民足君说 *Fumin Zujun Shuo*)," "the people abandoning the ruler (民弃君说 *Min Qi Jun Shuo*)," "gaining the people is equivalent to gaining the ruler (得民为君说 *Demin Weijun Shuo*)," and "the ruler being subject to the people (君为民主说 *Jun Wei Min Shuo*)." See Liu (2000).

Following interactions with the West in the late Qing period, in response to Western impacts in technology and thoughts, enlightened bureaucrats and progressives such as Li Hongzhang (李鸿章), Zeng Guofan (曾国藩), Zuo Zongtang (左宗棠), Feng Guifen (冯桂芬), Kang Youwei, Liang Qichao, Sun Yat-sen, etc., attempted to rescue the endangered Qing regime or reform China's millennia-old political system through initiatives like "learning from the West (采西学 *Cai Xixue*)," "manufacturing the Western-style goods (制洋器 *Zhi Yangqi*)," and "Embracing Chinese learning as the foundation and Western learning for practical applications (中学为体 西学为用 *Zhongxue Weiti Xixue Weiyong*)." However, all these attempts have failed to rescue China from the quandary of a hybrid regime. In contrast to the earlier Confucian (re)interpretations of *Minben* firmly placed within the unshakable framework of monarchy, from Kang Youwei and Liang Qichao to Sun Yat-sen, their moderate or radical reform or revolutionary propositions tried to gradually concretize *Minben*(*ism*) into practice. Whether advocating parliamentary democracy, mobilized participation under the imitation of the elitist principles within the imperial system or demanding the abolition of the imperial system for a radical republican revolution, *Minben* not only drew the public into the national affairs and politics via various social movements but also brought significant shocks and upheavals to the traditional imperial system that had persisted for thousand years.[4]

If one broadly considers the New Culture Movement, especially from the CCP's establishment to the period before the Reform and

[4] While the understanding of *Minben* underwent some transformations from the 1912 Xinhai Revolution to 1919 New Culture Movement, noteworthy distinctions also emerged within this evolutionary process. The moderate reformist faction, spearheaded by Kang Youwei, vehemently opposed autocracy and advocated for a republic. However, they posited that "while republicanism is aesthetically appealing, the timing is not propitious (共和虽美, 但今非其时 *Gonghe sui Mei, Dan Jin fei Qishi*)," espousing the concept of "enlightened despotism." This idea found support among enlightened bureaucrats and proponents of traditional-cultural continuity, exemplified by figures like Du Yaquan (杜亚泉). Conversely, the radical revolutionary faction, epitomized by Chen Duxiu, rebuffed the gradualism inherent in moderate reformism, contending that "ancient and modern, Eastern and Western, can never coalesce." The alike expressions of "governing in accordance with the will and desires of the people" and "prioritizing the people while disregarding the ruler" resonate with what can be characterized as the "ancient-style *Minben*," distinguishing it from contemporary democratic ideals. See Kang (1917, pp. 1, 48), Chen (1919), and Du (1914).

Opening Up, as a stage of China's democratic revolution, a new orientation of *Minben* can be re-observed. This shift involves combining the ancient tradition of *Minben* with modern democratic concepts, than fully embracing the Western liberal democracy but pursuing a Soviet-style communism. This includes the advocacy of Marxist class theory, where "the people" specifically refer to the proletariat with very exclusive advancement and correctness. However, early understandings of *Minben* were often associated with revolution during this period, with "revolutionary *Minben*" combining class struggle with original *Minben* and often utilized to mobilize the masses for revolution, displaying notable characteristics of dynamism, combativeness, and instrumentality.[5] During this period, democracy in China gradually shifted from the concepts of revolution and practice to the concept of legal systems.

After the establishment of new China, *Minben* did not diminish in its revolutionary nature. Instead, the concept of "continuing the revolution (继续革命 *Jixu Geming*)" became a decisive strategy for the CCP to achieve success, built upon the foundation of populism.

> Commencing with the nationwide seizure of power in 1949, the subsequent stage involved the anti-feudal land reform, followed by the initiation of agricultural collectivization immediately after the completion of the land reform. Subsequently, there was the socialist transformation of private industry, commerce, and handicrafts. The three major socialist transformations in terms of the ownership of the means of production were completed by 1956. Following this, there was a socialist revolution on political and ideological fronts last year, and this revolution could be considered largely concluded before July 1 of this year. However, the issues have not been fully resolved, and in the coming quite extended period, the methodology of rectification through criticism and self-criticism will be employed annually to continue readdressing these problems.[6]

[5] In the aforementioned context, notable elements include Li Dazhao's proletarian "plebeian democracy" (distinct from bourgeois "plebeian democracy"), Mao Zedong's initiation of the workers' movement, and the revolutionary strategy of rural encirclement of cities. Mao Zedong conceptualized the populace as the "masses," progressing from being merely the focal point of revolution to evolving into a fundamental ideology for the governance of the Chinese Communist Party, epitomized in the "mass line." Li (1959a, 1959b), Mao (1990), and Schram (1989).

[6] Mao (1999, pp. 349–350).

Yet, from the late 1950s to the late 1970s, *Minben* ideals, misconstrued in the understanding and evaluating class contradictions, the relationship between capitalism and socialism, and imperialism and modern revisionism, resulted in political and social turbulence like the "Great Leap Forward (大跃进 *Da Yuejin*)," the expansion of the struggle against the rightists, and the Cultural Revolution. *Minben*, along with the practical implementation of populist approaches, turned into tools to incite and compel the masses to deeply engage in politics, revolution, and large-scale mass movements. This *Minben*, established on the foundation of populist (broad/direct) democracy, not only failed to ensure the exercise of basic rights by the people but also placed them in the vortex of fervent nationalism and class struggle.

The Reform and Opening Up, as a significant juncture, did not, though, completely reverse the revolutionary nature of *Minben* but was gradually replaced by a reform agenda with development as its main focus, becoming institutionalized and legalized.[7] From Deng Xiaoping to Xi Jinping, successive leaderships have (re)interpreted the essence of Chinese democracy based on *Minben*, gradually forming a distinctive form of democracy with *Chinese characteristics*. In the political realm, Deng Xiaoping described the position and role of the people as "respecting the masses, loving the people, always paying attention to the interests and wishes of the broadest masses, taking 'whether the people support or not,' 'whether the people agree or not,' 'whether the people are happy or not,' and 'whether the people consent or not' as the starting point and destination of formulating various policies."[8] The people are the subject of history, the entity that the CCP can rely on, learn from, and draw ideological nourishment from.[9] To realize the people's central role, it is necessary

[7] After the Third Plenary Session of the Eleventh Central Committee, the revolutionary emphasis on the class struggle, while still present, underwent a gradual attenuation. In its stead, the Reform and Opening Up policy emerged, with development as its guiding principle, primarily focused on the liberation and advancement of productive forces.

[8] Jiang (1993).

[9] See, for example, Deng Xiaoping. *Guanche Tiaozheng Fangzhen,~baozheng Anding tuanjie [Implementing Adjustment Policies and Ensuring Stability and Unity]*. In Deng Xiaoping Wenxuan, Selected Works of Deng Xiaoping, Vol 2. Renmin Chubanshe, People's Publishing House, 1993. p. 368; Deng Xiaoping. *Zhongguo Gongchandang Dishierci Quanguo Daibiao Dahui Kaimuci [Opening Speech of the Twelfth National Congress of the Communist Party of China]*. In Deng Xiaoping Wenxuan, Selected Works of Deng Xiaoping, Vol 3. Renmin Chubanshe, People's Publishing House, 1993. p. 4;

to follow the mass line—"the masses are the source of our strength, the mass line and the lens of the masses are our treasures handed down via generations. Party organizations, party members, and party cadres must unite with the masses and must never be in opposition to the masses. If any party organization seriously deviates from the masses and cannot correct it decisively, it will lose the source of strength, it will surely fail, and it will be abandoned by the people."[10]

Deng Xiaoping's *Minben* perspective and the democratic nature of the methodology that to realize populism are reflected in his emphasis on placing *Minben* at the legal and institutional levels. "To safeguard the people's democracy, it is necessary to strengthen the legal system, to institutionalize democracy, to legalize it, so that this system and law do not change with the change of leaders, nor do they change with the change of leaders' views and attention."[11] Also, Deng's idea on *Minben* is deeply rooted in strong materialistic and pragmatic undertones. Reemphasizing the liberation and development of productive forces, with economic development at its core, the promotion of a market economy, the strategy of enriching the country first to drive subsequent prosperity, and the "three-step" development plan all reflect a focus on the well-being of the people rather than a democracy. This orientation is, of course, tied to China's initial stage of the socialist development during the early period of Reform and Opening Up, where the immediate priority was to elevate living standards.

During Jiang Zemin's era, the "Three Represents (三个代表 *Sange Daibiao*)" began to downplay the CCP's elitism in terms of ideology, embracing a broader spectrum of the population (no longer limited to the traditional workers and peasants) as the main force in China's democracy. The CCP evolved into the core representing the interests of the broad emerging social classes in the new era. The principles of "governing for

Deng Xiaoping. *Gaoji Ganbu yao Daitou Fayang Dang de Youliang Chuantong [Senior Cadres Should Take the Lead in Carrying forward the Party's Fine Traditions*, Vol 2. In Deng Xiaoping Wenxuan, Selected Works of Deng Xiaoping, Vol. 2. Renmin Chubanshe, People's Publishing House, 1993. p. 228.

[10] Deng Xiaoping Wenxuan, Vol 2. p. 211.

[11] Deng Xiaoping. Jiefang Sixiang, Shishi Qiushi, Tuanjie Yizhi Xiangqian Kan [Emancipate the Mind, Seek Truth from Facts, Unite and Look Forward (December 13, 1978). In *Deng Xiaoping Wenxuan, Selected Works of Deng Xiaoping*, Vol. 2. Renmin Chubanshe, People's Publishing House, 1993. pp. 146–147.

the people," "using power for the people's benefit, being emotionally connected to the people, and seeking benefits for the people" continue the top-down decision-making pattern of "*for* the people" in the mass line. The fourth generation of the central leadership, led by Hu Jintao and Wen Jiabao, expanded the meaning of modern *Minben*. In addition to emancipating productive forces and vigorous economic development, the policies benefiting the people during the Hu-Wen era and the leaders' people-centric governance approach reflected the crucial significance of *Minben* in the gradually forming landscape of China's democracy.

Xi Jinping's era goes beyond traditional Confucian ideas of benefiting the people and elevates the people to a level where their roleplay is critical to the destiny of the nation and the survival of the Communist Party. "The nation is the people, and the people are the nation."[12] In summary, the traditional Chinese idea on *Minben* did not, in a way, give rise to the theory and practice of modern Chinese democracy. On the contrary, democracy took root and sprouted in China by tracing and exploring ancient *Minben* elements after the influence and inbreaking of Western democratic ideas. This logical sequence is often inverted in many discussions on the relationship between *Minben* and modern Chinese democracy. Whether objectively responding to the Western influences during modern China to utilize democracy as a tool or subjectively seeking a Chinese counterpart distinct from Western liberal democracy, the pursuit of democracy in China is a very recent development. "Modern Chinese democratic thought did not directly emerge from thinkers like Huang Zongxi (黃宗羲) but started from the transmission of Western ideas and institutions. It is the result of tracing China's inherent democratic idea after the introduction of Western democratic ideas."[13] The modern pursuit of democracy in China is the outcome of national consciousness, Western impacts, and the search for tradition (*Minben*) working together.

Philosophically, *Minben*—whether in ancient or modern contexts—stands distinct from democracy. Despite being a prominent feature of traditional Chinese thought, especially within Confucianism, the essence of *Minben* is encapsulated in the phrase: "The people are the foundation

[12] Report of General Secretary Xi Jinping at the 20th National Congress of the Communist Party of China, October 16, 2022. Available at https://www.gov.cn/zhuanti/zggcddescqgdbdh/sybgqw.htm (Sccessed December 4, 2023).

[13] Chen (1997, pp. 206–207).

of the nation, and the foundation solidifies the nation."[14] The relation between *Minben* and democracy, however, is not a simple equivalence. To comprehend this relationship, one must not only grasp the shared aspects of *Minben* and democracy but also acknowledge the authoritarian aspect of it, particularly within Confucian despotism.[15] Simultaneously, one must consider the interplay between *Minben* and modernity, wherein traditional Chinese *Minben* oscillates between the ideas of "the people as the foundation" and the paradoxical embrace of monarchic absolutism.

Minben could only manifest on the basis of benevolent governance by authoritarian rulers, as it is articulated: "In essence, traditional Chinese *Minben* advocates are simultaneously proponents of monarchy." Therefore, the transition from traditional *Minben* to modern democracy requires not only absorbing the essence of "*Minben* democracy" but also confronting the anti-democratic traits inherent in *Minben*. Only through this process could *Minben* be intertwined with democracy and modernity.

Lastly, there is the relationship between *Minben* and Chinese-style democracy. While Chinese-style democracy centers around *Minben* (or termed people's democracy), its connotations extend beyond *Minben*. Modern Chinese-style democracy, grounded in the value of "putting the people first," is supplemented by well-established procedural safeguards that facilitate the public participation, consultation, supervision, and decision-making. Simultaneously, *Minben* has departed from the

[14] In the aftermath of the New Confucian movement, particularly prominent in the 1980s and 1990s, which aimed to reinstate tradition in the context of China's modernization, the *Minben* has become synonymous with "Chinese-style democracy." Advocates of New Confucianism endeavored to tackle the challenges posed by Western universal values by reclaiming China's traditional, especially Confucian, philosophical foundations. Concurrently, they also aimed to integrate these principles into a global context using a distinctive Chinese approach. This seemingly contradictory stance is evident in the emphasis of "New Confucians (新儒家 *Xin Rujia*)" on both the "cultural conservatism" and a "political embrace of globalization," showcasing a clear rejection of Western culture and values while actively utilizing Confucian cultural resources to interpret or transform China. The debate within the "New Confucians" discourse revolves around how to connect traditional Confucianism with modern democratic politics. The options range from shaping China into a "Confucian state" where politics and education are intertwined, to a replica of liberal democracy known as "Confucian-style democracy," or even a "Confucian-style modernization" model. As of now, a consensus on the conclusion remains elusive. For detailed exploration of "New Confucians" perspectives on *Minben* and modern democracy, see Jiang (2003), Kang (2006), Fukuyama (1995), Tan (2003), O'Dwyer (2003), Zhang (2003), and King (2018).

[15] See, for example, Li (2003).

political framework of ancient Chinese monarchic despotism and has been practiced within the modern Chinese political system. This practice encompasses two dimensions: firstly, improving and refining the CCP's governance style and philosophy, overcoming bureaucracy, and promoting clean governance; secondly, comprehensively (re)constructing a moderately prosperous society, advancing political civilization, and governing the country based on the rule of law.

Examining closely, both traditional and transformed modern *Minben* uphold the value proposition of "putting people first." However, they still struggle to effectively curb some phenomena such as bureaucratic tendencies, corrupt practices, and nepotism within governance. In practice, *Minben* often coexists paradoxically with "officialism" or "monarchism." Democracy emphasizes bottom-up people's participation and individual sovereignty, while the essence of *Minben* is rooted in benevolent governance from the top down. Therefore, the modern transformation of traditional *Minben* involves more than a simple absorption of its people-centric ideals or a shift away from despotic foundations. It is crucial to contemplate how to reconcile conflicting factors between people's participation and individual sovereignty in modern democracy with the essence of *Minben*. This process is essential for strengthening the persuasive power and theoretical depth of Chinese democracy in discourse.

Minben, People's Democracy, and Chinese Democracy

Minben could trace its roots back to various dynasties in imperial China. Whether characterized by benevolent or tyrannical rulers, it consistently remained the core of the monarchs, demonstrating concern, fear, and value for the well-being of the people. Conversely, *Minben* also constituted a key form of relative constraint on monarchical power from the bottom up. However, the pursuit of democracy in China is a relatively late thing, broadly divided into two stages: the exploration of democracy in the modern era (from the Opium Wars to the establishment of the People's Republic of China) and the generation of Chinese democracy in the contemporary era (from the founding of the People's Republic of China to the present).

During the modern era, the exploration of democracy either suppressed or abandoned the ancient *Minben* ideology.[16] *Minben* and democracy were not initially interconnected. It was only after the establishment of the CCP that, while continuing the traditional *Minben* ideology, it adopted and localized Marxist democratic views, forming the Chinese democratic model of people's democracy. Although, in the period from the founding of the nation to before the era of economic reforms, the people's democracy was mistakenly understood and practiced as the direct (mass) democracy or populism, post-economic reforms saw successive leaders enrich and develop the content of the people's democracy, creating a modern democratic model with *Chinese characteristics*. This discussion particularly emphasizes the relationship and transformation between ancient *Minben* and modern democracy, as well as the relationship between *Minben* and the Chinese-style people's democracy, especially within the CCP's democratic discourse after the economic reforms.

Minben originated and is deeply rooted in the ancient Chinese autocratic political system. It not only differs significantly from modern democracy but also distinguishes itself from constitutional monarchy, which integrates monarchical and constitutional principles, where the head of state has symbolic significance and is bound by the constitution and laws. Ancient autocratic rulers in China were acutely aware of the very importance of the people as the main labor force in maintaining autocratic rule and national stability within the basic economic framework of traditional agrarian society. Reflections in the economic and social spheres were also reflected in politics, valuing the role of "the people" in politics. Fundamentally, ancient *Minben* was essentially a manifestation of

[16] Especially during the period from the Xinhai Revolution to the New Culture Movement, many revolutions were eager to sever ties with traditional Chinese thought and instead embraced Western ideas and systems, like democracy, republicanism, and representation. In his works, among many, Hu Shi criticized traditional *Minben* for emphasizing feudal hierarchical notions that hindered individual and societal development, advocating for the necessity of modernization and Westernization in China. Interestingly, in many of Hu Shi's English writings, he openly admitted that traditional Chinese thought, and culture remained a crucial resource for China's continuity and differentiation from the West, making it difficult, or even impossible, to completely abandon the dichotomy between modernity and tradition. See Zhou (2001). Of course, many intellectuals, deeply rooted in China's unique national and cultural features, argue that "traditional Chinese politics is not necessarily against democracy; it is just another form of democracy, a 'De Mo ke La Dong (transliteration of democracy)'." See Liang (1990).

the ruler's well-being. Not only were the people were being marginalized politically, but they were also considered lowly, ignorant, and subservient in theory—objects to be tamed, enslaved, and ruled. The crucial role of "the people" in autocratic rule compelled rulers to prioritize them. The logic of autocratic rule is evident in statements like "The ruler is for the people, and the people are the foundation of the state." All subsequent discussions on *Minben*, such as "The people are the foundation of the state," "The people are precious, and the altars of the state come next; the ruler is lightest," and "The ruler is like a boat, and the common people are like water; water can carry the boat, but it can also capsize it," are products of the autocratic system. Rights of the people needed to be realized through the autocratic monarch rather than by the people themselves.[17] This is fundamentally different from modern democracy, which considers the people as active subjects of rights.

In the context of this theoretical immersion, *Minben* not only manifests itself in Chinese traditions, especially Confucian morality and ethics, but also in the proactive engagement of Confucianism in worldly affairs, bringing the people into the dimension of practical political endeavors. In political practices guided by *Minben*, the distinction between *for* the people and *by* the people constitutes the key features differentiating *Minben* from democracy, Chinese democracy from Western democracy. In essence, the rights of the people derive from the bestowed authority of the rulers from top to bottom, rather than being considered "inalienable human rights." *Minben* rooted in a patriarchal or paternalistic system cannot fundamentally address the issues of restraining the power of rulers and achieving a proper distribution of rights between rulers and the people. Even the ancient concept of "benevolent governance," aimed at further improving livelihoods, enhancing well-being, and understanding the will of the people, was essentially an idealized monarchic political model, often referred to as "enlightened despotism," falling within the category of authoritarianism. While such a system, characterized by the coexistence of authoritarian rule and *Minben*, demonstrated flexibility in

[17] In despotism, *Minben* manifests in two dimensions: from a value judgment idea, the interests of the people constitute the core values of the nation and society. However, from a factual perspective, the monarch's authority could only be consolidated through the endorsement of the people. Hence, in terms of political systems, *Minben* and democracy are inherently contradictory. From a philosophical perspective, *Minben* ideology harbors the seeds of transition from a monarchical system to a democratic one. See, Li (2009, 2016).

self-adjustment and longevity, it remains incongruent with the modern democratic politics and cannot be equated with contemporary Chinese democracy.[18]

Therefore, to achieve a modernized transformation of *Minben* and connect it with democracy, two fundamental issues must be clarified. First, the monarchical authoritarian system that nurtured ancient *Minebn* must be eradicated to align with the political environment of modern democracy. Second, while *Minben* can serve as a distinctive source and foundation for Chinese democracy in terms of paradigms, ethics, theory, and practice, careful reconsideration is required on how to integrate the two. As King Yeo-Chi (金耀基) pointed out:

> What is the rationale behind our country's political system being both authoritarian and enlightened? One bold hypothesis is that the mighty current of Confucian *Minben*, rooted in the spirit of the humanism, has washed away the poison of authoritarianism. It can be a significant error to assert that the main spirit and contribution of Confucian political thought are populism.[19]

Against this background, people's democracy has gradually emerged as the mainstream discourse in Chinese democracy. It continues the core of traditional *Minben* while incorporating a Marxist view of democracy (indigenized) and considering the national conditions of China. Following the political turbulence characterized by movements and revolutions in the period after the founding of the People's Republic until 1978, democracy gradually shifted from a tone of movement and revolution to development. The "development democracy" encompasses three crucial meanings.

Firstly, it concerns the relationship between democracy and productivity. Some statements like the "poverty is not socialism," "socialism cannot persist in a prolonged state of stagnation," and "to talk about socialism, the development of productive forces is paramount" by Deng indicate the interconnection between democracy, socialism, livelihoods,

[18] In contemporary Western Chia studies, the analysis of the resilience of Chinese authoritarianism persists along this trajectory. See Nathan (2017) and Fewsmith (2019).

[19] King (1993, p. 2).

and economic development.[20] While democracy is crucial to socialism, poverty and underdevelopment are not inherent attributes of socialism. In assessing the standard of a country's political system, Deng reemphasized, "The key lies in three aspects: first, whether the political situation in the country is stable; second, whether it can enhance the unity of the people and improve their lives; third, whether productive forces can experience sustained development."[21] Deng's assessment of the political system indicates the ultimate goal of political future in China, namely, the relation between the economy and democracy. This political logic aligns with both the Marxist historical materialism and the traditional Chinese political tradition rooted in *Minben*.[22]

Secondly, the establishment of democracy is built upon the emancipation of thought and political system reform. In his speech that titled *Liberate the Mind, Seek Truth from Facts, Unite as One, and Look Forward*, Deng reemphasized the relationship between democracy and the emancipation of thought, stating that "democracy is an essential condition for further emancipating thought"[23] and "we need centralized and unified leadership, however, there must be sufficient democracy to achieve correct centralization."[24] The emancipation of thought that naturally points towards the emancipation of individuals' thinking and the protection and respect for individual rights. From the late 1970s to the 1980s, discussions on the "criterion for truth" created conditions for the liberation of thought. The debate on the "criterion for truth" showed the confrontation between the ultra-left ideological line within the Party and the reformists. This debate did not entirely negate Mao's achievements but, through a compromise, "reinstated Comrade Mao's ideological line of seeking truth from facts, theoretical integration with reality, and starting everything from the actual conditions."[25]

[20] *Deng Xiaoping Wenxuan [Selected Works of Deng Xiaoping]*, Vol. 2. Renmin Chubanshe, People's Publishing House, 1994. pp. 310, 312, 314.

[21] Deng Xiaoping. "Zenyang Pingjia Yige GUojia de Zhengzhi Tizhi [How to Evaluate a Country's Political System]." In *Deng Xiaoping Wenxuan, Vol. 3, Selected Works of Deng Xiaoping*, Renmin Chubanshe, People's Publishing House, 1993. p. 213.

[22] See Lin (2012).

[23] Deng Xiaoping. Jiefang Sixiang, Shishi Qiushi, Tuanjie Yiqie Xiangqiankan." p. 144.

[24] Ibid.

[25] *Sanzhong Quanhui Yilai Zhongyao Wenxian Xuanbian [The Selected Documents Since the Third Plenary Session of the Eleventh Central Committee]*, Vol. 1. Renmin Chuabnshe,

Simultaneously, the exploration of the market in the economic sphere overturned the confinement in socialist dogma, where the market and socialist ideology were considered rather incompatible. Decisions to develop rural economies directly undermined the foundation of the "One Big Two Committees (一大二公 *Yida Ergong*)" people's commune system of the ultra-left line in rural areas. The rectification of unjust, false, and wrongful cases initiated by reformists within the Party, such as Hu Yaobang (胡耀邦), was a powerful exposure and counterattack against authoritarianism. It provided vivid example for the CCP to reflect on history, correct mistakes, and subsequently move toward democratization.[26] The emancipation of thought inevitably propels political system reform. Deng Xiaoping, around the time of the Thirteenth National Congress, repeatedly emphasized the importance of political reform[27]

People's Publishing House, 1982. p. 161. During the concluding session of Tenth Party Congress's Central Work Conference, Hua Guofeng (华国锋) delivered a self-critique, encapsulating some persistent issues in the discourse on truth. The implementation of the "two whatevers (两个凡是 *Liangge Fanshi*)" presented a formidable quandary for the destiny of both the Party and the country. The "two whatevers" not only impeded Deng Xiaoping's resumption of duties but also obstructed the collective mourning for Premier Zhou Enlai, hampered the rectification of the Tiananmen Square incident, hindered the engagement of esteemed revolutionary figures like Comrade Chen Yun in central work, impeded the commemoration of comrades Zhu De, Chen Yi, and He Long, obstructed the rectification of many unjust, erroneous, and fabricated cases, exploited flawed documents to propagate misguided theories, shielded Kang Sheng, obstructed the exposure and criticism of the Gang of Four, opposed Deng Xiaoping, and diverged from the central political guidelines.

[26] See also Du (2010). The intellectual emancipation prevalent during the 1980s, characterized by some debates on the intra-party democracy, re-enlightenment, the discourse on capitalism versus socialism, opposition to the bourgeois liberalization, and the eradication of the spiritual pollution, unfolded concurrently with advancements in ideological liberation. Proponents of intra-party democracy and reform, exemplified by figures like Hu Yaobang and Zhao Ziyang (赵紫阳), played pivotal roles. However, their divergence on political and democratic reform is noteworthy. Hu sought to catalyze rapid economic development, thereby fostering a comprehensive political reform and democratization in China. In contrast, Zhao inclined towards a cautious and incremental model of partial reform. See more Zhao et al. (2009).

[27] In June 1986, while providing insights into the economic landscape, Deng Xiaoping emphatically asserted, "Without reforms to the political system, our ability to adapt to the prevailing circumstances remains compromised. Political system reform ought to be emblematic of the broader reform agenda, as the success of all other reforms hinges upon the restructuring of the political system." Subsequently, in September of the same year, during a presentation by the Central Finance and Economics Group, Deng reaffirmed the strategies for political reform in China. Furthermore, in June 1987, during diplomatic

and, in *Reform of the Party and State Leadership System*, criticized the existing political system for its bureaucracy, excessive concentration of power, and paternalism.[28] Although these political reforms were confined to aspects like separating the Party and government, decentralizing power, streamlining institutions, and primarily focused on administrative reforms to improve efficiency, optimize government structure, and stimulate production enthusiasm, they nevertheless facilitated the development of democracy in China within the strong conservative political atmosphere of the ultra-left forces.

Lastly, the institutionalization and legalization of democracy are also included in the agenda. For a considerable period after the founding of the new China, democracy and its practices were entangled with the personality cults, populism, and class struggles, lacking institutionalization and legalization. After 1978, Deng, in the closing session of the 1978 Central Work Conference, stressed, "To safeguard people's democracy, it is necessary to strengthen the legal system. Democracy must be institutionalized and legalized, ensuring that this system and law do not change with changes in leadership or shifts in views and attention of leaders."[29] The Third Plenary Session of the Eleventh Central Committee also pointed, "To safeguard people's democracy, it is necessary to strengthen the socialist legal system, therefore institutionalize and legalize democracy, ensuring stability, continuity, and great authority of this system and law."[30]

In the late 1970s to the entire 1980s, the institutionalization and legalization of democracy mainly manifested in three aspects: constitutional amendments, the separation of Party and government, and reforms in the electoral representative system. Given the prior situation where political power often operated beyond constitutional constraints before the

engagements with representatives from Yugoslavia and a discourse delivered to foreign dignitaries from Bangladesh in July of the same year, Deng emphatically underscored the pivotal importance of political system reform within the Chinese context.

[28] See Deng Xiaoping. Dang he Guojia Lingdao Zhidu Gaige [Reform of the Party and State Leadership System]. In *Deng Xiaoping Wenxuan, Selected Works of Deng Xiaoping*, Vol. 2. Renmin Chubanshe, People's Publishing House, 1994. p. 327.

[29] *Deng Xiaoping Wenxuan [Selected Works of Deng Xiaoping]*, Vol. 2. Renmin Chubanshe, People's Publishing House, 1994. p. 146.

[30] *Sanzhong Quanhui Yilai Zhongyao Wenxuan Xuanbian Selected Documents Since the Third Plenary Session of the CPC Central Committee]*, Vol. 1. Renmin Chubanshe, People's Publishing House, 1982. p. 819.

Opening Up and Reform, the 1982 Constitution gradually embedded political power within its framework, stating, "No organization or individual may have privileges beyond the Constitution and the law."[31] This rectification of the relationship between the constitution and politics, coupled with the balance aimed at safeguarding people's democracy, democratic centralism, and the principles of legality, ensured a relatively stable and progressively developing social system. The separation of politics and law in China, along with the intricate relationship between the Party and the government, has remained ambiguous since new China's establishment. The delineation of powers and their interconnection in both the Party constitution and the national constitution lacked clarity for a significant period. The constitutions of 1954, 1978, and 1982 failed to explicitly designate the CCP as the supreme authority in China.[32] Despite the Party constitution, which designates the Party as the highest authority, this provision remains unacknowledged in China's constitution. Notwithstanding the ambiguity and complexity of this relationship, an informal understanding regarding the division of functions persisted within the CCP's non-formalized politics. The CCP neither monopolizes all aspects nor fully integrates into the state. As Zhao Ziyang emphasized in 1987, "The nature, functions, organizational forms, and working methods of the Party and the state power organs are different."[33]

Furthermore, the People's Congress system and the electoral process underwent restoration and development following the Reform and Opening Up. Key developments include the *Organic Law of the People's Congresses and Local People's Governments of the People's Republic of*

[31] During the initial post-founding era of new China, the constitutions of 1954 and 1975 functioned as foundational legal documents. Although these documents aimed to establish a socialist democratic political system that within the highest legal framework, they were significantly impacted by disruptions caused by the Cultural Revolution and the emphasis on class struggle campaign. Both constitutions, to varying extents, persisted in emphasizing the significance of class struggle. The constitutional amendments of 1978, while temporarily reinstating certain correct principles and systems from the 1954 constitution, nonetheless exhibited notable leftist errors and failed to conduct a comprehensive reassessment of the Cultural Revolution.

[32] The constitution enacted in 1975 amalgamated the Party and the state into a Revolutionary Committee.

[33] In his discourse during the preparatory session of the Seventh Plenary Session of the Twelfth Central Committee of the Chinese Communist Party, Zhao Ziyang initially introduced the concept of "separation of Party and government."

China and the *Election Law of the People's Congresses and Local People's Congresses of the People's Republic of China*,[34] both ratified during the second session of the Fifth National People's Congress (NPC) in July 1979. Through electoral system reforms and expanded suffrage, the empowerment-oriented "democratic elections" are recognized as a major impetus for democratization in China at the grassroots level.[35]

The shift from the "revolution" to "development" characterized the primary theme of democratic development in the 1980s. In the 1990s, the exploration of China's democratic development path prioritized economic growth and political stability.[36] Deng Xiaoping's early 1990s idea of the "not arguing (不争论 *Bu Zhenglun*)"—"Not arguing is for the sake of getting things done"[37]—incorporated elements of

[34] During the same timeframe, pivotal legislations were enacted, notably including the *Organic Law of the People's Courts of the People's Republic of China*, the *Organic Law of the People's Procuratorates of the People's Republic of China*, and the *Resolution of the Standing Committee of the National People's Congress on Issues Concerning the Validity of Laws and Decrees Formulated Since the Founding of the People's Republic of China*. These enactments entailed some corresponding adjustments and provisions pertaining to the NPC system and the electoral framework. See *Renmin Daibiao Dahui Zhidu Zhongyao Wenxian Xuanbian [Selected Documents on the System of the National People's Congress]*, Vol. 2. Zhongguo Minzhu Fazhi Chubanshe/Zhongguo Wenxian Chubanshe, China Democratic Legal System Press/Central Literature Publishing House, 2015.

[35] In line with the accounts of Chinese elections in the 1980s provided by Li Meng et al. in their work *The Developmental Course of the Electoral System in New China*, it is noteworthy that despite notable deficiencies in election quality and procedures, elections conducted at various levels of the People's Congress in all levels, particularly the experimental direct elections at the county level, have, to some extent, delved into and enhanced the foundational political system in China—namely, the People's Congress system. See Li (2013). Detailed election data can be referenced in the report issued by the General Office of the Standing Committee of the National People's Congress on the status of direct elections at the county level nationwide. Available at http://fgcx.bjcourt.gov.cn:4601/law?fn=chl601s029.txt&truetag=2586&titles=&contents=&dbt=chl (Accessed December 5, 2023).

[36] In examining the legitimacy of Chinese regime since the Reforms and Opening Up, Kang Xiaoguang acknowledges that democratic rule of law constitutes a long-term goal for legitimizing the Chinese political authority. Nevertheless, he observes that under the authoritarian system, the focal points remain the emphasis and pursuit of economic and performance achievements. Naturally, discussions concerning democratic rule of law, fairness, and justice are relatively subdued. See Kang (1999).

[37] *Deng Xiaoping Wenxuan [Selected Works of Deng Xiaoping]*, Vol. 3. Renmin Chubanshe, People's Publishing House, 1993. p. 374.

capitalism, such as a market economy, private ownership, and a joint-stock system, into China's socialist building. Simultaneously, it definitively addressed fundamental political issues in Chinese socialism, including the CCP's affiliations that with the capitalist and socialist elements.[38] With technocrats like Jiang Zemin (江泽民) entering the decision-making echelons, less ideological constraints and support from beneficiaries of the economic reform, particularly the new middle-class constituencies, led to a more pragmatic approach to political reform and democracy in China. Alongside the rapid development of the market economy in the 1990s, there was an urgent need to formulate a discourse representing both the workers and peasantries (traditional CCP's political discourse) while accommodating emerging social classes. The concept of the "Three Represents (三个代表 *Sange Daibiao*)" broke new ground by acknowledging an elite alliance while emphasizing popular rights. This transformation saw the CCP evolve from a class party that representing the proletariat to an "all-encompassing party" or "ruling party" that includes both the elites and the masses.[39]

The market economy serves as an effective institutional arrangement for advancing the productive forces and improving people's lives. Hence, the "Three Represents" must first "strive to comply with the laws of the

[38] Deng Xiaoping's "not arguing" policy played a pivotal role in propelling China's comprehensive national strength, particularly its swift economic development. Between 1992 and 1997, in conjunction with substantial openings in policies toward foreign investment, township, and private enterprises, China's economic system underwent a transition from the scarcity era of planned economy to the surplus era of a market economy. The open stock market also facilitated the primitive accumulation of capital. The township economic model, as exemplified by coastal cities like south Jiangsu Province and Shandong, experienced rapid growth. The State-owned Enterprise Reform after the 15th National Congress in 1997 adeptly navigated between Coaseanism and Keynesianism, achieving a progressive transformation of corporate property rights. Most significantly, Deng's "not arguing" and subsequent Southern Tour speech also suppressed orthodox leftist ideology and its impact on official ideology and control forces.

[39] Tian Lihong. "Zhonggong 'Sange Daibiao' Lilun de Tichu Beijing yuqi Yingxiang [The Background and Impact of the Introduction of the CCP's'Three Represents' Theory]." *Gongdang Wenti Yanjiu, Journal of Communist Party Studies (Taiwan)* 28.2 (2011): 103. In the late 1990s, the escalating differentiation of social interests, driven by the market economy, became markedly conspicuous. Against this backdrop, Jiang Zemin, in replacing the politically charged term "class" with "stratum," not only attenuated the ideological reverberations of socialist class struggle but also eliminated impediments for the conceptualization of the "Three Represents."

development of productive forces, embody the requirements for continuously advancing the emancipation and development of social productive forces, especially embody the requirements for advancing the development of advanced productive forces, and continuously improve the living standards of the people through the development of productive forces."[40] Thus, the "Three Represents" alleviated China's challenges on the global stage in terms of the economic globalization and the new technological revolution.

At the domestic level, it readdressed the economic structural adjustments brought about by the market economy and the ensuing complex ideological struggles. The 15th National Congress of the CCP integrated the construction of Chinese socialist culture into the basic program of the primary stage of socialism in China, along with the construction of the Chinese socialist economy and politics. The cultural construction is considered an important task that dialectically unifies the promotion of the development of productive forces with the improvement of the comprehensive quality of individuals, particularly emphasizing the advancement of the development of the most extensive interests of the people.[41] Traditional Chinese culture, the dualism of ancient and modern, East and West, and its tense relationship with ideology, saw relaxation. Advanced culture provided spiritual and intellectual support for the development of market economy and social progress. When the market and development became mainstream discourses and provided material support for China's socialist construction, the construction of people's democracy and spiritual civilization could be better carried out.

The iron logic of market economy, driving rapid economic development in China, has concurrently engendered various issues like uneven

[40] Jiang (2001).

[41] Li (2001, p. 35). In this period, cultural construction steadfastly adhered to the Marxism, Mao Zedong Thought, and Deng Xiaoping Theory as guiding ideologies. There existed a high degree of vigilance and even outright rejection towards Western liberal culture. Li Lanqing highlighted that, "Some have proposed the elimination of the guiding position of the Marxism in ideological and cultural aspects, advocating the diversification of guiding ideologies... Regardless of the direction from which these statements and viewpoints come, they are all incorrect." See also Jiang Zemin. "Jianchi Sixiang Yuanze [Adhering to the Four Cardinal Principles]." In *Jiang Zemin Wenxuan, Selected Works of Jiang Zemin*, Vol. 3, Renmin Chubanshe, People's Publishing House, 2006. p. 231.

(re)distribution of social wealth, wealth disparity, corruption, and environmental pollution. Consequently, in alignment with the "Three Represents," the focus on "scientific development (科学发展 *Kexue Fazhan*)" in the economic sphere and "harmonious development (和谐发展 *Hexie Fazhan*)" in the social and political realms that became the reform priorities of the first decade of the twenty-first century. In October 2003, during the 16th Third Plenary Session, Hu Jintao delivered a speech that titled *Establishing and Implementing the Scientific Development Concept*, underscoring the idea that "growth does not equate to development."[42] The decision on *Improving the Socialist Market Economy System* systematically elucidated the meaning of the "Scientific Development Concept (SDC 科学发展观 *Kexue Fazhan Guan*)", saying: "adhere to comprehensive consideration, coordinate various interest relationships in the reform process, uphold a people-centered approach, thus establish a comprehensive, coordinated, and sustainable development perspective, promote the comprehensive development of the economy, society, and individuals."[43]

The SDC is regarded as a pivotal ideological development since the 16th National Congress of the CCP. It not only adjusted China's market economy reform and extensive development models but also ideologically connected with the "people-oriented" democratic concept. The 17th National Congress Report stated, "The primary essence of the SDC is development, with its core being people-oriented."[44] The assertion in the report, "People's democracy is the life of the socialism," elevated the relationship between people's democracy and socialism to a new level. The 16th and 17th National Congresses emphasized, "the Party's leadership, people as masters, and governing the country according to law" are the fundamental paths to achieving socialist democratic politics.[45]

In 2004, Hu Jintao officially introduced the concept of a "harmonious society" at the 16th Fourth Plenary Session, describing it as "achieving

[42] Hu (2005).

[43] "Zhonggong Zhongyang Guanyu Wanshan Shehui Zhuyi Shichang Jingji Tizhi Ruogan Wenti de Jueding [The Decision of the Central Committee of the Communist Party of China on Several Issues Concerning the Improvement of the Socialist Market Economic System]." In *Shiliuda Yilai Zhongyao Wenxian Xuanbian, Selected Important Documents Since the 16th National Congress (Part 1)*. Zhongyang Wenxian Chubanshe, Central Literature Publishing House, 2005. p. 465.

[44] Hu (2008).

[45] Jiang (2002).

social harmony and building a beautiful society, which has always been an ideal society that humanity tirelessly pursues." "Harmony" and "stability"—according to Professor Yu Keping (俞可平)—are the "primary values" in Chinese politics, the core goals of the public governance.[46] The "harmonious society" is not only a continuation of the lofty Confucian ideal of "great harmony under heaven (天下大同 *Tianxia Datong*)" but also the ultimate social ideal of people's democracy. The people-oriented SDC and the harmonious society built on it are not only an ideological shift for the CCP in the new era but are also demonstrated through the "people-friendly and caring grassroots route" by the new generation of top leaders.[47] This is evident in various political reforms aimed at improving people's livelihoods and advancing social security during the 16th and 17th National Congresses, such as Hu Jintao's proposal of the "New Three People's Principles (新三民主义 *Xin Sanmin Zhuyi*)" and "two actions (二为 *Erwei*),"[48] as well as Wen Jiabao's talks on democratic constitutionalism, universal values, and political reforms.[49]

During this period, human rights were enshrined in the constitution, and laws protecting individual rights and private property, such as the *Property Rights Law*, were passed. To note, a service-oriented accountable government was established on this basis. The very White Paper on

[46] Yu (2008).

[47] See "21 Shiji Jingji Baodao [21st Century Business Herald]." November 11, 2003.

[48] The "New Three People's Principles" advocate that, at all levels of leadership, officials should maintain a profound engagement at the grassroots level. They are urged to establish connections with the masses, attentively listen to their voices, show genuine concern for their hardships, and consistently prioritize the well-being of the people. Officials are expected to employ their authority for the betterment of the populace, develop an emotional attachment to the concerns of the people, and actively pursue the interests of the public. The "Two Actions" underscores that leadership officials must nurture a correct understanding of power, aligning themselves with the principles of serving the party for the greater public good and governing with the people in mind. This necessitates sincere efforts to wield power in the best interest of the people, exemplifying a dedication to hard work and diligence. Such dedication may extend to the point of sacrificing personal rest for the collective welfare.

[49] In terms of political reform, the conceptual advancements made by Hu and Wen, as opposed to the Jiang-Zhu era, are evident in their heightened acceptance and recognition of values such as judicial independence and constitutional democracy. Within the distinctive political framework of the CCP's centralized authority, the role of "enlightened" leaders in propelling political system reform is undeniably more consequential. Refer to Zong (2002). See also Gilley and Nathan (2003).

China's Democracy Construction, published by the State Council Information Office in October 2005, directly addressed China's democratic issues for the first time since the founding in China, providing a more specific interpretation of the concept and practice of people's democracy.[50] In the discourse pertaining to the change of people's democracy, particularly within modern contexts, the CCP conceptualizes it as a manifestation of "performance democracy." This conception entails the attainment of national and ethnic democracy in China primarily through good governance, with a pronounced emphasis on material considerations, in contrast to the emphasis on "individualistic democracy." Within the framework of Xi Jinping's 24-character socialist values, national prosperity occupies a preeminent position. Guided by this perspective, the realization of people's democracy necessitates a departure from the Western paradigm, which accentuates disorderly elections and cumbersome deliberations inherent in the liberal democracy, especially as it undergoes a gradual distortion. Consequently, the salient feature of people's democracy, under the CCP's leadership, becomes conspicuously evident. This leadership embodies a fundamental attribute that distinguishes people's democracy in China from other democratic modalities. The organic unity of Party leadership, people's self-governance, and governance according to the law hinges on the steadfast commitment to "upholding the CCP's leadership."[51] In Xi's discourse, the CCP's leadership is all-encompassing, as exemplified by the principle of "the Party leads in government, military, civilian, and academia, in the east, west, south, north, and center (党政军民学 东西南北中 党领导一切 *Dang Zheng Jun Min Xue, Dong Xi Nan Bei Zhong, Dang Lingdao Yiqie*)."[52] This comprehensive leadership ensures the broadening and deepening of people's democracy. Strengthening the Party's leadership at all levels is not a mere abstraction but a tangible commitment that must manifest in various facets.[53]

There are two crucial aspects of people's democracy in the Xi Jinping era. Firstly, development, especially economic development, has been the primary focus for over 40 years since the beginning of Reform

[50] See more of the *China's Democracy Construction* by Information Office of the State Council of the People's Republic of China. Available at: http://www.gov.cn/2005-10/19/content_79553.htm (Accessed December 5, 2023).

[51] Xi (2015, p. 19).

[52] *Xi Jinping on the Governance of China*. p. 85.

[53] Xi (2015, p. 11).

and Opening Up. However, the people-oriented development philosophy of "relying on whom for development and for whom to develop" has gradually become the core content of Chinese democratic politics. Key initiatives such as building a moderately prosperous society in all respects, achieving common prosperity, and eliminating poverty are all vital measures to advance development and people's democracy simultaneously. Secondly, although people's democracy has always been a core concept in the construction of China's democratic politics by the CCP, Chinese democracy still lacks a comprehensive theoretical discourse. Xi's introduction of the "Whole-Process People's Democracy (全过程人民民主 *Quanguocheng Renmin Minzhu*)" endeavors to render people's democracy more accessible. However, this conceptual framework strives to encompass both the ideal and the real, procedure and substance, institution, and all facets within a singular toolkit. However, this endeavor proves illusory, placing the people's democracy in a quandary amid the ascendancy of Chinese authoritarianism.

In summary, traditional *Minben* serves as a pivotal intellectual and cultural underpinning for the modern "people-oriented" democratic ideals in China. Within the official and academic discourses, *Minben* is often portrayed as a manifestation of Chinese democracy, one that not only aligns with Western liberal democracy but may even surpass it. The logic underlying this modern democratic approach in China is indeed a commendable and robust argument. Nevertheless, it is imperative to acknowledge that while ancient populism "endured the oppression of authoritarian rule, and its spirit could not be extinguished,"[54] it has consistently coexisted with the passive democracy and authoritarianism. In essence, despite the modern democratic logic and norm, the political structure and influence of the Chinese imperial system present challenges for traditional populism to evolve into a modern democratic system. Instead, it remains in a state of distrust, disdain, and pity from the ruling authority, which is non-institutionalized and under unstable autocratic rule.[55]

[54] Liang Qichao. *Xianqin Zhengzhi Sixiangshi [History of Political Thought in Pre-Qin Dynasty]*. Dongfang Chubanshe, Oriental Publishing House, 2014. p. 5.

[55] In the discourse of many modern non-democratic regimes, the proclamation of "people-oriented" governance often serves as a façade for authoritarian rule, concealing the reality of despotism beneath a veneer of apparent democracy—expressed as a purported

So, starting from the late Qing Dynasty, benevolent Chinese, including enlightened officials, took the initiative to reform Chinese traditions. They advocated for a fusion of "Chinese learning as the foundation and Western learning for practical application" or selectively adapting Chinese tradition to address Western challenges. This marked the awakening stage of modern Chinese democracy, wherein the people no longer depended on or were confined by the autocratic monarch and the state (or at least began to awaken to the very perception of their relationships). Although nearly all democratic attempts in modern China culminated in failure, the enduring connection between traditional populism and modern democracy remained unaltered.

References

"Zhonggong Zhongyang Guanyu Wanshan Shehui Zhuyi Shichang Jingji Tizhi Ruogan Wenti de Jueding [The Decision of the Central Committee of the Communist Party of China on Several Issues Concerning the Improvement of the Socialist Market Economic System]." In *Shiliuda Yilai Zhongyao Wenxian Xuanbian, Selected Important Documents Since the 16th National Congress (Part 1)*. Zhongyang Wenxian Chubanshe, Central Literature Publishing House, 2005.

Andrew Nathan and Bruce Gilley. *China's New Rulers*. New York Review of Books Press, 2002.

Backer, Larry Catá. "Linking People to Governing Institutions Through Leninist Political Parties: 全过程民主 (Whole Process Democracy), Socialist Consultative Democracy, and"中国新型政党制度 (China's New Political Party System)." Socialist Consultative Democracy, and "中国新型政党制度 (China's New Political Party System)", June 11, 2022.

Chen Duxiu. "Zai Zhiwen 'Dongfang Zazhi' Jizhe" [Re-Interrogating the "East Magazine" Reporter]. In *Xin Qingnian, New Youth*, Vol. 6, No. 2, Feb 15, 1919.

Chen, Jidong, Jennifer Pan, and Yiqing Xu. "Sources of Authoritarian Responsiveness: A Field Experiment in China." *American Journal of Political Science* 60.2 (2016): 383–400.

Chen, Xulu. Fuxiang Oucun [Thoughts Occasionally Exist], Vol. 4. In *Chen Xulu Wenji, Collected Works of Chen Xulu*. Huadong Shifan Daxue Chubanshe, East China Normal University Press, 1997.

respect for popular sovereignty. This phenomenon bears striking similarities to the historical Chinese concept of prioritizing the well-being of the people. See Przeworski et al. (1999).

Deng Xiaoping Wenxuan [Selected Works of Deng Xiaoping], Vol. 2. Renmin Chubanshe, People's Publishing House, 1994.

Deng Xiaoping. Gaoji Ganbu yao Daitou Fayang Dang de Youliang Chuantong [Senior Cadres Should Take the Lead in Carrying forward the Party's Fine Traditions. In *Deng Xiaoping Wenxuan, Selected Works of Deng Xiaoping*, Vol. 2. Renmin Chubanshe, People's Publishing House, 1993.

Deng Xiaoping. Zhongguo Gongchandang Dishierci Quanguo Daibiao Dahui Kaimuci [Opening Speech of the Twelfth National Congress of the Communist Party of China]. In *Deng Xiaoping Wenxuan, Selected Works of Deng Xiaoping*, Vol. 3. Renmin Chubanshe, People's Publishing House, 1993.

Deng, Xiaoping Wenxuan [Selected Works of Deng Xiaoping], Vol. 2. Renmin Chubanshe, People's Publishing House, 1994.

Deng, Xiaoping. "Zenyang Pingjia Yige Guojia de Zhengzhi Tizhi [How to Evaluate a Country's Political System]." In *Deng Xiaoping Wenxuan, Selected Works of Deng Xiaoping*, Vol. 3. Renmin Chubanshe, People's Publishing House, 1993.

Deng, Xiaoping. Guanche Tiaozheng Fangzhen, Baozheng Anding Tuanjie [Implementing Adjustment Policies and Ensuring Stability and Unity]. In *Deng Xiaoping Wenxuan, Selected Works of Deng Xiaoping*, Vol. 2. Renmin Chubanshe, People's Publishing House, 1993.

Diamond, Larry, Juan Linz, and Seymour Martin Lipset. *Democracy in Developing Countries, Volume 3: Asia*. Lynne Rienner, 1989.

Diamond, Larry. "Is the Third Wave of Democratization Over?: The Imperative of Consolidation." *Assessment* (1997): 121–139.

Dittmer, Lowell. "Chinese Informal Politics." *The China Journal* 34 (1995): 1–34.

Du, Guang. "Yiwei Weida de Minzhu Zhuyizhe: Jinian Hu Yaobang Tonzhi Shishi Ershi Zhounian [A Great Democrat: Commemorating Comrade Hu Yaobang's 20th Anniversary of Passing]." In *Hu Yaobang and Political Reform in China—Reflections of 12 Elder Communist Party Members*. Zhongchen Shuju, Morning Bell Press, 2010.

Du, Yaquan. Jiexu Zhuyi [Continuity-ism]. In *Dongfang Zazhi, Dongfang Magazine*, Vol. 11, No. 1, July 1, 1914.

Duverger, Maurice. *Political Parties: Their Organization and Activity in the Modern State*. Metheun & Co. Ltd., 1959.

Fewsmith, Joseph, and Andrew J. Nathan. "Authoritarian Resilience Revisited: Joseph Fewsmith with Response from Andrew J. Nathan." *Journal of Contemporary China* 28.116 (2019): 167–179.

Fukuyama, Francis. "Confucianism and Democracy." *Journal of Democracy* 6.2 (1995): 20–33.

Gao, Minzheng. "Dangnei Minzhu yu Renmin Minzhu, Jiujing Shui Daidong Shui-Jian yu Hu Wei, Yang Guangbin Jiaoshou Shangque [Intraparty Democracy and People's Democracy: Who Propels Whom-Discussion with Professors Hu Wei and Yang Guangbin]." *Tansuo yu Zhengming, Exploration and Debates* 4 (2013): 29–34.

Gilley, Bruce, and Andrew Nathan. *China's New Rulers: The Secret Files*. Second. New York Review of Books, 2003.

He, Baogang. "'Orderly Political Participation' in China." In *The Palgrave Handbook of Local Governance in Contemporary China* (2019): 347–363.

He, Baogang. ""Orderly Political Participation" in China." In *The Palgrave Handbook of Local Governance in Contemporary China*. Palgrave Macmillan, 2019. pp 347–363.

He, Zengke. "Jianjin Zhengzhi Gaige yu Minzhu de Zhuanxing [Progressive Political Reform and the Transformation of Democracy] (Part I, II)]." *Beijing Xingzheng Xueyuanbao, Journal of Beijing Administrative College* 1/4(2004): 1–5, 10–14.

Heurlin, Christopher. *Responsive Authoritarianism in China*. Cambridge University Press, 2016.

Hu, Jintao. "Qieshi Gaohao Shenru Xuexi Shijian Kexue Fazhan Guan Huodong, Ba Guanche Luoshi Kexue Fazhan Guan Tigao dao Xinde Shuiping [Effectively Carry Out the Activities of In-Depth Study and Practice of the Scientific Development Concept and Raise the Implementation of the Scientific Development Concept to a New Level]." *Renmin Ribao, People's Daily* September 20, 2008.

Hu, Jintao. "Shuli he Luoshi Kexue Fazhan Guan [Establishing and Implementing the Scientific Outlook on Development]." In *Shibada Yilai Zhongyao Wenxian Xuanbian, Selected Important Documents Since the 16th National Congress (Part 1)*. Zhongyang Wenxian Chubanshe, Central Literature Publishing House, 2005.

Huntington, Samuel P. *Political Order in Changing Societies*. Yale University Press, 2006.

Jiang, Qing. *Zhengzhi Ruxue [Political Confucianism]*. Sanlian Shudian, Sanlian Bookstore 2003.

Jiang, Zemin. "Quanmian Jianshe Xiaokang Shehui, Kaichuang Zhongguo Te'se Shehui Zhuyi Jianshe Xinjumian [Building a Moderately Prosperous Society in an All-Round Way and Creating a New Situation in the Construction of Socialism with Chinese Characteristics]." *Report at the 16th National Congress of the Communist Party of China*, 2002.

Jiang, Zemin. "Zai Qingzhu Zhongguo Gongchandang Chengli 80 Zhounian Dahui hang de Jianghua [Speech at the Conference to Celebrate the 80th Anniversary of the Founding of the Communist Party of China]." *Renmin Ribao, People's Daily* July 2, 2001.

Jiang, Zemin. Yong Deng Xiaoping Tongzhi Jianshe You Zhongguo Te'se Shehui Zhuyi Lilun Wuzhuang Quandang [Arming the Whole Party with Comrade Deng Xiaoping's Theory of Building Socialism with Chinese Characteristics]. In *Xuexi "Deng Xiaoping Wenxuan" Disanjuan Baogaohui Shang de Jianghua, Speech at the Report Meeting for Studying the Third Volume of "Selected Works of Deng Xiaoping,"* November 2, 1993.

Kang, Xiaoguang. "Jingji Zengzhang, Shehui Gongzheng, Minzhu Fazhi yu Hefaxing Jichu: 1978 Nian Yilai de Bianhua yu Jinhou de Juese [Economic Growth, Social Justice, Democratic Rule of Law, and the Foundations of Legitimacy: Changes since 1978 and Future Choices]." *Zhanlue yu Guanli, Strategy and Management* 4 (1999): 72–81.

Kang, Xiaoguang. "Wo Weishenme Zhuzhang 'Ruhua'-Guanyu Zhongguo Weilai Zhengzhi Fazhan de Baoshou Zhuyi Sikao [Why I Advocate 'Confucianization'—Conservative Reflections on China's Future Political Development]." cited in Qiu Tao. "Ping Ruhua Zhongguo Lun [On 'Confucianizing' China]." *Gaoxiao Lilun Zhanxian, University Theoretical Frontline* 6 (2006): 37–42.

Kang, Youwei. "Heping Gongyi [On Republican Peace]." In *Buren, Buren*, Vol. 9–10, December 1917.

King, Ambrose Y. C. *China's Great Transformation: Selected Essays on Confucianism, Modernization, and Democracy*. The Chinese University of Hong Kong Press, 2018.

King, Yeo-Chi. *Zhongguo Minben Sixiang [Chinese People-centered Thought]*. Taiwan Shagwu Yinshuguan, Taiwan Commercial Press, 1993.

Li Xiantang. "Shilun Rujia Minben Sixiang de Zhuanzhi Zhuyi Shizhi [On the Essence of Authoritarianism in Confucian People-Oriented Thought]." *Lishi Jiaoxue, History Teaching* 5 (2003): 21–25.

Li, Cunshan, "'Mingui Junqing Shuo Jiexi-Yu Li Junping Xiansheng Shangque [Analyzing the "People Esteem, Monarch Light" Theory—A Discussion with Mr. Li Junping]." *Shehui Kexue Luntan (Xueshu Pinglun Juan), Social Science Forum (Academic Review Volume)* 1 (2009): 5–17.

Li, Cunshan. "Dui Zhongguo Wenhua Minben Sixiang de Zairenshi [Revisiting the Concept of Minben in Chinese Culture]." *Kongzi Yanjiu, Confucius Studies* 6 (2016): 5–15.

Li, Dazhao. Minyi yu Zhengzhi [Minyi and Politics]. In *Li Dazhao Xuanji, Selected Works of Li Dazhao*. Renmin Chubanshe, People's Publishing House, 1959a.

Li, Dazhao. Pingmin Zhuyi [Plebeian Democracy]. In *Li Dazhao Xuanji, Selected Works of Li Dazhao*. Renmin Chubanshe, People's Publishing House, 1959b.

Li, Dazhao. Pingmin Zhuyi [Populism]. In *Li Dazhao Xuanji, Selected Works of Li Dazhao,* Renmin Chubanshe, People's Publishing House, 1959c.

Li, Lanqing. "'Sange Daibiao' Zhongyao Sixiang shi Woguo Wenhua Gongzuo de Zhinan [The Important Thought of the 'Three Represents' Serves as the Guiding Principle for China's Cultural Work]." In *Guanjian Zaidang: Gaoceng Lingdao tan "Sange Daibiao" [The Key Lies in the Party—Senior Leaders Discuss the 'Three Represents']*, Shiwuda yilai Zhongda Wenti Ganbu Luncong, Series on Major Issues Concerning Cadres Since the Fifteenth National Congress, Vol. 1. Zhongyang Wenxian Chubanshe, Central Literature Publishing House, 2001.

Li, Meng et al. *Xin Zhongguo Xuanju Zhidu Fazhan Licheng [The Developmental Course of the Electoral System in New China]*. Shijie Zhishi Chubanshe, World Knowledge Press, 2013.

Liang Qichao. "Guyi Yuankao [An Examination of the Ancient Council]," Vol. 10. *Shiwu Bao, Current Affairs* November 5, 1896.

Liang, Shuming. "Zhongguo Wenhua Yaoyi [Essence of Chinese Culture]." In *Liang Shuming Quanji, Liang Shuming Collected Works,* Vol. 3. Shandong Jiaoyu Chubanshe, Shandong Education Press, 1990.

Lin, Shangli. "Minzhu yu Minsheng: Renmin Minzhu de Zhongguo Luoji [Democracy and People's Livelihood: The Chinese Logic of People's Democracy]." *Beijing Daxue Xuebao (Zhexue Shehui Kexueban), Journal of Peking University (Philosophy and Social Sciences Edition)* 1 (2012): 112–122.

Lin, Shangli. "Renmin, Zhengdang Yu Guojia: Renmin Minzhu Fazhan de Zhengzhixue Fenxi [People, Political Parties and the Country: Political Science Analysis of the Development of People's Democracy]." *Fudan Xuebao (Shehui Kexueban), Journal of Fudan University (Social Science Edition)* 5 (2011): 1–10.

Liu, Zehua, ed. *Zhongguo Chuantong Zhengzhi Zhexue yu Shehui Zhenghe [Traditional Chinese Political Philosophy and Social Integration]*. Zhongguo Shehui Kexue Chuban She, China Social Sciences Press, 2000.

Lu, Xiaobo. "Cong Shoucheng dao Nengdong: Zhongguo Gongchandang yu Minben Zhuyi de Zhuanxiang [From Conservation to Proactivity: The Chinese Communist Party and the Shift towards *Minben* Ideology]." *Jilin Daxue Shehui Kexue Xuebao, Journal of Jilin University Social Sciences* 58 (2018): 5–23, 203.

Mainwaring, Scott. *Rethinking Party Systems in the Third Wave of Democratization: The Case of Brazil*. Stanford University Press, 1999.

Mao, Zedong. Minzhong de Dalianhe [The Great Union of the Masses]. In *Mao Zedong Zaoqi Wengao, Mao Zedong's Early Manuscripts*. Hunan the Central Committee Document Research Office edited, Renmin Chubanshe, People's Publishing House, 1990.

Mao Zedong Wenxuan Diqi Juan [Seventh Volume of the Selected Works of Mao Zedong]. *Renmin Chubanshe*. People's Publishing House, 1999.

Martinelli, Alberto. *Global Modernization: Rethinking the Project of Modernity*. Sage, 2005.

Metzger, Thomas A. *Escape from Predicament: Neo-Confucianism and China's Evolving Political Culture*. Columbia University Press, 1977.

Nathan, Andrew J. "China's Changing of the Guard: Authoritarian Resilience." In *Critical Readings on the Communist Party of China (4 Vols. Set)*. Brodsgaard, Kjeld Erik, ed. Brill, 2017.

O'Dwyer, Shaun. "Democracy and Confucian Values." *Philosophy East and West* 53.1 (2003): 39–63.

Perry, Elizabeth J. *Anyuan: Mining China's Revolutionary Tradition*, Vol. 24. University of California Press, 2012.

Przeworski, Adam, Susan C. Stokes, and Bernard Manin, eds. *Democracy, Accountability, and Representation*. Vol. 2. Cambridge University Press, 1999.

Qiaoan, Runya, and Jessica C. Teets. "Responsive Authoritarianism in China—A Review of Responsiveness in Xi and Hu Administrations." *Journal of Chinese Political Science* 25.1 (2020): 139–153.

Sanzhong Quanhui Yilai Zhongyao Wenxian Xuanbian [The Selected Documents Since the Third Plenary Session of the Eleventh Central Committee], Vol. 1. Renmin Chuabnshe, People's Publishing House, 1982.

Sanzhong Quanhui Yilai Zhongyao Wenxuan Xuanbian [Selected Documents Since the Third Plenary Session of the CPC Central Committee], Vol. 1. Renmin Chubanshe, People's Publishing House, 1982.

Schraeder, Peter J. "Understanding the 'Third Wave' of Democratization in Africa." *The Journal of Politics* 57.4 (1995): 1160–1168.

Schram, Stuart Reynolds. *The Thought of Mao Tse-tung*. Cambridge University Press, 1989.

Schubert, Louis, Thomas R. Dye, and Harmon Zeigler. *The Irony of Democracy: An Uncommon Introduction to American Politics*. Cengage Learning, 2015.

Smith, Ewan. "On the Informal Rules of the Chinese Communist Party." *The China Quarterly* 248.S1 (2021): 141–160.

Society for Research on the History of Modern Japanese Thought edited. Jindai Riben Sixiangshi [History of Modern Japanese Thought], Vol. 2. translated by Li Min et al., Shangwu Yinshu Guan, The Commercial Press, 1991.

Tan, Sor-hoon. *Confucian Democracy: A Deweyan Reconstruction*. SUNY Press, 2003.

Wang, Shaoguang. "Zhongshi Zhengdao Siwei Haishi Xishi Zhengti Siwei [Chinese-Style Political Thinking or Western-Style Political Thinking]." *Renmin Luntan, People's Forum* 8 (2012): 64–66.

Xi, Jinping. Guanyu Quanmian Yifa Zhiguo Lunshu Zhaibian [Excerpts of Xi Jinping's Essays on Comprehensive Rule of Law]. Edited by *Documentation Research Office of the Central Committee of the Communist Party of China*. Zhongyang Wenxian Chubanshe, Central Literature Publishing House, 2015.

Xi, Jinping. *Zai Qingzhu Zhongguo Gongchandang Chengli 100 Zhounian Dahui Shang e Jianghua [Speech at the Conference to Celebrate the 100th Anniversary of the Founding of the Communist Party of China].* Renmin Chubanshe, People's Publishing House, 2021.

Xiao, Gongqin. "Gaige Yilai Zhongguo Zhengzhi de "Qu Liangji Chongtu Hua" Jiqi Lishi Yiyi [The 'Depolarization' of Chinese Politics Since the Reform and Its Historical Significance]." Available at https://m.aisixiang.com/data/18779-3.html (Accessed December 5, 2023).

Xu, Yaotong. "Dangnei Minzhu he Renmin Minzhu de Guanxi [The Mutual Relationship between Intraparty Democracy and People's Democracy]." *Mao Zedong Yanjiu, Mao Zedong Studies* 2 (2017): 32–41.

Yoshino, Sakuzo. *Minshushugi Ronshut [Collected Essays on Democracy]*, Vol. 8. Tokyo, 1947.

Yu, Keping. "Toward an Incremental Democracy and Governance: Chinese Theories and Assessment Criteria." In *Democracy and the Rule of Law in China.* Brill, 2010. pp. 1–33.

Yu, Keping. "Zhongguo Zhili Bianqian 30 Nian (1978–2008) [30 Years of Changes in Chinese Governance (1978–2008)]." *Jilin Daxue Shehui Kexue Xuebao, Journal of Social Sciences of Jilin University* 3 (2008): 5–17+159.

Zhang, Wei-Bin. *Taiwan's Modernization: Americanization and Modernizing Confucian Manifestations.* World Scientific, 2003.

Zhao, Ziyang et al. *Prisoner of the State: The Secret Journal of Zhao Ziyang.* Simon & Schuster, 2009.

Zhou, Zhiping, ed. *Hu Shi Weikan Yingwen Yigao [Unpublished English Manuscripts of Hu Shi].* Liaojing, Liaojing, 2001.

Zong, Hairen. "Hu Jintao: Juqing Ruozhong, Shoucheng Youyu [Hu Jintao: Handling Lightly, Preserving Excess]." and "Wen Jiabao: Mianli Cangzhen, Juzhong Ruoqing [Wen Jiabao: Hidden Needle in Cotton, Handling Heavily]." In *Disi Dai, The Fourth Generation (Chapter One and Chapter Three).* Hong Kong Mingjing Press. 2002.

Whole-Process People's Democracy

The concept of Whole-Process People's Democracy (WPPD) represents the latest articulation of democracy in China in the new era, with people's democracy at its core. Proposed by Xi Jinping as an umbrella concept, it incorporates various elements into a comprehensive toolbox. At a time when the competition over democratic discourse between China and the West is intensifying, the WPPD is not only described as inheriting and continuing the theories of Marxist democracy and the practical experiences of democratic exploration by the CCP, but it also refines and elevates past democratic discourses. This makes it a form of democracy that considers both procedure and substance, process and outcome, theory and practice. Although only four years have passed since the introduction of the concept of WPPD, considerable research has been conducted on its theory and practice.

Comprehending WPPD: Conceptualization and Definition

The WPPD was initially introduced by Xi Jinping during his inspection of the Gubei Civic Center in Hongqiao Street, Changning District, Shanghai in 2019. The Gubei Community, that established in the 1990s, boasts a population that exceeding 30,000 residents, with over half originating from overseas, marking its distinction as a inaugural international

R. Li, *Democratizing China's Political Imaginaries*,
https://doi.org/10.1007/978-981-97-3670-6_3

community. In 2015, the Legislative Affairs Commission of the Standing Committee of the National People's Congress (NPC) in China established a Grassroots Legislative Contact Point (*Jiceng lifa lianxidian* 基层立法联系点 GLCP) in the Gubei Community. Over the past four years, nearly 2,000 residents have actively engaged in diverse legislative opinion solicitation and consultation activities. The CCP regards this form of participation as a manifestation of *authentic* democracy. Xinhua Commentary, in turn, underscores that "democracy is not a mere ornament or display but a tool for addressing tangible issues that people wish to resolve."[1] The CCP persists its pragmatic approach to the democracy, emphasizing its practical utility. Western-style democracy, that characterized by an excessive focus on elections, is viewed as hypocritical and marginalizing the people's voices.

Shortly after the proposal of the WPPD in 2021, the phrase of "adhere to the WPPD in China's politics" was formally integrated into the legal framework through the *Decision of the National People's Congress on Amending the Organic Law of the National People's Congress of the People's Republic of China*, which was adopted during the Fourth Session of the Thirteenth National People's Congress. This decision thus explicitly states, "we are following a pathway of socialist political development with Chinese characteristics, and the people's democracy is a 'Whole-Process People's Democracy'."[2] Subsequently, Xi Jinping reconciles the "people-oriented" narratives in the WPPD during the commemoration of the 100th Anniversary of the Founding of the Chinese Communist Party in 2021, and assigning a significant historical mission to the WPPD.

> In embarking on this new journey, we must place unyielding reliance upon the "people" as the architects of history. It is imperative that we should resolutely uphold the fundamental objective of wholeheartedly serving the populace and standing in unwavering solidarity with their aspirations. To this end, the implementation of the mass line, which respects the pioneering spirit of the people and embraces a development paradigm centered around their needs, and assumes the paramount significance. Our

[1] Xi Jinping's speech on his inspection of the grassroots legislative liaison point of the Standing Committee of the National People's Congress in Hongqiao Street, Shanghai, November 2019, https://www.gov.cn/xinwen/202211/03/content_5723913.htm (Accessed June 19, 2023).

[2] Ibid.

endeavor must be to nurture a holistic people's democracy throughout the entire process, one that ensures social equity and justice. Our unwavering focus should be channeled towards effectively readdressing the challenges stemming from the imbalanced and inadequate development, with immediate attention to the pressing concerns of the citizenry. Through the promotion of comprehensive individual development and the attainment of substantial progress in the pursuit of shared prosperity for all, we shall chart a course toward collective advancement.[3]

The same year, in October, Xi emphasis at the Work Conference of the Central People's Congress, "the WPPD in our country not only has a complete system and procedures, but also encompasses participatory practices."[4] This, however, indicates that the WPPD is not only theoretically reliable but also empirically feasible. In China: Democracy that Works promulgated by the State Council Information Office in 2021, the WPPD was packaged with a classic definition:

Our country's whole-process people's democracy is a unification of the process democracy and result democracy, procedural democracy and substantive democracy, direct democracy and indirect democracy, and people's democracy and the will of the state. It is a democracy that covers the entire chain, all aspects, and full coverage, and is the broadest, most genuine, and most effective socialist democracy.[5]

Then, *The Resolution of the Central Committee of the Communist Party of China on the Major Achievements and Historical Experience of the Party's Centennial Struggle*, passed during the CCP's Sixth Plenary Session of the Nineteenth Central Committee, incorporated the WPPD into the ten clarifications of Xi Jinping's Thoughts on the Socialism

[3] Xi Jinping's speech at the meeting celebrating the centenary of the founding of the Communist Party of China, https://www.gov.cn/xinwen/2021-07/06/content_5622641.htm (Accessed June 19, 2023).

[4] Xi Jinping's systematic and incisive exposition on the major concepts and practical requirements of the WPPD at the work conference of the Central People's Congress, October 2023, https://www.gov.cn/xinwen/202303/03/content_5744265.htm (Accessed June 19, 2023).

[5] Xi Jinping: Hold High the Great Banner of Socialism with Chinese Characteristics and Work Together to Build a Modern Socialist Country in an All-round Way—Report at the Twentieth National Congress of the Communist Party of China, https://www.gov.cn/xinwen/2022-10/25/content_5721685.htm (Accessed June 19, 2023).

with Chinese Characteristics for the New Era. This inclusion emphasizes that "the principal contradiction in our society lies between the people's ever-increasing aspirations for a better life and the imbalanced and inadhttps://www.gov.cn/zhengce/2021-11/16/content_5651269.htmequate development."[6] Thus, it underscores the imperative to adhere to the people-centered development ideology, promote the WPPD, and make substantial progress in advancing the comprehensive development of individuals and the shared prosperity of the entire populace. In 2022, the WPPD found its place in the report of the 20th National Congress and was enshrined in the CCP's Constitution during the same congress, and states that:

> The WPPD constitutes an indispensable hallmark of the China's socialist democratic politics, and embodying the most comprehensive, authentic, and efficacious manifestation of the democratic principles. Our unwavering commitment lies in traversing the trajectory of the socialist political evolution, distinguished by *Chinese characteristics*, while upholding the guiding role of the CCP. Our overarching objective is to ascertain the populace genuinely assumes the mantle of sovereignty and that we administer the nation in strict accordance with the rule of law. To realize this ambition, it is imperative that we refine the framework facilitating popular sovereignty; foster a methodical that engagement of the citizenry in the political affairs; safeguard their entitlement to partake in democratic processes, encompassing elections, consultations, decision-making, administration, and oversight, all executed in the bounds of legality. Central to our endeavor is the unleashing of the untapped potential, zeal, and creative faculties of the people, thereby fortifying and propelling a thriving, steadfast, and cohesive political milieu.[7]

At the Central People's Congress Working Conference in 2021, Xi comprehensively expounded upon the significance, characteristics, advantages, and practical requisites of the WPPD. It entails the inclusive engagement of all individuals, encompassing the entire populace as active

[6] *Resolution of the Central Committee of the Communist Party of China on the Major Achievements and Historical Experience of the Party's Centennial Struggle*, passed by the Sixth Plenary Session of the Nineteenth Central Committee of the Party, (Accessed June 19, 2023).

[7] Report at the Twentieth National Congress of the Communist Party of China, https://topics.gmw.cn/node_147767.htm (Accessed June 29, 2023).

participants, thereby underscoring a continuous public involvement both prior to and following the decision-making processes. This encompassing participation spans a wide spectrum of topics and manifests itself across all facets, illustrating a comprehensive, systematic, and holistic engagement approach. Furthermore, the WPPD also places particular emphasis on the complete continuum of the public participation, wherein the democratic process remains uninterrupted and manifests itself in the interplay and coexistence of the democratic election, decision-making, consultation, management, and supervision. Lastly, the WPPD underscores the inherent efficacy of participation outcomes, not only esteeming procedural democracy but also accentuating the results realized through the democratic process. It is intrinsically intertwined with decision-making and governance objectives, displaying a distinct focus on problem-solving and the attainment of tangible outcomes.

Xi Jinping also links the WPPD with the Chinese-style modernization (中国式现代化*Zhongguishi Xiandaihua*), which emerged as a prominent aspect of China's centennial goals, as endorsed during the CCP's 20th National Congress in 2022: "the WPPD is deemed indispensable for Chinese-style modernization."[8] In a remarkably short span of less than three years (from 2019 to 2023), the CCP has effectively formulated and propagated a *distinctive* discourse on Chinese democracy, effectively incorporating the WPPD into China's legal framework (with the potential for inclusion in China's Constitution), Xi Jinping's Thoughts, and the Party Constitution. This democratic discourse is intricately interwoven with the broader context of Chinese-style modernization, particularly the political modernization. This timely narrative carries a direct implication, particularly amid the backdrop of the intensifying US-China confrontation. As underscored in various speeches by Xi, Western-style vote-centered democracy is, in practice, fraught with dysfunction, often resulting in political polarization, governance failures, and social unrest. In contrast, the WPPD in China is fully integrated into the entire democratic process.

This mapping offers a straightforward insight into the evolution of the concept of WPPD and its alignment with broader narratives in China. However, several critical dimensions have yet to be adequately addressed. Firstly, the WPPD that draws upon a rich tapestry of influences,

[8] Ibid.

including the Marxist tradition of democracy, people-oriented (*Minben* 民本) democratic perspectives from Confucianism, as well as various democratic ideas stemming from both Chinese historical sources and Western classical democratic thought. Paradoxically, this rich tapestry of influence has resulted in a conceptualized vagueness that hinders its empirical application. For instance, while WPPD is envisioned as a multidisciplinary practice that spans the state and society, encompassing elements within the structures of the CCP and the NPC, legislative processes, and the grassroots community self-governance, empirical studies in these areas remain notably scarce.

Secondly, there exists a paucity of in-depth examinations at the meso and micro levels within the framework of WPPD. While significant attention has been directed towards the rather overarching narrative, such as the incorporation of the WPPD into the *NPC's Organizational Law* and *Rules of Procedure*, while the dynamics of the middle and grassroots ground, and how they are implementing WPPD, as well as the mechanisms of bottom-up interactions that facilitate its implementation, remain largely unexplored. These more concrete studies represent a notable gap in the existing literature. Thirdly, current research on WPPD demonstrates a limited methodological diversity, primarily focusing on the theoretical (re)construction. Comparative studies, case analyses, and quantitative research endeavors in this domain are also relatively scarce.

The design of the WPPD is considered, on the one hand, as a reaction to the "narrow construal" of democracy in Western liberal democracies, which frequently confines democracy solely to the vote. As articulated by Schubert et al. (2015), "...political activities in the United States are also controlled by a small group, with the majority of political, economic, and social decisions made by a few elites rather than the broader population."[9] This lens gains particular significance within the context of intense competition in the discourse on democracy between China and the West, where mocking the West for highlighting the superior of the WPPD.[10]

[9] Schubert et al. (2015, p. 2).

[10] The comparison, measuring exercise, is built around three core propositions. a. The system's chronic defects are difficult to overcome; b. the practice of democracy is rather chaotic, and c. exporting the so-called democracy produces evil results). This entails two layers of significance. Firstly, the commendation of Chinese democracy aligns with Xi Jinping's unwavering position, asserting that China's democracy outshines that of the West. This enthusiastic acclaim is rooted in a perspective that deems Chinese democracy

In the WPPD, the term "people" refers to the "whole population" rather than the Western definition of voters possessing "sovereignty" exclusively during the elections. The latter, grounded in the competitive electoral system and the principle of "majority rule," could fluctuate with changes in the needs of a minority ruling class, contradicting the Marxist insistence on the class-based, fixed, and absolute majority rule to achieve the majority decision of the people.

On the other hand, the WPPD refines the traditional Chinese democratic model, which primarily relied on the government responsiveness.[11] It thus establishes a comprehensive closed-loop system comprising the so-called responsive democracy, participatory democracy, consultative democracy, and supervisory democracy. This "consensus democracy" not only counters the one-time decision-making democracy prevalent in the West but also signifies the evolution of Marxist democratic theory within the context of China. In contrast to the Western emphasis on political systems or forms of government, China's focus on the "political philosophy (*Zhengdao* 政道)"[12] places greater importance on listening to, absorbing, and providing feedback to public opinion during the policy-making process. Simultaneously, this process adheres to traditional Chinese political values such as harmony, stability, and order.[13] Therefore, the introduction of the WPPD refines and enriches the essence of democratic politics in contemporary Chinese socialism, encapsulating the refined essence of democracy in China for the new era.

as inherently superior (1) "a minority of self-righteous outsiders" have little legitimacy in judging the democratic character of a foreign system; (2) that the ideal of perfect democracy has yet to be attained, though systems may strive toward perfection; and (3) some inter-systemic dialogue at the international level should be undertaken "on the basis of equality and mutual respect" striving toward collective human progress. see Backer (2022).

[11] On the responsiveness of china's governance, see Qiaoan and Teets (2020), Heurlin (2016), and Chen et al. (2016).

[12] See Wang (2012).

[13] For example, the "orderly participation", see He (2019).

The WPPD in Grand Narrative: A Chinese Approach to Modernization

The concept of modernization or modernity has gradually solidified its position in sociology during the post-World War II political ideological competition. On the one hand, it is marked by the rapid rise of decolonization and post-colonial nations, and on the other hand, by the inclusion of similar nations into the sphere of influence through the competition between the United States and the Soviet Union. According to Martinelli's (2005) analysis of modernization in the second half of the last century, three major features characterize the global modernization at this stage. Firstly, it involves the transformation of capitalism, manifested as the globalization of the economy and the progression towards post-industrial society, namely, transitioning from labor organization in large assembly line factories (the Ford-Taylorism type) to automation. Secondly, it is represented by the rapid economic and power growth of Asian countries (primarily the Four Asian Tigers—South Korea, Taiwan, Singapore, and Hong Kong—including later mainland China, India, Thailand, and Malaysia), as well as some countries in Latin America. These countries explored different paths of modernization, establishing alliances between economic liberalism and national authoritarianism. Finally, by the late 1980s, some significant international events such as the dissolution of the Soviet Union, German reunification, and European economic recovery led the United States to become the sole superpower. Simultaneously, it accelerated the eastward expansion of the European Union, creating new opportunities for modernization in countries outside the Western world.[14]

While Western modernization has undoubtedly become the most successful and representative model as modernization approaches consensus, a prevailing misconception is that modernization is often associated with the West. The idea is achieving modernization—especially for developing countries—involves following the Western path. However, from the second half of the last century to the twenty-first century, many cases of developing countries emulating Western modernization in politics, economics, and society have mostly ended in failure. The main reason is that while modernization has somehow universal value, the paths to

[14] Martinelli (2005, p. 3).

achieving it are diverse, and neglecting to consider one's own practical absorption and adaptation can lead to incongruities.[15]

Against this backdrop, the opening up of diverse paths to modernization becomes a crucial issue for many developing countries. During the celebration of the 100th anniversary of the founding of the Communist Party of China, Xi therefore pointed out, "We adhere to and develop socialism with *Chinese characteristics*, promote the coordinated development of material civilization, political civilization, spiritual civilization, social civilization, and ecological civilization, and have created a new path of Chinese-style modernization, forging a new form of human civilization."[16] This is a rather new interpretation of Chinese-style modernization in Xi's discourse. While aligning with the inexorable global trend of modernization, it diverges from the Western trajectory of modernization. This divergence is manifested across various dimensions, encompassing political, economic, and societal realms.

The development of China's modernization has demonstrated nominal similarities with Western modernization in *instrumental* rationality, encompassing aspects like urbanization, industrialization, and technological advancement. However, in terms of axiological rationality, the former exhibits some distinctive characteristics. It is therefore characterized by the pursuit of a modernization that achieves the common prosperity for all the citizens, harmonizes material and spiritual civilization, fosters coexistence and harmony between humans and nature, and adheres to the path of peaceful development. Consequently, our modernization stands on a higher plane of axiological rationality and a loftier moral standpoint. Professor Hu Angang (胡鞍钢) thus summarizes the key features of Chinese-style modernization as follows:

[15] Some evidence emerging from the third wave of democratization, initiated in the 1980s, indicates that only a limited number of countries achieved stable and successful democratic transitions. Conversely, most countries, particularly in Africa, South America, and the Middle East Asia, either maintained their authoritarian regimes or experienced setbacks. The introduction of elections, party competition, and similar systems under immature conditions incurred substantial costs for both the country and society. These costs encompassed disorder and economic regression, far surpassing the advantages derived from the democratization process. See Schraeder (1995), Diamond (1997), and Mainwaring (1999).

[16] Xi (2021, pp. 13–14).

> In terms of the nature of the state, Chinese modernization is characterized as the modernization of a socialist state, distinct from the modernization of capitalist countries in the West. Considering the governance system, China follows a governance structure led by the CCP, implementing a system of the NPC, and engaging in multi-party cooperation and political consultation. This differs from Western countries that adopt presidential, parliamentary, two-party, or multi-party systems. Examining the philosophy of national governance, China centers its modernization on the well-being of all citizens, in contrast to the capital-centric modernization focusing on a tiny monopoly of capital groups. Concerning the developmental task, socialism's essence is emphasized, aiming to liberate and develop productive forces, eliminate exploitation, eradicate polarization, and ultimately achieve common prosperity. Regarding the development goal, it aspires to achieve the participation, development, prosperity, and shared benefits of the entire population, promoting a modernization characterized by the absence of severe social conflicts and political conflicts that among parties. In terms of the relationship with the outside world, China advocates building a community with a shared future for humanity, practicing win-win cooperation, as opposed to colonialism, imperialism, and hegemony.[17]

Chinese-style modernization is described as focusing on the modernization of "individuals," while Chinese democracy in modern days is also being portrayed as centered on human beings. In some respects, they mutually resonate to advocate for a new discourse endorsing this interconnectedness. In the context of monarchy, "democracy" constitutes the populace's role within the state system, whereas in a democratic system, it represents the institutional framework of the people within the state.[18] In China, the democratic centralism under the dictatorship of the proletariat serves as the state structure, while the system of the People's Congress ensures the democratic nature of Chinese-style modernization. Three critical aspects require emphasis regarding the relationship between the WPPD and Chinese-style modernization: the role of the WPPD in political modernization, and the pivotal roles of the CCP's leadership and common prosperity in the practical realization of the WPPD and Chinese-style modernization.

[17] Hu (2022, p. 25).

[18] See Marx (1970, p. 281).

The WPPD encompasses various dimensions, such as politics, economy, culture, and society, with its primary emphasis lying on the politics.[19] Political modernization is identified as an indispensable component of Chinese-style modernization, wherein the WPPD assumes a central role in political reform. This logic interconnects these key dimensions within a unified framework. China's pursuit of modernization traced to the early twentieth century, and its democratic endeavors throughout modern Chinese history, including institutional experiments, centralization and decentralization, party-state relations, and the balance between planned economy and market considerations, have all contributed to the formulation of a distinctive political model that reconciles general political principles with China's specific conditions.

Following the period of Reform and Opening Up, several key democratic discourses have emerged simultaneously, both theoretically and practically. These include electoral democracy, consultative democracy, grassroots democracy, and intraparty democracy, etc. While not unique to China, they incorporate distinct *Chinese characteristics* and serve as institutional safeguards for political reforms in China. Nevertheless, this equilibrium remains precarious, particularly in light of the burgeoning democratic demands precipitated by the highly developed economy in China. Come to twenty-first century, political modernization is characterized by "the convergence and mutual embedding of democracy and governance,"[20] further indicating an inexorable path towards the integration of the WPPD and governance within China's political modernization endeavor. Democratic governance not only affirms the WPPD as a rather "practical" and "effective" democratic model, but also catalyzes the modernization of governance structures and augments governance efficacy.

In contrast to Western models of modernization that primarily propelled by the market forces and democratization facilitated by the civil society, to date, China's trajectory of modernization and democratization is distinctly characterized by the guidance and leadership of the ruling party. This deviation is intricately linked to the lower level of societal organization, underdeveloped economic conditions, extensive participation

[19] Xi (2021, pp. 13–14).

[20] Zhang (2022, p. 96).

challenges, and an inadequate legal framework that is typically encountered by late-developing countries. Consequently, it tends to give rise to a modernization development dominated by political forces like the party, military, or government. Simultaneously, in the process of democratization in such context, the potential positive roleplay of the state or government emerges as a predominant force in supporting, reinforcing, or even leading post-statist forms of democratic governance.[21] Therefore, the Chinese model of modernization and democratic development, designed, controlled, and propelled by the CCP and its public authority, presents an alternative non-Western approach to modernization.

Functioning as a Marxist mission-oriented party with a strong inclination towards modernization,[22] the CCP, however, intertwines its intrinsic values, aspirational goals, and institutional designs with the construction of the state and political power. The former significantly influences and reshapes the latter's form and modernization process. If anything unique and distinctly Chinese feature China's modernization, the CCP's leadership emerges as the most salient. This tradition within Marxism is frequently described as the core advantage of the socialist system, representing the fundamental foundation and lifeline of both the party and the state, and binding the interests and destinies of people of all ethnic groups. As such, the Chinese-style modernization unfolds within the framework of the CCP's leadership, rooted in the fundamental value of "putting people first" and practiced through Deng Xiaoping's strategy of the "three-step (*Sanbuzou* 三步走)" plan. This attempt aimed to resolve the people's basic needs by the end of the 1980s, achieve a moderately prosperous society by the end of the twentieth century, and essentially attain modernization by the mid-twenty-first century. The 18th Party Congress formalized the "Two Centenary Goals (*Liangge Yibainian* 两个一百年)," calling for the comprehensive establishment of a moderately prosperous society by the centenary of the CCP in 2021 and the construction of a socialist modernized nation by the centenary of the New China in 2049.

In this phased pathway of Chinese-style modernization, democracy follows, albeit in a retrograde manner. Following the Post-Reform and Opening Up era, democracy in China gradually deviated from the notions

[21] See also Warren (2004).

[22] Zhao (2022).

of "great leap forward" and "mass democracy," distancing itself from abstract and feeble democratic ideals while eschewing organizational and movement-oriented methods to promote democracy. Instead, it adopts a rather pragmatic approach rooted in China's economic development and the realities of the socialist primary stage as outlined by Deng, simultaneously adjusting its relationship with traditional political culture. This approach was designed to integrate with other facets of modernization, such as the rule of law and governance, achieving a seamless unity of the CCP leadership, people's autonomy, and governance by law.

The essence of China's modernization lies in progressively achieving the common prosperity of the entire population. Common prosperity is not only in contrast to the wealth of a few individuals in the Western capitalist modernization process but also addresses the fundamental issues inherent in the capitalist system itself, specifically its inability to resolve polarization and proletarian poverty. Since the initiation of Reforms and Opening Up, the relationship between the common prosperity and people's democracy has been continuously strengthened. Deng Xiaoping emphasized, "The characteristic of socialism is not poverty but wealth, a wealth that belongs to all the people."[23] In 1978, the Third Plenary Session of the Eleventh Central Committee of the Party first proposed encouraging certain regions and individuals to become prosperous, breaking through the "poverty trap," solving subsistence problems, and achieving a moderately prosperous level. Since the 18th Party Congress, Xi Jinping has also emphasized, "The development we pursue is development that benefits the people, the prosperity we pursue is the common prosperity of the entire population."[24] By 2021, Xi declared that China had comprehensively built a moderately prosperous society at the celebration of the 100th anniversary of the founding of the CCP.

In the rhetoric of the CCP, common prosperity denotes a form of prosperity that transcends the enrichment of a few individuals, avoids egalitarianism, and eschews synchronous affluence. It signifies a state of prosperity that characterized by universal, differential, and incremental wealth accumulation. Common prosperity primarily entails material abundance, effectively elevating the living standards of the populace. However,

[23] Deng (1993, p. 265).

[24] *Xi Jinping Guanyu Shehui Zhuyi Shehui Jianshe Lunshu Zhaibian [Excerpts of Xi Jinping's Essays on the Construction of Socialist Society]*. Zhonggong Zhongyang Wenxian Chubanshe, Central Literature Publishing House, 2017. p. 35.

it extends beyond mere material wealth. As stated, "... common prosperity ensures societal stability. Economic development can only thrive within stable societal frameworks."[25] The interconnectedness among common prosperity, social equity, stability, and economic development is paramount. Additionally, "Achieving common prosperity is not solely an economic issue but a significant political matter that underpins the CCP's governance legitimacy."[26] Since the advent of Reform and Opening Up in 1978, realizing common prosperity and enhancing the well-being of the broadest population have perennially been a crucial source of legitimacy for the CCP's governance. Lastly, akin to the profound insights of Marx and Engels into the material and spiritual impoverishment of the proletariat under capitalism, the loftier goal of common prosperity lies in fostering spiritual enrichment among the masses. It serves as the foundation for realizing an ideal society where individuals could achieve comprehensive freedom and development, encapsulated in the dictum, "Enrich both the pockets and the minds."[27] Thus, common prosperity embodies a crucial manifestation of the people's democracy and reflects the multifaceted aspects of Chinese-style modernization encompassing politics, economy, culture, and spirituality.

Xi Jinping has departed from the policy during the Deng Xiaoping era of allowing some people to become rich first, instead opting for a departure from the laissez-faire capitalism initiated by Deng Xiaoping and former Premier Zhu Rongji (朱镕基), shifting towards a pursuit of a Mao-era mass egalitarian and constructing a system "coordinated distribution of initial distribution, redistribution, and third distribution." This policy is closely interlinked to the stability of Chinese politics, with three significant implications: the elimination of wealth and urban–rural disparities, as these pose major challenges to China's goal of achieving

[25] *Deng Xiaoping Nianpu (1975–1997) [Chronicle of Deng Xiaoping (1975–1997] (Part 2)*. Zhongyang Wenxian Chubanshe, Central Literature Publishing House, 2004. p. 1312.

[26] Shenru Xuexi Jianjue Guanche Dang de Shijiujie Wuzhong Quanhui Jingshen, Quebao Quanmian Jiancheng Shehui Zhuyi Xiandaihua Guojia Haokaiju [In-Depth Study and Resolute Implementation of the Spirit of the Fifth Plenary Session of the 19th CPC Central Committee to Ensure a Good Start in Building a Modern Socialist Country in an All-Round Way]. *Renmin Ribao, People's Daily* January 12, 2021.

[27] *Shibada Yilai Zhongyao Wenxian Xuanbian [Selection of Important Documents Since the 18th National Congress] (Part 2)*. Zhongyang Wenxian Chubanshe, Central Literature Publishing House, 2018. p. 50.

middle-income status and escaping the middle-income trap; the promotion of common prosperity holds crucial political significance, essentially constituting a populist strategy that aimed at revitalizing the very foundation of Chinese communist ideology, strengthening the CCP's legitimacy, and the personal authority of Xi Jinping; and the advancement of China's socialist authoritarian system's relative advantages in discourse, morality, material, and institutional aspects over Western liberal capitalist systems, disseminating the "Chinese model" worldwide.[28] In pursuing such policies, measures advocating for greater social equality, such as imposing heavy taxes on the rich and promoting state ownership while reducing private ownership, provide a new opportunity for aligning with the people and opposing those privileged elite.[29] Such efforts also inevitably serve to restrain China's emerging oligarchs from challenging Xi Jinping or the authority of the CCP in controlling China.

Then, why the WPPD? The utilization of WPPD by the CCP should not be facilely dismissed as mere a rhetorical innovation. Within the framework of "people's democracy," little novelty exists, given that the Marxist-Leninist indigenized democratic perspective in China has been denoted as "people's democracy" since the post-World War II era. However, the terminology "whole process" introduces a hitherto unaddressed feature in Chinese democratic discourse. Firstly, "whole process" amalgamates various democratic elements previously underscored in China, such as democratic participation, consultation, supervision, and management. While Western audiences are inclined to categorize this as a simplistic form of participatory democracy, it functions both as the CCP's rejoinder to the Western democracy, which is centered around elections and aims to showcase the advantages of the WPPD, and as a means of downplaying the significance of elections, thereby mitigating the chaos and challenges to the CCP's rule brought about by electoral processes.

Secondly, the WPPD reinforces China's governance-oriented democratic model, and accentuating outcome-oriented democracy. In contrast to the Western emphasis on the procedural democracy, especially the Schumpeterian electoral democracy, China tends to re-concretize and measure its democracy through governance performance. Despite the primary criticism from Western scholars directed towards the elusive and

[28] Wu (2022).

[29] Hass (2021).

vague nature of WPPD, China's response consistently focuses on offsetting these critiques by highlighting the CCP's accomplishments under the banner of good governance and its output.

In this toolkit, firstly, democracy is presented in a practical and visual format. For instance, China's notable achievement in further eradicating absolute poverty over the past four decades and the enhancement of the standard of living resulting from China's economic growth since the Reform and Opening Up. Despite the economic backlashes that faced by China, the momentum of its economy not only accrues credibility for the CCP but also substantiates the pragmatic efficacy of Chinese democracy. Secondly, the WPPD in a way reinforces a "consensus democracy" in China, even though non-democratic methods may be employed in the process of consensus building. For instance, Chinese democracy is being portrayed as a combination of electoral democracy and Xieshang Minzhu (Chinese version of "deliberative democracy"). However, the official discourse consistently interprets the "deliberative democracy" that in the West as consultative democracy, underscoring the consultative nature of democracy.

This consensus democracy in China, founded on consultation, diverges somewhat from the Scandinavian-style consensus democracy, which is grounded in compromise, accommodation, and inclusivity, as opposed to adopting an adversarial and exclusionary stance, as observed in Anglo-Saxon and Continental European counterparts.[30] This democracy, coined as "Eastern meritocracy"—in also contrast to Western meritocracy, which emphasizes the justice of distribution not only in political power but also in other public goods—wherein democracy is viewed as a governance approach to achieve positive outcomes. From this perspective, WPPD is not merely a superficial rebranding but a daring traverse through an all-encompassing grand discourse. In contrast to Western liberal democracy, it accentuates the pragmatic democratic model of China, grounded in good governance and outputs. Despite numerous pitfalls and the accompanying authoritarian controls in practice, this concept is, however, ambitious.

Therefore, only by contextualizing WPPD within a broader narrative can it be understood. Firstly, the WPPD seeks to readdress the paradox

[30] See Goodin (2006).

between development, order, and participation in the context of modernization transition. Under the framework of party-led democracy, while ensuring strong central authority and the foundation of social order, it is crucial to balance and expand the breadth and depth of citizen participation channels, enhance the responsiveness, transparency, and accountability of governments, and institutionalize democratic processes, procedures, and norms within the context of China's path to modernization and socialist construction. Civil rights are no longer seen as absolute and abstract but as rights that citizens genuinely enjoy. Secondly, while the ultimate goals and values of modernization and democratization are accepted and advocated in China, the pathways and models of modernization and democratization are diverse and adaptable. Lastly, the theory and practice of the WPPD and China's unique path to modernization embody both inheritance and innovation, encompassing various dimensions such as the Chinese tradition, party system, indigenized socialism, market economy, democracy, authority, and governance. This not only promotes the endogenous, autonomous, balanced, and orderly development of China's modernization but may also provide valuable reference for other developing countries to explore democratic political paths suitable for their national conditions and effectively promote economic and social development in the process of modernization.

References

Backer, Larry Catá. "Linking People to Governing Institutions Through Leninist Political Parties: 全过程民主 (Whole Process Democracy), Socialist Consultative Democracy, and 中国新型政党制度 (China's New Political Party System)." *Socialist Consultative Democracy, and "中国新型政党制度 (China's New Political Party System)"*, June 11, 2022.

Chen, Jidong, Jennifer Pan, and Yiqing Xu. "Sources of authoritarian responsiveness: A field experiment in China." *American journal of political science* 60.2 (2016): 383–400.

Deng Xiaoping Nianpu (1975–1997) [Chronicle of Deng Xiaoping (1975–1997)] (Part 2). Zhongyang Wenxian Chubanshe, Central Literature Publishing House, 2004.

Deng Xiaoping Wenxuan [Selected Works of Deng Xiaoping], Vol. 3. Renmin Chubanshe, People's Publishing House, 1993.

Diamond, Larry. "Is the Third Wave of Democratization Over?: The Imperative of Consolidation." *Assessment* (1997): 121–139.

Goodin, Robert E. "Input Democracy." In *Power and Democracy: Critical Interventions*. Fredrik Engelstad and Øyvind Østerud, eds. Farnham: Ashgate, 2006. pp. 79–100.

Hass, Ryan. *Assessing Chinas Common Prosperity Campaign*. Brookings Institution, 2021.

He, Baogang. "'Orderly Political Participation' in China." In *The Palgrave Handbook of Local Governance in Contemporary China*. Yu, Jianxing, and Sujian Guo, eds. Palgrave Macmillan, 2019. pp. 347–363.

Heurlin, Christopher. *Responsive authoritarianism in China*. Cambridge University Press, 2016.

Hu, Angang. "Zhongguoshi Xiandaihua Daolu de Tezheng he Yiyi Fenxi [Analysis of the Characteristics and Significance of the Chinese Modernization Road]." *Shandong Daxue Xuebao (Shehui Kexueban), Journal of Shandong University (Philosophy and Social Sciences Edition)* 1 (2022): 21–38.

Mainwaring, Scott. *Rethinking Party Systems in the Third Wave of Democratization: The Case of Brazil*. Stanford University Press, 1999.

Martinelli, Alberto. *Global Modernization: Rethinking the Project of Modernity*. Sage, 2005.

Marx, Karl. *Critique of Hegel's Philosophy of Right*. Cambridge University Press, 1970.

Qiaoan, Runya, and Jessica C. Teets. "Responsive Authoritarianism in China—A Review of Responsiveness in Xi and Hu Administrations." *Journal of Chinese Political Science* 25.1 (2020): 139–153.

Report at the Twentieth National Congress of the Communist Party of China. Available at https://topics.gmw.cn/node_147767.htm (Accessed June 29, 2023).

Resolution of the Central Committee of the Communist Party of China on the Major Achievements and Historical Experience of the Party's Centennial Struggle, passed by the Sixth Plenary Session of the Nineteenth Central Committee of the Party. Available at https://www.gov.cn/zhengce/2021-11/16/content_5651269.htm (Accessed June 19, 2023).

Schraeder, Peter J. "Understanding the 'Third Wave' of Democratization in Africa." *The Journal of Politics* 57.4 (1995): 1160–1168.

Schubert, Louis, Thomas R. Dye, and Harmon Zeigler. *The Irony of Democracy: An Uncommon Introduction to American Politics*. Cengage Learning, 2015.

Shibada Yilai Zhopngyao Wenxian Xuanbian [Selection of Important Documents Since the 18th National Congress (Part 2). Central Literature Publishing House, 2018.

Wang, Shaoguang. "Zhongshi Zhengdao Siwei Haishi Xishi Zhengti Siwei [Chinese-Style Political Thinking or Western-Style Political Thinking]." *Renmin Luntan, People's Forum* 8 (2012): 64–66.

Warren, Mark E. "What Kind of Civil Society Is Best for Democracy?" *Portuguese Journal of Social Science* 3.1 (2004): 37–47.

Wu, Guoguang. "China's Common Prosperity Program: Causes, Challenges, and Implications." *The Asia Society Policy Institute* March 2022.

Xi Jinping Guanyu Shehui Zhuyi Shehui Jianshe Lunshu Zhaibian [Excerpts of Xi Jinping's Essays on the Construction of Socialist Society]. Zhonggong Zhongyang Wenxian Chubanshe, Central Literature Publishing House, 2017.

Xi Jinping: *Hold High the Great Banner of Socialism with Chinese Characteristics and Work Together to Build a Modern Socialist Country in an All-Round Way—Report at the Twentieth National Congress of the Communist Party of China*. Available at https://www.gov.cn/xinwen/2022-10/25/content_5721685.htm (Accessed June 19, 2023).

Xi Jinping. *Zai Qingzhu Zhongguo Gongchandang Chengli 100 Zhounian Dahui shang de Jianghua [Speech at the Conference to Celebrate the 100th Anniversary of the Founding of the Communist Party of China]*. Renmin Chubanshe, People's Publishing House, 2021.

Xi Jinping's Speech at the Meeting Celebrating the Centenary of the Founding of the Communist Party of China. Available at https://www.gov.cn/xinwen/2021-07/06/content_5622641.htm (Accessed June 19, 2023)

Xi Jinping's Speech on His Inspection of the Grassroots Legislative Liaison Point of the Standing Committee of the National People's Congress in Hongqiao Street, Shanghai. November 2019. Available at https://www.gov.cn/xinwen/202211/03/content_5723913.htm (Accessed Jun 19, 2023).

Xi Jinping's Systematic and Incisive Exposition on the Major Concepts and Practical Requirements of the WPPD at the Work conference of the Central People's Congress, October 2023. Available at https: //www.gov.cn/xinwen/202303/03/content_5744265.htm (Accessed June 19, 2023).

Zhang, Aijun: "Mudi yu Shouduan: Quanguohcneg Renmin Minzhu yu Guojia Zhili Guangxi Zaigoujian [Goals and Means: Reconstructing the Relationship Between the Whole Process People's Democracy and National Governance]." *Lilun Jianshe, Theory Construction* 2 (2022): 94–102.

Zhao, Dapeng. "Mission-Oriented Political Parties and the Self-Revolution of the Communist Party of China: Basic Logic, Motive Mechanism, and Risk Response." *Governance Studies* 38.3 (2022): 80.

Intrapart Democracy

Intraparty Democracy, Supervision, and People's Democracy

The intraparty democracy constitutes initiative by the CCP to implement democratic practices from top to bottom, and from within to without. As early as the 11th National Congress in 1977, Hua Guofeng discussed the political reform in China following the dismantling of the "Gang of Four (四人帮 *Sirenbang*)," introducing the concepts of "Party democracy" and "people's democracy."[1] Subsequently, in the political report of the 12th National Congress in 1982, Hu Yaobang again employed the term "intraparty democracy" to underscore the rolepaly of democracy within the framework of "democratic centralism."[2] In the political report of the 13th National Congress in 1987, Deng Xiaoping elaborated on the relationship between intraparty democracy and people's democracy, stating, "To gradually promote people's democracy through intraparty democracy is a practical and effective path to develop socialist democratic politics." In the subsequent preliminary elections of the 13th Central Committee, intraparty elections were conducted by establishing a 5% quota for the number of candidates.

[1] Hua (1977).
[2] Hu (1982).

R. Li, *Democratizing China's Political Imaginaries*,
https://doi.org/10.1007/978-981-97-3670-6_4

The primary attempt of intraparty democracy in the 1980s was to achieve the overarching strategic goal of Reform and Opening Up by reinstating democratic practices within the Party, fostering liberated thinking, and rectifying disorder. Since the 1990s, intraparty democracy has evolved in response to societal developments, propelling the internal transformation of the CCP through the standardization and innovation of intraparty institutions. This transformation seeks to enhance the CCP's leadership and governance responsibilities. By the early twenty-first century, Jiang Zemin's "July 1st Speech (七一讲话 *Qiyi Jianghua*)" in 2001 and the *Decision on Strengthening and Improving Party Conduct under the framework of the Sixth Plenary Session of the 15th Central Committee* reiterated the concept of "promoting people's democracy via intraparty democracy" and elevated intraparty democracy to a significant driving force for China's democratic development. The 16th National Congress report in 2002, for the first time, elevated intraparty democracy to the level of the "Party's life," emphasizing that "intraparty democracy is the life of the party and plays an important exemplary and driving role in people's democracy." *The Decision on Strengthening the Party's Governing Capability* adopted at the Fourth Plenary Session of the 16th Central Committee in 2004 further incorporated intraparty democracy, driven by intraparty elections at the grassroots level, into the construction of the CCP's governing capability.

In the political report of the 17th National Congress in 2007, Hu Jintao reiterated the assertion of "expanding the intraparty democracy to drive people's democracy." Subsequently, documents such as the *Decision on Major Issues Concerning Further Strengthening and Improving Party Building in the New Situation* adopted at the Fourth Plenary Session of the 17th Central Committee in 2009 and the political report of the 18th National Congress in 2012 all expounded on the development prospects of the pathway to democratization in China, emphasizing "driving people's democracy through intraparty democracy."[3]

[3] During the Xi Jinping era, particularly in the aftermath of the 19th National Congress of the Communist Party of China and subsequent events, the advocacy for intraparty democracy has gradually diminished. In the report of the 19th CPC National Congress, the reference to intraparty democracy is confined to the section addressing of "the significant strides taken in the past five years in the construction of democracy and the rule of law," portraying it as a "political achievement." In 2018, Xi Jinping, in a speech delivered at the Central Commission for Discipline Inspection plenum, remarked, "As the comprehensive and strict governance of the Party deepens, there have been some noises within

Intraparty democracy is a form of democracy promoted within the context of the CCP's single-party governance. Its practical implementation revolves around how the CCP internally manages, governs, and supervises its members. This form of democracy differs from partisan competition and supervision in multi-party systems in the West. As early as 2002, the *Regulations on the Selection and Appointment of Party and Government Leading Cadres* issued by the Central Committee of the Chinese Communist Party aimed to further strengthen the intraparty democratic construction by standardizing the selection and appointment of the CCP and government cadres. The *Regulations on Intraparty Supervision and the Regulations on Safeguarding the Rights of Party Members* issued in 2004 also enumerated the rights of the CCP members in political life, including the right to information, participation, election, and supervision, all based on the principle of "the CCP governs the Party and exercises strict self-discipline (党要管党 从严治党 *Dang Yao Guandang, Congyan Zhidang*)." More specifically, the *Regulations on the Term of Office for Leading Cadres* issued by the Central Committee in 2006, as well as the *Regulations on the Exchange of Leading Cadres and the Regulations on Temporary Avoidance of Office for Leading Cadres*, detailed some relevant provisions on the tenure, transfer, and avoidance of office for party cadres from the perspectives of institutionalization, standardization, and proceduralization.

In 2008, the Central Committee of the Chinese Communist Party issued the *Provisional Regulations on the Term of Office for Delegates to the National Congress of the Communist Party of China and Local Congresses at All Levels*. In 2009, the Central Committee promulgated the *Provisional Regulations on Holding Party and Government Leading Cadres Accountable*. In 2010, the *Methods for Reporting Matters Concerning*

the Party. Some argue, 'In the past five years, the emphasis on Party centralization and unity has been sufficient; in the future, we should focus on developing intra-party democracy.' Such absurd talks have surfaced, stemming from political confusion and muddled thinking, while others harbor ulterior motives, lacking personal integrity, attempting to deceive their way through." Notably, the 20th National Congress report in 2022 omits any reference to intraparty democracy. See The Central Compilation and Translation Bureau of the CPC Central Committee, ed. *Xi Jinping Guanyu Quanmian Congyan Zhidang Lunshu Zhaibian [Selected Excerpts from Xi Jinping's Discourses on Comprehensive and Strict Governance of the Party]*. CPC Central Literary Press, 2021. See also the political report of the 20th National Congress, available at http://www.gov.cn/zhuanti/zggcddescqgdbdh/ (Accessed December 29, 2023).

the Selection and Appointment of Party and Government Leading Cadres (Trial), *the Methods for Holding Party and Government Leading Cadres Accountable (Trial)*, *the Methods for Local Party Committees to Report on the Selection and Appointment of Cadres* and *Accept Democratic Evaluation (Trial)*, and *the Methods for Inspection upon Leaving Office by Party Secretaries of Municipal and County Party Committees (Trial)* continued to specify detailed regulations on the selection, appointment, transfer, departure, and supervision of the CCP and government cadre. These documents, though unevenly implemented, serve as official references for analyzing the CCP's intentions, approaches, and effectiveness in further advancing intraparty democracy.

In addition, intraparty democracy serves as a manifestation of "self-supervision within the Party," aiming to achieve effects comparable to mutual supervision among competitive political parties in the West. This supervisory approach, focused on preventing and penalizing power corruption, is not only subject to regulation within the Chinese legal framework, including statutes such as the Criminal Law, Administrative Supervision Law, Civil Servant Law, Judges Law, and Procurators Law; but is also governed by an intricate set of party regulations and disciplines. These encompass the *Regulations on Disciplinary Actions of the Communist Party of China*, the *Regulations on Intra-Party Supervision of the Communist Party of China*, *Guidelines on Integrity and Self-discipline for Party Members in Leadership Positions*, *Regulations on the Handling of Cases by Disciplinary Inspection Organs of the Communist Party of China*, *Regulations on the Examination of Cases by Disciplinary Inspection Organs of the Communist Party of China*, *Implementation Rules on the Examination of Cases by Disciplinary Inspection Organs of the Communist Party of China*, *Provisions on the Handling of Violations of the Interim Regulations on Party and Government Cadres' Selection and Appointment*, *Temporary Provisions on Disciplinary Actions Against Party Members and Leading Cadres for Serious Bureaucratic Errors*, *Temporary Provisions on Disciplinary Actions Against Party Members for Violations of Discipline in Foreign-related Activities*, and *Temporary Provisions on Disciplinary Actions Against Party Members and Relevant Individuals for Involvement in Prostitution and Whoring*, among others.

Beyond the aforementioned traditional constraints and supervision mechanisms, the CCP employs numerous informal rules (customs) to administer penalties for violations committed by the CCP members.[4] Historically, however, this "self-supervision" has been predominantly confined to top-down organizational supervision within the CCP. While the *Regulations on Intra-Party Supervision of the Communist Party of China* explicitly identify Party members as the "subject and master" of the CCP, propelling intraparty democracy and internal supervision, democratic supervision at the same level, from bottom to top, and external to the Party, remains highly limited and challenging in its ability to impose constraints and supervision, especially on some higher-level CCP organizations, particularly the top leaders of the Party and government. This limitation primarily stems from the Chinese political inclination towards emphasizing "centralization" over "democracy," with a lingering influence of "personalized leadership." For instance, the leadership groups established by the CCP after the 18th National Congress disrupted the consensus-oriented collective decision-making model and expanded the influence of leadership authority and individual preferences to some extent.[5]

Simultaneously, against the background that of increasing power and commercialization of strict hierarchical relationships within the CCP, the top-down supervision often exhibits a movement-oriented and deterrent effect, such as the extensive anti-corruption campaign within the Party since the 18th National Congress. However, this also highlights the instability and non-sustainability of the unidirectional supervisory channel.

The *Chinese Communist Party Constitution* stipulates, "Party organizations at all levels should exchange information, mutually support, and supervise each other."[6] To date, this provision stands as the most authoritative statement in the Party constitution regarding hierarchical

[4] Smith (2021).

[5] Agencies, like the Central Comprehensive Deepening Reform Leading Group, the Central Financial and Economic Leading Group, and the Central Leading Group for Responding to the Coronavirus-19 Epidemic, have not only reshaped the intraparty decentralized governance model of the Hu-Wen era, colloquially known as the "Nine Dragons Managing Water (九龙治水 *Jiulong Zhishui*)," but have also, albeit not in the traditional sense of checks and balances, consolidated ultimate decision-making authority in the hands of Xi. For a comprehensive analysis of the consensus-driven and collective decision-making processes within the CCP's leading groups, see Chen (2015).

[6] *Zhongguo Gongchandang Dangzhang [Constitution of the Communist Party of China]*. Renmin Chubanshe, People's Publishing House, 2012. p. 11.

relationships within the CCP. Building upon this foundation, the *Regulations on the Intra-Party Supervision* require the Party Committees at all levels to "express opinions and suggestions on the work of higher-level Party Committees and discipline inspection committees and conduct supervision."[7] However, ordinary Party members, as the main body of bottom-up supervision, find it challenging to assume the responsibility of supervision, especially in the absence of institutional channels and safeguards for exemption.

In such circumstances, this "supervision" serves merely as a reference for upper-level decision-making, lacking binding force and feedback from top to bottom. Regarding external supervision, the Regulations stress that "intraparty supervision should be combined with external supervision," and "the Party Committees at all levels should support and ensure that the People's Congresses, governments, procuratorial organs, judicial organs, and others at the same level supervise the state organs and public officials in accordance with the law, People's Political Consultative Conferences carry out supervision in accordance with their stipulated regulations, while auditing organs conduct supervision in accordance with the law."[8] Notwithstanding the presence of this internally closed loop, intraparty regulations and disciplines frequently manifest ambiguity and conflicts with certain external supervisory mechanisms, laws, and regulations, for example. This is particularly evident in instances related to significant political events, giving rise to a gray area delineating the boundaries between external and intraparty supervision. Also for peer supervision, like the Party Congresses supervising the Central Committees, the Central Committees supervising the Standing Committees, the Party Committees at various levels supervising their peer Discipline Inspection Committees, and the Discipline Inspection Committees at various levels supervising their peer Standing Committees, Central Committees, and Standing Committees, is not addressed in the Regulations, and its implementation is often impeded by complex power relations and impediments to interests among peers.

[7] *Zhongguo Gongchandang dangnei Jiandu Tiaoli [Regulations on Inner-Party Supervision of the Communist Party of China]*. Falv Chubanshe, Law Press, 2016. p. 33.

[8] Ibid., p. 40.

In the late 1980s to the early 1990s, amid discussions on "new authoritarianism (新权威主义 *Xin Quanwei Zhuyi*)" and democratization, discourses on intraparty democracy had already surfaced. However, some disparities regarding the definition of intraparty democracy, its implementation, distinctions between interparty democracy and multiparty alternation in the Western competitive elections, and the correlation between intraparty democracy and people's democracy manifested significantly among the CCP's conservative and moderate factions, radical democratic factions, and between the CCP's top leadership and external intellectuals. The CCP's majority tends to favor a more conservative, moderate, and gradual approach to promote the intraparty democracy.[9] This inclination is primarily rooted in the prolonged rule and unique leadership position of the CCP, signifying that bypassing the CCP and establishing an alternative system for the democratization process is impractical. In this context, intraparty democracy emerges as a preferable choice within the existing political framework to drive political reforms, particularly democratization.

Furthermore, an abrupt adoption of radical democratic methods is considered unlikely to swiftly overturn prevailing conditions of "unipolar decision-making" and "rule by a single leader" within the CCP. Such an approach may pose a threat to the CCP's rule. Therefore, the CCP elites find it more feasible to gradually promote democratic elections within the Party and thus accommodate diverse intellectual groups. In summary, while the CCP's mainstream acknowledges the imperative of political reforms in China, the conditions for implementing the Western-style multipartism, representative of liberal democracy, are deemed immature and prone to causing social crises and instability. Immediate acceptance of diverse popular democracy is also deemed unattainable for the CCP.[10]

[9] The CCP and its propaganda departments tend to endorse a more measured and incremental model of intraparty democracy. This model is an extension and refinement of Deng Xiaoping's 1980s theories regarding the *Reformation of the Party and State Leadership System* and other theories related to the CCP's development. It takes into consideration the imperative need for political reform in China, the practical feasibility of advancing intraparty democracy in the current stage, and the alignment of intraparty democracy with the ideological framework and party-building theories of the CCP. Consequently, the objective is to attain the highest level of legitimacy by reconciling intraparty democracy with the CCP's ideology and party-building theories.

[10] Some non-party-affiliated intellectuals or societal elites with official backgrounds, such as Yu Keping advocating for "incremental democracy (增量民主 *Zengliang Minzhu*)"

Nevertheless, external intellectuals, especially those overseas and individuals with dissenting views, advocate for a more radical stance. They argue that the CCP should lift the ban on other political parties, permit the legitimate existence of dissenting groups within the Party, and therefore achieve democratization by establishing a legal mechanism for intraparty competition among different factions-an approach known as the "multi-faction discourse (党内多派论 *Dangnei Duopai Lun*)." They posit that any form of intraparty democracy or political reform that lacking a foundation in competitive, orderly, and power-constraining principles may lead the CCP towards a one-party dominant autocrat. However, in terms of acceptability and practicality, the gradual and moderate approach to intraparty democracy appears more readily acceptable. In essence, political reforms in China, including intraparty democracy, need to be considered within the framework of ensuring political stability, consolidating the CCP's governance, and reducing decision-making errors. The 15th Central Committee's Fifth Plenum report stipulates the need to "strengthen the construction of democratic politics, promote scientific and democratic decision-making, and expand citizens' orderly political participation," with the initial mention of orderly political participation indicating the CCP's intent to develop a controlled form of democracy while ensuring political stability and order.[11]

and He Zengke proposing "progressive democracy (渐进民主 *Jianjin Minzhu*)," align inadvertently with the trajectory of intraparty democracy. See Yu (2010) and He (2004).

[11] The *Proposal of the Central Committee of the Communist Party of China on Formulating the Tenth Five-Year Plan for National Economic and Social Development* approved during the Fifth Plenary Session of the Fifteenth Central Committee of the Communist Party of China, introduced the conception: "To expand the orderly political participation of citizens and guide the masses in lawfully managing their own affairs." The subsequent report of the Sixteenth National Congress further underscored the imperative: "To strengthen democratic institutions, enrich democratic forms, and expand the orderly political participation of citizens." During the Second Plenary Session of the Sixteenth Central Committee, it was emphasized: "There is a need to vigorously reinforce institutional development, continuously refine the various systems of socialist democratic politics, enrich democratic forms, and expand the orderly political participation of citizens." The Seventeenth National Congress report continued to articulate more specific directives, advocating for "the expansion of orderly political participation by citizens at all levels and in all fields, mobilizing and organizing the people to lawfully manage state and social affairs, as well as economic and cultural endeavors, on the widest scale." The paramount goal of "orderly" political participation, as articulated in official discourse, is to uphold the authority of the CCP and enhance governance, with empowering public participation in politics relegated to a secondary goal. In practice, citizen participation, predominantly

While intraparty democracy holds undeniable significance, its ultimate goals resides in advancing people's democracy through intraparty democratic processes, aiming to achieve democratization in China. Deng Xiaoping, on the eve of the 11th Central Committee's Third Plenum, underscored the imperative to "adopt various measures to continue the efforts to expand intraparty democracy and people's democracy. Without democracy, there is no socialism, and no modernization of socialism."[12] Deng's classification of democracy into intraparty democracy and people's democracy suggests an inevitable trajectory of democratic map in China. However, does this necessarily imply a straightforward sequential or gradual relationship between the two? Some superficial analyses of intraparty democracy posit that the future of China's democracy is contingent upon the sequence of "intraparty democracy driving people's democracy,"[13] thus suggesting that the development of intraparty democracy should precede that of people's democracy. This perspective is exemplified by the political upheaval triggered by attempts to implement "mass democracy" and "people's democracy" during Mao's Cultural Revolution, transpiring at an "immature" stage. This viewpoint not only implies a judgment on the sequence of democratic development but also alludes to the comparison of the merits and drawbacks of different forms of democracy.

Irrespective of the form of democracy or democratization, it mirrors the escalating democratic aspirations of the populace and the intricate interplay between democratic rights, such as public participation, and the establishment of national institutions alongside political reform. Additionally, it encapsulates the positive correlation between modernization and democratization that emanates from the evolution of a market economy. In the Chinese context, intraparty democracy emerges as a judicious choice within the system to advance democracy, and representing the

orchestrated by official entities, tends to exert a predominant influence on participation rules, forms, and outcomes, prioritizing stability and order. See He (2019).

[12] *Deng Xiaoping Wenxuan [Selected Works of Deng Xiaoping]*, Vol. 2. Renmin Chubanshe, People's Publishing House, 1994. p. 168.

[13] Typical examples include, Xu (2017). However, there are some authors who argue that the assertion that "intraparty democracy propels people's democracy" is inconsistent with the current reality of democratic development in China. They contend that it should be "people's democracy propelling intraparty democracy." This analysis is grounded in the democratic achievements that already realized in Chinese society, with accomplishments in grassroots elections surpassing those in intraparty democracy. See also Gao (2013).

most pragmatic avenue for actualization. Nevertheless, this does not imply that the burgeoning democratic demand within the society will acquiesce and await intraparty democracy by adhering to a very sequence of "intraparty democracy first, followed by social democracy" or "social democracy first, followed by intraparty democracy." Conversely, if intraparty democracy lags behind the people's democracy, the latter may further exert compelling pressures on the former or lead to the suppressions of people's democracy, thereby engendering alternative and disorderly chaos.

Can it be asserted that China will never embrace democracy or democratization if the CCP rejects intraparty democracy? This idea presents a formidable challenge, given the interdependence of intraparty democracy and people's democracy, suggesting a mutual coordination than a sequential intent.[14] While the advancement of intraparty democracy is feasible through specific measures, such as implementing competitive elections within the Party, internal supervision, and the separation of Party and government functions, its underlying rationale resides in the amalgamation of interests among diverse social strata and interest groups facilitated by internal Party diversification. This approach achieves a comparable political function to a multi-party system without adhering to the Western multi-party model. Despite a temporary deceleration in political reform following the late 1980s, the lenient political sphere of the early twenty-first century acknowledged intraparty democracy as the most pragmatic and pivotal institutional solution in many visions of Chinese democratization.

The emergent people's democracy was initially deemed as the rightful trajectory for democratic advancement in China; however, this ideal gradually waned in subsequent phases. Operating as a Leninist party characterized by an elevated concentration of power, the CCP forsook potential intraparty democratic implementation strategies, such as the adoption of the "separation of Party and government" paradigm during Zhao Ziyang's tenure, and the incorporation of the Japanese party model

[14] While the early contributions of Lipset and Huntington regarding the nexus that between economic development, modernization, and democratization have undergone reassessment and even revision in some later works of Francis Fukuyama, the positive and affirmative correlation between market economy and political order, modernization, and democratization persists across an extended historical trajectory. See Diamond (1989), Diamond et al. (1989), and Fukuyama (2011).

featuring "intra-party factions." The inevitable deductions that formulated by both intraparty and extra-party factions, spanning radicals and moderates, and grounded in "normative judgments," frequently neglect the consideration of China's "positive judgments." The CCP has exercised prudence in its approach to diverse intraparty democratic proposals, and a discernible shift towards more centralized power structures in Party construction and governance presents specific challenges to the advancement of intraparty democracy.

Intraparty Democracy: Boundaries and Future

Given the divergence of the Leninist Party model in China from the Western multi-party system, emulation of the latter is not a straightforward option. Simultaneously, China aspires to achieve outcomes reminiscent of the Western model, marked by alternating and competitive governance, particularly in terms of constraining and supervising power. In this context, intraparty democracy emerges as the exclusive means to realize this objective. Democracy, often delineated in conceptual, institutional, and democratic political life, lacks a clear demarcation between political parties and the general public. Within the very framework of the CCP and its members, several considerations demand attention for the actualization of intraparty democracy. Firstly, the distinctive nature of intraparty democracy is evident, as the term itself implies a form of democracy unique to the Party. It is underscored that general democracy cannot be somehow indiscriminately applied to intraparty democracy, nor can the intraparty democracy of one party be uncritically transposed onto another.[15] Nevertheless, akin to the nuanced features that inherent in Chinese democracy, which concurrently reflects universal values, one must acknowledge the relations and interplay between the uniqueness and universality of democracy within the CCP. The democratic rights of Party members, internal democratic elections, and the supervision and constraint of power do not inherently differ due to variations in the party model.

Nonetheless, debates persist concerning the democratization of the CCP, including the scope and boundaries thereof. Lin Shangli, the former

[15] Lin (2011).

Secretary of the Policy Research Office of the CPC Central Committee, posits that:

> The evolution of intraparty democracy, grounded in the principles of general democracy and democratic progress, may alter the internal structure and functions of the CCP, conceivably eroding the essence of the CCP. The promotion of intraparty democracy necessitates careful consideration not only of the inherent characteristics of intraparty democracy itself but also of the distinctive nature of the CCP. It is contended that general democracy cannot effectively regulate intraparty democracy, and the intraparty democracy observed in parties with dissimilar natures should not be forcibly imposed upon the CCP. For the CCP, the ultimate goal however lies in creating a political environment that is simultaneously "centralized" and "democratic," disciplined yet liberating, marked by a unified collective will alongside individual satisfaction, vibrancy, and dynamism. This however ensures the enduring vitality of the CCP's organization and system.

But the contention that the intraparty democracy might alter the nature of the CCP and potentially compromise and even jeopardize its leadership is unsubstantiated. Amid the global backdrop of democratization and the prevalence of the multi-party systems in the West, intraparty democracy emerges as an inevitable consequence of party evolution. For instance, the adoption of the "one person, one vote" system in the UK's Labour Party and Conservative Party, the implementation of faction-based elections and a representative model within Japan's Liberal Democratic Party, as well as the selection of presidential candidates through party conventions by the Republican and Democratic parties in the United States. It is noteworthy, however, that Western liberal democratic systems prioritize the interparty democracy than intraparty democracy. Nonetheless, both models share the common objective of achieving state and societal democratization through political party mechanisms. Duverger's (1959) concept of "one-party pluralism" may offer insightful theoretical perspectives. Intraparty factional competition within a single yet dominant party, for instance, can realize political democracy without necessitating competition and election between multiple parties. Importantly, the realization of intraparty democracy need not necessarily be contingent upon the factional model. Nonetheless, the exploration of a trajectory that promotes the democratization of national political life through intraparty democracy (-tization), while preserving the fundamental nature of the CCP, could serve a distinctive feature of China's politics, distinguishing it from the Western democratic trajectory.

If this holds true theoretically and is practicable in application, then when considering intraparty democracy in China, one then could seek a framework for achieving Chinese democracy under the premise of one-party rule by the CCP. Hence, the underlying logic, as perceived by the author, is that in circumstances where the CCP has amassed sufficient power to dominate, intervene, or even suppress any other form of democracy, such as recent erosions of grassroots democracy, bottom-up or external forces driving democratization evidently struggle to propel Chinese democracy. Under a highly idealized assumption, willingly or unwillingly embrace of intraparty democracy by the CCP, regardless of the mode adopted, should constitute the sole path towards realizing Chinese democracy. Discussions concerning democratization in China should therefore revolve around this central tenet.

Secondly, if the intraparty democracy is to be truly established, its foundation must derive from institutionalization and the rule of law, rather than relying solely on political mobilization, such as the so-called movement-style anti-corruption or maintaining ambiguous boundaries between the CCP's rule and law. Specifically, a careful reexamination of the nuanced variability is needed when considering the public participation (political engagement), electoral processes (authorization of power), and supervision mechanisms (oversight of power) within the CCP. Traditional analyses surrounding intraparty democracy often focus on democratizing the organizational life of the Party by integrating the subjectivities of its members and their active involvement, thereby rendering it a more closed loop. However, it is imperative to acknowledge that intraparty democracy is not a closed-door game; both the ordinary party members and the general public ought to be actively engaged in such a process. As articulated in the 19th National Congress of the Chinese Communist Party, which underscores the imperative of "strengthening constraints and supervision on the operation of power, allowing the people to supervise power, therefore ensuring the power operates in the sunlight."[16]

[16] The 19th National People's Congress of the Communist Party of China, available at https://www.12371.cn/special/19da/bg/ (Accessed June 3, 2024). A more concrete proposal would suggest that the extent of Party members' and the public's participation in intraparty democracy should be contingent upon specific circumstances. For instance,

The full participation of both the party member and the public, along with the bestowment of the sovereignty, constitutes the threshold of intraparty democracy. Competitive elections are typically contrasted with "non-competitive elections" prevalent in Chinese politics. However, competitive elections do not inherently align with the Western models of the party competition and electoral processes. Given the CCP's single-party rule, such elections may entail the direct election of Party representatives at local levels, the adoption of the "two-vote system (两票制 *Liangpiao Zhi*)"[17] in party branch elections, or the direct selection of township leadership, among other mechanisms. Participation pertains to the thresholds for engaging in politics, while elections, regardless of their form, address the issue of authorization, and supervision addresses concerns of power constraints. Intraparty democracy can only function when these requests are met. This transformative process cannot solely, or perhaps even predominantly, rely on politically organizational mobilization, such as efforts to mobilize for intraparty elections, rectification campaigns within the party, or anti-corruption within party structures. It is imperative that intraparty democracy be established on a foundation of institutionalization and legal frameworks rather than the rule of man.

decisions pertaining to significant directional issues affecting the entire Party and each individual member, such as the formulation of Party programs and amendments to Party constitutions, should thus mobilize the broadest possible participation within the Party. Regarding the authorization level of democratic elections, the closer to the grassroots level (e.g., below the county level), the more direct elections should be expanded, whereas at higher levels (e.g., provincial and above), indirect elections may be more appropriate. In terms of exercising power, democratic processes should primarily rely on various forms of oversight (e.g., public opinion monitoring, oversight by other political parties, oversight by social organizations, oversight by party members, representatives, and intra-party oversight mechanisms). See Wang (2011).

[17] The two-vote system, also known as the mixed election, combines both proportional representation and majoritarian representation in electoral procedures. While there may be variations in its implementation across different regions, commonly, it involves grassroots election processes such as party branch recommendations, self-nominations by party members, and nominations by higher-level organizational departments. These processes are subject to qualification review by the party committee, leading to the identification of several preliminary candidates. Subsequently, the voting public with suffrage casts confidence votes to select provisional candidates for party branch secretaries and committee members. Then, official candidates are elected from this pool in the party members' assembly. Finally, party members with suffrage vote to elect branch secretaries and committee members. Candidates elected through this process are deemed satisfactory by the public, party members, and higher-level party committees.

This institutionalized exploration revolves around safeguarding the democratic rights primarily of the CCP members, such as enhancing the transparency of intraparty affairs, ensuring the CCP members' right to information, and expanding the scope of participation in intraparty affair, among others. It can also manifest in other feasible institutional choices, such as fully leveraging the Party Congress as the fundamental institution of intraparty democracy, namely, dispersing intraparty power. This however entails a rational division of powers that between the Party Congress and the Party's Central Committee, Standing Committee, Secretary's Office, Working Conference, and Expanded Conference, among others. However, as a form of institutional design attempting to prevent excessive concentration of intraparty power, the very role of the Standing Committee of the Party Congress in intraparty democracy lies in whether there exists a meaningful relationship of power authorization between the representatives and the represented. Otherwise, the *permanence* of representatives merely suggests an increase in meetings and burdensome tasks, counteracting efforts to enhance intraparty democracy, thus reducing the Standing Committee to a mere flower vase. Consequently, the empowerment of intraparty elections could be achieved through a bottom-up pilot approach, incrementally decentralizing the highly centralized monopoly on the personnel appointments within the party. For instance, semi- or quasi-competitive elections at the grassroots and local party levels are exemplified by the aforementioned "two-vote system" and the direct election of local party committee secretaries and key members by party representatives.

This differs from traditional grassroots democracy endeavors aimed at bottom-up promotion of democratization in China, as well as from "deliberative democracy" attempts to foster constructive decision-making or limited empowerment through re-establishing connections both within and outside the party for "deliberation." These conceptualizations represent a form of quasi-infiltration and hybrid reassignment of portions of the CCP's power and authority.

Once the power authorization is resolved, the institutionalization of intraparty democracy pivots towards regulating the exercise and supervise of power within the CCP. This primarily involves the redistribution of power relations among various party departments. For example, the decision-making power is exercised by the party representative assemblies, while the executive authority is wielded by the party committees elected by representative assemblies at all levels, and supervision power is exercised by disciplinary inspection committees at the same level elected by representative assemblies. Besides decentralizing power within the party, the formation of "factions" also serves as a primary means of implementing intraparty democracy, As Mao once articulated, "Outside the Party, there is no other party; Emperors' thinking. Inside the Party, there are no factions; myriad anomalies."[18] Factions do not denote factional groups based on personal interests or cronyism but rather "opinion groups" dissenting from party policies. The formation of factions does not imply a zero-sum game aimed at severing the CCP but aims to effectively combat the undemocratic phenomena of "one-man rule" and highly centralized power. Regarding supervision, apart from routine intraparty power supervision, the role of Disciplinary Committees should be highlighted. This necessitates reforming the dual leadership system of Disciplinary Committees, coordinating the relation between Disciplinary Committees at all levels and superior ones and Party Committees at the same level thus to maximize the supervisory role of Disciplinary Committees. This involves refraining from placing Disciplinary Committees, originally designed as supervisory bodies, in a position of being supervised, thereby hindering their effectiveness.[19]

The relationship between party regulations has also long been criticized. Evidentially, they do not equate to laws, and other political norms (such as customs and informal rules) cannot replace legal norms. However, from the perspective of the CCP's strategy, it shows no sign to integrate those party regulations into laws but rather to maintain both simultaneously. This approach underscores the necessity to delineate the boundaries between the two without confusion, which should be achieved through the interconnection of political procedures and legal procedures. "To reestablish political and legal responsibility, it is therefore imperative

[18] Mao (1966).

[19] While it may present an alternative approach to the supervision of power within the party through the establishment and enhancement of specialized supervisory and inspection institutes, as ambitiously advocated by Xi Jinping in his political reform agenda aimed at "caging power," a deeply paradox emerges from the reality that institutions wielding power and exercising supervisory authority are all party-affiliated. Thus, reconciling the dilemma of "locking the cage of power while still managing the hands holding the keys" may pose a formidable challenge to intraparty democracy.

to assert the non-substitution and non-subordination between party regulations and law. Only through such clarity can an accountability system be established."[20]

Therefore, the delineation of intraparty democracy within China and the CCP is founded on two factual bases: firstly, the CCP's ruling position, and secondly, the feasibility and practical pathways towards achieving it.[21] The propositions advanced in the Sixteenth National Congress, proclaiming "Intraparty democracy is the lifeblood of the CCP," and those of the Seventeenth National Congress, asserting "People's democracy is the lifeblood of socialism," are intricately linked, both aiming to underscore the distinctive features of socialist democracy vis-à-vis capitalist democracy. The question of whether intraparty democracy or people's democracy takes precedence is not presently contested. However, in the very short term, given the ruling position of the CCP and the escalating democratic consciousness and demands within Chinese society, the immediate priority lies in achieving intraparty democracy. The realization of it is not contingent upon whether there is a single-party or multi-party system; rather, it hinges on whether people can exercise their right to govern. A multi-party system serves as a means rather than an end. The approach to intraparty democracy in China aims to explore a third path that is suitable for China's development, one that "navigates between a one-party authoritarian system and a multi-party democratic system."[22]

The ultimate goal of intraparty democracy is not only to promote the people's democracy and even the democratization of China, but also to facilitate political reforms in China, thereby building a justified theoretical and practical framework for socialist politics *with Chinese characteristics*. Since the initiation of the Reform and Opening Up, discontent and criticism towards China's development have primarily focused on the slow progress of political reform, including intraparty democracy, which has failed to align with the changes brought about by the market-oriented economic reforms in various economic and social dimensions. However, there is a consensus, which advocates for a incremental approach, as

[20] Wei and Dong (2016).

[21] Indeed, there are many other propositions attempting to achieve Chinese democracy or democratization. However, disregarding these two fundamental facts—for example, the overthrow of the CCP or proposals that are empirically unachievable—would inevitably render the realization of such endeavors challenging.

[22] Page (2002).

emphasized by Deng Xiaoping: "We should not adopt a leap-forward approach to democratic development but instead adhere to a step-by-step, leadership-guided way, following a path of gradual democratic development." This idea is also highlighted in documents such as the White Paper on Democracy in China.

> The construction of socialist democratic politics in China is a historical process characterized by the continuous enhancement of the degree and level of people's participation in decision-making. The attainment of a comprehensive democratic form is not achievable overnight. The CCP and the Chinese people unwaveringly promote the coordinated development of socialist material civilization, political civilization, spiritual civilization, and the construction of a harmonious society. They persistently study new situations and problems in the construction of democratic politics, explore and innovate new mechanisms and approaches to further realizing people's participation in decision-making, and develop socialist democracy in a guided, step-by-step, and orderly manner in accordance with the objective laws of socialist democratic political development.[23]

There have been notable explorations of intraparty democracy, particularly noteworthy after 1978. For instance, during the 13th National Congress of the Party in 1987, the Central Committee introduced a differential election system whereby the candidates exceeded the available seats by 5%. Subsequently, at the 17th National Congress of the Party in 2007, this differential election ratio for Central Committee members was further expanded to 8.3%, and for alternate Central Committee members to 9.6%. Also, a democratic recommendation method was first implemented in the nomination of Political Bureau member candidates. More experiments at the grassroots level have involved competitive elections of party cadres, including reforms such as competitive elections and term limits, which have challenged the traditional CCP's rules regarding the election and appointment of party cadres, particularly the first hands.

On the contrary, radical proposals such as intraparty democracy, as perceived by the CCP, often delve into the fundamental yet sensitive issues of Chinese politics—namely, the interplay between democracy and centralization, and between intraparty democracy and party unity, traditionally conceived as paradoxical and potentially jeopardizing the CCP's

[23] White Paper on Democracy in China (2005).

monopoly. It is important to note, however, that they are not diametrically opposed and irreconcilable. The authority and hegemonic position of the CCP need not necessarily derive from a highly centralized authoritarian system; conversely, historically, undemocratic phenomena such as "paternalism" and "one-man rule" have precipitated significant calamities in China. Likewise, democracy does not inevitably culminate in anarchism, societal disarray, and governmental ineptitude, thereby ultimately leading to the CCP's downfall, as asserted by many Western China observers. The overarching objective of democracy is precisely to transmute coercive power into authority imbued with guiding principles and moral legitimacy. Hence, intraparty democracy assumes an exceedingly significant role, whether in the internal reconsolidation of the CCP itself or in the broader political evolution of China; however, this progression necessitates gradual and protracted advancement.

At that juncture, the demonstrative impact of the intraparty democracy would inherently act as a catalyst for the emergence of people's and social democracy. Consequently, discourses concerning their interrelation would transmute into a secondary proposition, ultimately resolving itself through the overarching democratization of China. Therefore, the intraparty democracy assumes primary importance—indeed, it is not an overstatement to assert its existential significance—for the CCP itself, with its implications for other democratic modalities, such as broader political reforms within China, being secondary in nature. The realization of the principle of people's sovereignty hinges upon achieving a delicate equilibrium between universality and particularity in democratic forms, including intraparty democracy, thereby laying the groundwork for the manifestation of "Chinese-style democracy," "Chinese-style politics," or "the Chinese path." However, conventional analyses of Chinese political development, particularly since the assumption of power by Xi Jinping in 2012, are inadequate. In last decade, intraparty democracy has conspicuously receded from the party's discourse and the agenda of political reform, supplanted by a subset operating under the purview of the WPPD. Instead of the envisaged decentralization of power and the fostering of factionalism, as well as the empowerment of party members and the populace through diverse mechanisms, a political milieu characterized by pronounced centralization of power, personality cult, and the predominance of an individual figure has begun to emerge, deviating markedly from the trajectory of intraparty democracy. A mode of democracy instigated top-down from within the system by the CCP itself is gradually eclipsing traditional conceptions of intraparty democracy.

References

Chen, Ling: "Zhongguo Gaoling Lingdao Xiaozu de Yunzuo Jizhi [The Operational Mechanism and Evolution of China's Senior Leadership Group]." In *Zhonggong de Zhili you Shiying: Bijiao de Shine Governance and Adaptation of the Chinese Communist Party: A Comparative Perspective*, Yu Keping, Thomas Heibler, and Björn Alpermann, eds. Zhongyang Bianyi Chubanshe, Central Compilation and Translation Press, 2015.

Deng Xiaoping Wenxuan [Selected Works of Deng Xiaoping], Vol. 2. Renmin Chubanshe, People's Publishing House, 1994.

Diamond, Larry. "Beyond authoritarianism and totalitarianism: Strategies for democratization." *Washington Quarterly* 12.1 (1989): 141–163.

Diamond, Larry, Juan Linz, and Seymour Martin Lipset. *Democracy in Developing Countries*, Vol. 3: Asia. Lynne Rienner, 1989.

Duverger, Maurice. *Political Parties: Their Organization and Activity in the Modern State*. Metheun & Co. Ltd., 1959.

Fukuyama, Francis. *The origins of political order: From prehuman times to the French Revolution*. Farrar, Straus and Giroux, 2011.

Gao, Minzheng. "Dangnei Minzhu yu Renmin Minzhu, Jiujing Shui Daidong Shui-Jian yu Hu Wei, Yang Guangbin Jiaoshou Shangque [Intraparty Democracy and People's Democracy: Who Propels Whom-Discussion with Professors Hu Wei and Yang Guangbin]." *Tansuo yu Zhengming, Exploration and Debates* 4 (2013): 29–34.

He, Baogang. ""Orderly Political Participation" in China." In *The Palgrave Handbook of Local Governance in Contemporary China*. Palgrave Macmillan, 2019. pp. 347–363.

He, Zengke. "Jianjin Zhengzhi Gaige yu Minzhu de Zhuanxing [Progressive Political Reform and the Transformation of Democracy] (Part I, II)." *Beijing Xingzheng Xueyuanbao, Journal of Beijing Administrative College* 1/4 (2004): 1–5, 10–14.

Hu, Yaobang. "Hu Yaobang Zai Zhongguo Gongchandang Di Shierci Quanguo Daibiao Dahui Shang de Baogao [Hu Yaobang's Report at the Twelfth National Congress of the Communist Party of China]." Available at National Congresses of the Communist Party of China, 1982, http://cpc.people.com.cn/GB/64162/64168/64565/65448/4526430.html. (Accessed December 28, 2023).

Hua, Guofeng. "Shiyida Shang de Zhengzhi Baogao [Political Report at the Eleventh National Congress]." Available at National Congresses of the Communist Party of China, 1977, http://cpc.people.com.cn/GB/64162/64168/64563/65449/4526439.html. people.com.cn/GB/64162/64168/64563/6544 9/45264 39.html. (Accessed December 28, 2023).

Lin, Shangli. "Renmin, Zhengdang Yu Guojia: Renmin Minzhu Fazhan de Zhengzhixue Fenxi [People, Political Parties and the Country: Political Science Analysis of the Development of People's Democracy]." *Fudan Xuebao (Shehui Kexueban), Journal of Fudan University (Social Science Edition)* 5 (2011): 1–10.

Mao, Zedong. Zai Bajie Shiyizhong Quanhui Bimushi Shang de Jianghua [Speech at the Closing Ceremony of the Eleventh Plenary Session of the Eighth Central Committee of the Communist Party of China]. August 12, 1966. Available at https://www.marxists.org/chinese/maozedong/1968/5-206.htm (Accessed December 28, 2023).

Page, Jeremy. "China Open Up Political Debate to Strengthen Party." Reuters News, July 20 (2002).

Smith, Ewan. "On the Informal Rules of the Chinese Communist Party." *The China Quarterly* 248.S1 (2021): 141–160.

The Central Compilation and Translation Bureau of the CPC Central Committee, ed. *Xi Jinping Guanyu Quanmian Congyan Zhidang Lunshu Zhaibian* [Selected Excerpts from Xi Jinping's Discourses on Comprehensive and Strict Governance of the Party]. CPC Central Literary Press, 2021.

The Political Report of the 20th National Congress. Available at http://www.gov.cn/zhuanti/zggcddescqgdbdh/ (Accessed December 29. 2023).

Wang, Changjiang. "Dui Zhonggong Dangnei Minzhu Zhidu de Xiong Sheji [Systematic Design of the Inner-Party Democratic System of the Chinese Communist Party]." Available at https://www.aisixiang.com/data/41859.html. 2011 (Accessed December 28, 2023).

Wei, Bingfeng, and Dong, Jing. "Guowuyuan Canshi Zhu Weijiu: Zhizhengdang Yingdang Chengwei Zunshou Xianfa Falv de Moran [State Council Counselor Zhu Weiqiu: The Ruling Party Should Become a Model in Abiding by the Constitution and Laws]." Available at http://politics.people.com.cn/GB/17348297.html. 2016 (Accessed December 28, 2023).

White Paper on Democracy in China, 2005. Available at https://www.gov.cn/200510/19/content_79553.htm (Accessed December 28, 2023).

Xu, Yaotong. "Dangnei Minzhu he Renmin Minzhu de Guanxi [The Mutual Relationship Between Intraparty Democracy and People's Democracy]." *Mao Zedong Yanjiu, Mao Zedong Studies* 2 (2017): 32-41.

Yu, Keping. "Toward an Incremental Democracy and Governance: Chinese Theories and Assessment Criteria." In *Democracy and the Rule of Law in China*. Brill, 2010. pp. 1–33.

Zhongguo Gongchandang Dangnei Jiandu Tiaoli [Regulations on Inner-Party Supervision of the Communist Party of China]. Falv Chubanshe, Law Press, 2016.

Zhongguo Gongchandang Dangzhang [Constitution of the Communist Party of China]. Renmin Chubanshe, People's Publishing House, 2012.

Grassroot Democracy

The grassroots democracy has long been esteemed as a potent catalyst for nurturing bottom-up democratization within China, particularly via grassroots elections—such as village and community elections—which are often contrasted with Western electoral and autonomous practices. Tracing back through Chinese history, prototypes, and practices of grassroots autonomy can be discerned, evident in the feudal system of the Western Zhou dynasty (西周) and the system of prefectures and counties following the Qin dynasty (秦朝). Whether through feudal fragmentation or imperial centralization, the grassroots—albeit subject to variations in conceptualization—have historically retained a degree of relative freedom and autonomy; the adage "the emperor's power does not extend to the counties (皇权不下县 *Huangquan Bu Xia Xian*)" is frequently invoked to demarcate the boundary between state and society. In contemporary Chinese politics, grassroots democracy constitutes a focal point for both Western and Chinese observers endeavoring to comprehend the intricacies of Chinese-style democracy, notwithstanding the erosion of grassroots autonomy in recent decades under centralized governance.

R. Li, *Democratizing China's Political Imaginaries*,
https://doi.org/10.1007/978-981-97-3670-6_5

Grassroots Elections, Autonomy, and Democracy

The democratization practices in China, as epitomized by rural self-governance, find their roots in the advocacy and promotion undertaken at the upper echelons of the CCP. This initiative can be construed as a deliberate attempt by the CCP to address the dual crises of governance capability and legitimacy encountered in rural areas since the inception of Reform and Opening Up. From the New China to the pre-reform era, rural regions underwent agricultural collectivization within the People's Communes system (人民公社制 *Renmin Gongshezhi*).[1] The state exercised considerable control over peasants via these communes, overseeing collective labor and planned distribution.

Subsequent to the Reforms and Open Up (1978–mid-1980s), the overhaul of rural landownership—Household Responsibility System (家庭联产承包责任制 *Jiating Lianchan Chengbao Zeren Zhi*) and the restructuring of rural grassroots governance from the three-tier system of "People's Commune —the Production Brigade (生产大队 *Shengchan Dadui*)—the Production Team (生产小队 *Shengchan Xiaodui*)" to the "Township People's Government (乡人民政府 *Xiangrenmin Zhengfu*)—the Village Committee (村民委员会 *Cunmin Weiyuanhui*)—the Village Group (村民小组 *Cunmin Xiaozu*)" expedited the disintegration and demise of the People's Commune. Nonetheless, the establishment of a new grassroots system remained incomplete, resulting in the waning influence of grassroots, particularly at the village-level administrative organizations, and the near-collapse of rural society. A 1994 report by the CCP Central Committee revealed that 75% of grassroots party organizations in rural areas were incapacitated, failing to fulfill their political functions.[2] Concurrently, tensions surfaced in the relations between village cadres and the masses, marked by abuses of power and pervasive corruption among the former, further compounding the state's crisis

[1] During the contemporaneous epoch at the grassroots level, the "urban unit system (城市单位制 *Chengshi Danweizhi*)" functioned as the underpinning structure. Within this system, urban denizens found themselves subordinated to their corresponding units, and the entire spectrum of public organizational endeavors, inclusive of the apportionment of public resources, mandated strict adherence to this unitary framework. This part however predominantly engages in an exploration of village self-governance as the preeminent manifestation of grassroots democracy.

[2] See Liu and Guan (1998).

of governance capability and legitimacy in vast rural regions. All these necessitated the reconstruction of a new grassroots political system.

During the late 1980s and early 1990s, the political and economic reforms in Chinese rural regions were nuanced. On the one hand, economic reforms precipitated significant differentiation within the peasant class, further eroding the community-based interest protection mechanisms previously established in rural regions. Consequently, peasants became more directly subject to state control, and the state's penetration and governance capability in rural areas markedly intensified.[3] However, concurrently, the patron-client relationships (e.g., Wan, 2023) between rural cadres and the villagers, instead of ameliorating during these economic reforms, manifested in a renewed form of political patronage relationships, diminishing the state's control over rural cadres and enabling them to pursue their own interests on a broader scale.[4] Moreover, there emerged a state-promoted (albeit limited) force that gradually bolstered villagers' self-governance and the implementation of state policies through the establishment of rural autonomous organizations, commonly referred to as "grassroots democracy." For a considerable period, grassroots democracy, grounded in villagers' autonomy and elections, was regarded as the principal impetus for bottom-up democratization in China.[5]

The grassroots governance model, initiated by peasants in Yishan County (宜山县) and Luocheng County (罗城县), Guangxi Autonomous Region in the early 1980s via the spontaneous formation of villagers and committees, achieved a rather delicate equilibrium amid grassroots governance, social stability, peasants' participation, and economic development in China. This model served as a catalyst for emulation nationwide. At the central level, the new constitution officially acknowledged the legal status of villagers' committees as grassroots mass autonomous organizations in rural areas in December 1982. Subsequently, in October

[3] See for example, Shue (1990) and Kelliher (1992).

[4] See for example, Oi and Little (1994) and Unger (1994).

[5] This encompasses both domestic and foreign scholars, media, as well as political elites from both China and in the West. See, for example, Chen (1998), Wang (1998), Xu (2009), Yu (2008), Wang and Yang (2007), Weiping and Chen (2011). Grassroots democracy encompasses democratic elections, supervision, management, and decision-making. However, in the practical experiences of the 1990s, it primarily referred to grassroots democratic forms with elections as the main component.

1983, the Central Committee of the Communist Party of China and the State Council issued the *Notice on Separating Politics and Economics, Establishing Township Governments*, advocating for the establishment of villagers' committees. The momentum continued with the passage of the *Organic Law of Villagers' Committees* (Trial Implementation) by the Standing Committee of the National People's Congress in November 1987, solidifying its position as a guiding document for grassroots democratic practices in China.[6] By the close of 1992, many provinces in China had more or less engaged in democratic practices through the grassroots elections. By 1994, twenty provinces had conducted two rounds of village committee elections, and subsequent years witnessed the commencement of the third or even fourth rounds of elections in many provinces.

Despite the interlink of the "villager autonomy" in the late 1980s and early 1990s with bourgeois liberalization, CCP's top leaders demonstrated unwavering commitment to promoting grassroots democratic experiments and practices. In 1987, Peng Zhen (彭真), the Chairman of the Standing Committee of the National People's Congress at the time, articulated during the 23rd session of the sixth Standing Committee of the National People's Congress: "Implementing mass autonomy at the grassroots level means that the people handle their own affairs by law and directly exercise democratic rights... Establishing robust villagers committees and residents' committees is a significant reform in the country's political system, holding profound and far-reaching significance for eliminating feudal remnants of thought, changing old traditions, and realizing the people's ownership of their affairs."[7] Other Party elders, including Bo Yibo (薄一波) and Cui Naifu (崔乃夫), the Minister of Civil Affairs at the time, joined the ranks supporting villager autonomy. In August

[6] The *Organic Law of Village Committees* has undergone several iterations. The inaugural version, initially conceived as a pilot edition, received approval on November 24, 1987, during the 23rd session of the Standing Committee of the Sixth National People's Congress, taking effect on June 1, 1988. The second rendition was ratified and enacted as the extant version on November 4, 1998, during the 5th session of the Standing Committee of the Ninth National People's Congress, concomitantly annulling the antecedent iteration. The third iteration was amended and adopted during the 17th session of the Standing Committee of the Eleventh National People's Congress on October 28, 2010, subsequently entering official implementation. The fourth and latest version underwent revision and approval during the 7th session of the Standing Committee of the Thirteenth National People's Congress on December 29, 2018, followed by its subsequent promulgation and implementation.

[7] Peng (1991, p. 125).

1990, during the National Symposium on Village-level Construction held in Laixi City (莱西), Shandong Province, Song Ping (宋平) emphatically stated, "Stop debating the *Organic Law of Village Committees*; it should be implemented." Subsequently, in September 1990, the Ministry of Civil Affairs issued the *Notice on Carrying Out Demonstrative Activities of Villager Autonomy in Rural Areas Nationwide*, outlining plans to gradually expand grassroots autonomy practices nationwide over a 10-year period.[8]

In the 1990s, grassroots democracy in China garnered official and academic recognition primarily in response to the imperative need for political reform that following the very conservative political transformations of the 1980s. Characterized by anti-bourgeois liberalization, debates on electoral democracy, and the conservative political reforms of the "not arguing" 1990s, it became apparent that a form of political change that was gradual, controllable, and less disruptive, such as grassroots democracy, was essential. Despite persistent opposition to grassroots autonomy since the 1980s, the central leadership resisted pressures and facilitation for its practices to be further implemented nationwide, starting from Guangxi and Guizhou. This advocacy was subsequently formalized and legalized through constitutional amendments, laws, regulations, and ordinances.[9] While grassroots democracy advocates for direct democracy in village autonomy and elections, it remains a form of democracy guided and constructed by the state and the CCP. Two paradoxes emerge: first, how to navigate the relationship between grassroots democracy and central authority while maintaining the one-party rule of the CCP; second, grassroots autonomous organization, though not a primary political entity, possesses administrative attributes. Consequently, how to check-and-balance the official intervention and grassroots autonomy to booster grassroots democracy becomes a central challenge.

[8] See Bai (2001).

[9] The legal regulations encompass not only the aforementioned constitutional amendments but also extend to the *Law on Village (Residential) Community Organizations* (revised draft). Additionally, they incorporate provisions and directives pertaining to village elections and village self-governance disseminated by the Ministry of Civil Affairs. For example, *Notice on Carrying out Demonstration Activities for Village Self-Governance in Rural Areas Nationwide* (September 26, 1990), the *Notice on Further Strengthening the Construction of Village Committees* (February 27, 1995), and the *Supplementary Notice on Implementing the "Law on Village Committee Organizations"* issued by the General Office of the Ministry of Civil Affairs (December 18, 1998). See, Lang (2009).

These paradoxes, however, intricately probe the foundational dimensions of Chinese politics—the interplay between centralization and democracy. Contrary to its initial goals, the autonomy granted to villages in the 1990s notably augmented the burden on peasants. In 1993, Jiang Zemin advocated a resolute initiative to bolster the country's 800,000 rural grassroots organizations within a span of 3–5 years, ensuring the fulfillment of their designated roles.[10] Yet, a subtle transition unfolded in the relationship between grassroots party entities and village autonomous organizations. Article 37 of the *Organic Law of the Village Committees of the People's Republic of China* mandates that "the people's government should furnish requisite conditions for the village committee to assist the government in executing its functions." The *Regulations on the Work of Communist Party Organizations in Rural Grassroots Organizations of the People's Republic of China* bifurcates decision-making powers at the village level into two realms. While critical matters pertaining to village economic construction and social development rest with the CCP's branch, other affairs are/should delegated to the village committee, village assembly, or collective economic organization. However, legally and practically, the village Party branch retains the de facto supreme yet decision-making authority. This involves the amalgamation of power in the village-level Party branch, the village committee, the assembly of villagers' representatives, and the villagers themselves. Simultaneously fortifying the grassroots organizations in rural areas while advancing democratic autonomy poses a formidable challenge. The Central Committee's No.1 Document in 2020 further mandated that the ensuing round of village and community organization elections adopt a "one shoulder carry (一肩挑 *Yijiantiao*)" system wherein one person assumes both the secretary and hand roles. This approach heightens the tension between the CCP's comprehensive leadership in the grassroots organizations and the rural areas' autonomy.

In order to rectify shortcomings, such as the absence of a clear demarcation between the CCP and government within village committees, undue interference of state authority in grassroot autonomy, and the transformation of village committees into localized "second government"

[10] *Jiang Zongshuji Zhua Dangjian Zhongyao Huodong Jilue [Memorandum on General Secretary Jiang's Emphasis on Party Building]*. Renmin Chubanshe, People's Publishing House, 1998. p. 344. A substantial reorganization ensued, leading to the replacement of 136,000 village party branch secretaries, 128,000 village committee directors, and the resolution of issues within over 25,000 township party committees. Zhong (1998).

under the aegis of the CCP, diverse initiatives have been undertaken at the grassroots. One noteworthy endeavor involves the implementation of "incremental democracy (增量民主 *Zengliang Minzhu*)" to augment the village election system through the "two-vote system (两票制 *Liangpiaozhi*)."[11] Originating from Qingdui Village (青堆村) in Luodian Town, Guangshui City, this system entails villagers initially casting a vote of confidence during the election of the village party branch and branch secretary. Subsequently, following the endorsement of villagers through a public opinion poll, party members proceed to cast their votes. This "two-vote system" has subsequently been disseminated in various regions, including Hequ County (河曲县) in Shandong and Suizhou (随州) in Hubei. In Gua Yuan Village (瓜园村), Zengdu District, Suizhou, a "two-session system (两会制 *Lianghuizhi*)" has been instituted. The decision-making process for significant village matters involves the collaborative proposals by the village committee, formulation of proposals by the party assembly, approval via voting by the village representative assembly, and supervision of execution by a village affairs supervision group.

These explorations have also precipitated adjustments in the village representative assembly system. In 1999, in Fengyang County (凤阳县), Anhui Province, the practice of involving non-party masses in the election of village party branches was introduced. Candidates were initially selected based on party internal deliberations and democratic recommendations. Subsequently, non-party villager, constituting over 80% of eligible voters, evaluated the preliminary candidates through anonymous assessments. The final candidates were then determined by the township party committee based on the evaluation results. In 1998, the town of Buyun (步云乡) in Suining City, Sichuan Province, pioneered the first direct election of township leaders nationwide, thereby elevating grassroots elections to the township level.[12]

[11] See, for example, Yu (2000).

[12] In the early twenty-first century, amid the pervasive trend of "public recommendation and election (公推公选 *Gongtui Gongxuan*)" for village branch secretaries, Sichuan Province initiated comprehensive reforms in the municipalities of Daxian, Nanchong, Bazhong, Suining, and Meishan. Spanning from late 2001 to early 2002, the turnover elections witnessed the Sichuan Provincial Party Committee Organization Department advocating for the adoption of "public recommendation and election" in one-third of townships. By early 2002, excluding three autonomous ethnic minority prefectures,

The existence of a conflict between national power and grassroots autonomy does not necessarily presuppose the manifestation of a boundary dispute and ambiguity between the two. Historical analyses of their relationships indicate the dynamic of power and reciprocal development between the state and local (grassroots) levels from diverse perspectives. These encompass considerations of "imperial power constrained within county boundaries," "officials and civilian society (吏民社会 *Limin Shehui*)," "centralized and simplified governance (集权简约治理 *Jiquan Jianyue Zhili*)," and "unitary rule and diverse governance (一元统治与多样性治理 *Yiyuan Tongzhi yu Fuoyang Zhili*)."[13] In this dynamic landscape of village autonomy exploration during the 1990s, both top-down official experimentations and bottom-up spontaneous reforms were employed to address the aforementioned challenges. Against the backdrop of a pioneering central atmosphere, many villages formulated detailed regulations and systems, such as *Village Rules and Agreements*, *Village Committee Work System*, *Village Cadres Term Goal Responsibility System*, *Village Affairs Transparency System*, *Village Economic Cooperative Work System*, and *Village Economic Account Transparency System*. These explorations and legislations not only provide assurances for villagers to participate in grassroots politics but also establish a legal foundation for village cadres to govern villagers in accordance with laws and regulations.

In contrast to subsequently occurring urban resident self-governance—a state-dominated, planned, administrative, and weakly autonomous form

Sichuan Province had collectively elected 5,447 township leaders through public recommendation and election, constituting 17.5% of the total township leadership. In 2004, experimental initiatives for the direct public recommendation and election of township party secretaries unfolded in 30 counties (cities, districts) across ten cities and prefectures, culminating in the direct election of 45 township party secretaries. See Ren and Zhang (2018).

[13] Authors endorsing the perspective of rural autonomy include Fei Xiaotong (费孝通), Wen Tiejun (温铁军), and other proponents. Conversely, scholars such as Xiao Gongquan (萧公权), Zhai Tongzu (翟同祖), and Qin Hui (秦晖) posit that traditional Chinese villages lack autonomy, contending that imperial power permeates rural regions through local officials for governance. Noteworthy scholars like Weber, Michael Mann, Huang Zongzhi (黄宗智), and others assert that China has historically manifested a governance model characterized by robust authoritarian central power and feeble foundational local power, constituting a paradigmatic manifestation of "centralized minimalist governance." Fu Yiling (傅衣凌), Zhou Lian (周黎安), and their counterparts advocate for a perspective highlighting the amalgamation of unity and diversity within the Chinese imperial system. These perspectives delve into the intricate relations between state power and local autonomy.

of grassroots autonomy—the village self-governance holds greater significance for the promotion of grassroots democracy in China. Nevertheless, the anticipated effectiveness of grassroots democracy, built upon the foundation of village autonomy, remains uncertain. Within the context of the China's "democratic centralism," the emphasis on "autonomy" does not necessarily mandate the withdrawal of the state/party/government from the scene. That said, as long as the relations and boundaries between the two are well coordinated, grassroots democracy can still find a place in China's democratization process. In scrutinizing the modalities of self-governance within rural villages during the 1990s and the early twentieth century, albeit marked progressions under official auspices, an inherent predicament persists. This quandary progressively metamorphoses into a manifestation of "gifted democracy" (Zheng, 1998). This variant of democracy may be conceptualized as an "elite bestowal upon society," as opposed to a system organically crafted by diverse societal forces in alignment with their intrinsic aspirations.

The CCP has, for a long time, undertaken a dual tactic aimed at fortifying governance effectiveness and augmenting ruling legitimacy. Primarily, it endeavors to attain these goals by advocating village autonomy, conferring greater self-governing powers upon peasants, and amplifying the functions of the CCP's grassroots organizations, all while preserving the CCP's centralized power structure. It simultaneously aspires to incrementally achieve Chinese bottom-up democratization by further instituting grassroots democracy grounded in village autonomy, characterized by processes that are gradual, smooth, and controllable. This significance extends beyond the mere democratic sense, accentuating the capacity of village autonomy to delineate a public sphere and civil society outside the state—an indispensable facet for the construction of modern nation. Besides the concentrated endeavors of the CCP's upper echelon, especially the intraparty reformists, in facilitating grassroots democracy and the consequential emancipation of grassroots productivity, notably in economic realms, authors' discourse, and empirical investigations within both Chinese and Western academia have offered supplementary perspectives on the observation of grassroots democracy in China, such as Kevin J. O'Brien, Tianjian Shi, Jean C. Oi, Yong Xu, Keping Yu, Dingjian Cai, Mingshi Niu, Tiejun Wen, Daniel Kelliher, Gunter Schubert, and Allen C. Choate. As traverse into the twenty-first century, the challenges confronting grassroots democracy in China transcend the aforementioned contradictions and historical legacies. They encompass, however, intricacies such as urbanization, townification, rural labor migration, and brain drain, all of which constitute formidable obstacles to the flourishing of grassroots democracy.

Entering of the twenty-first century, grassroots democracy exerted an increasingly conspicuous influence on the reform of China's political system, giving rise to a plethora of discernible transformations. Reform initiatives initiated at the village and township levels have (in)directly instigated reforms within local governments. Concurrently, the evolution of grassroots democracy has precipitated alterations within some Party grassroots organizations. The election processes in urban community resident committees have witnessed significant progress, and the advocacy endeavors championing the rights of urban residents have cultivated an enhanced awareness of civil rights amid the grassroots populace. Commencing in 2002, some town(ship)s in Hubei underwent comprehensive election reforms, encompassing the election of township leaders and Party secretaries.[14] In 2003, Pingba Town (坪坝镇) in Chengkou County, Chongqing, implemented a "comprehensive political system reform," which entailed the establishment of a permanent representative system for the township People's Congress and Party representatives, balance of the relationship between the government and the People's Congress, and reforms addressing the interrelationships among township party committees, governments, People's Congresses, and the public. Several townships in Sichuan have taken a step further in 2013, wherein Party Secretaries are directly elected by all Party members. In Wenzhou (温州), Zhejiang, honest talk (恳谈 *Kentan*) and participatory budgeting have facilitated a seemingly radical participation and deliberation, ushering China's grassroots towards a semblance of democracy.

In this period, grassroots democracy primarily pivoted around grassroots elections. Between 2005 and 2007, (in)direct elections were conducted in 623,690 villages nationwide, achieving an average completion rate of 99.53%. Approximately 95.85% of villages instituted secret balloting booths, and the success rate of elections averaged approximately 85.35% among participating villages. The mean participation rate in the village committee elections across the nation stood at 90.97%. In 17 provinces, pilot projects or more extensive implementations experimented

[14] In early 2003, Xian'an (咸安区) in Hubei province undertook extensive explorations in grassroots reforms, focusing notably on the rationalization of township institutions and the reconfiguration of governmental functions. See Li (2011).

with "sea selection (海选 *Haixuan*)," whereby candidates were directly elected by villagers via voting.[15] Notwithstanding persistent challenges such as intervention by township governments, procedural deficiencies, and a lack of transparency in the election process, the village committee elections have consistently manifested as a pivotal facet of grassroots democracy in China. Notably, two fresh features arose. Firstly, the ascendancy of "elites" like "capable people" and the "rich" in elections has engendered the gradual formation of oligarchic politics, particularly conspicuous in economically developed southeast coast regions.[16] However, concomitant phenomena like bribery, regional protectionism, and conflicts of clan power still remain and persistently erode the grassroots autonomy.

Secondly, concerning with electoral processes, grassroots democracy has presently expanded to encompass a comprehensive framework that integrates democratic consultation, in addition to the hitherto widely practiced democratic elections, management, supervision, and decision-making. Since the 18th National Congress, democratic consultation in Chinese grassroots has experienced rapid growth, transforming into an indispensable form of democracy in the local governance. This evolution underscores leadership via consultation, thereby endorsing the populace as the ultimate masters of the country. Nevertheless, a predominant characteristic of most grassroots consultation practices is their "government-led: nature, often contingent upon the personal proclivities of local cadres." Also, challenges manifest in incomplete consultation procedures, divergent consultative and deliberative capabilities among participants, and a relatively insufficient level of standardization of the process. Consequently, grassroots consultation, as a facet of democracy, is confronted with significant challenges.

[15] Wu (2008).

[16] This advantage is not solely evident in economics; it also extends to dimensions of social resources and clan influence, for example. See Lin (2011), Avenarius and Zhao (2012), and Madsen (2022).

Following the 18th National Congress, the CCP has displayed increased prudence and vigilance of the competitive elections.[17] Followingly, there has been a strategic transition away from the direct pressure associated with elections, with a redirected focus towards the modernization of grassroots governance systems and capabilities. This strategic maneuver seeks to fortify the CCP's leadership at the grassroots level while simultaneously extending its legitimacy. Noteworthy is the reemphasis placed on "political consciousness, overall situation awareness, core consciousness, and alignment consciousness (政治意识、大局意识、核心意识、看齐意识 *Zhengzhi Yishi, Daju Yishi, Hexin Yishi, Kanqi Yishi*)" in the grassroots governance. Then, grassroots democracy is primarily characterized and portrayed by the simultaneous implementation of "consultative democracy" and "democratic centralism." This nuanced approach highlighted the practical manifestation of Chinese democracy at the grassroots level. This tactical transformation however emanates from a discerning analysis of corruption instances within grassroots elections and the CCP's reflective scrutiny of the inherent pitfalls associated with unreservedly adopting the "Western democratic model," as observed in specific third-world countries. A heightened awareness prevails regarding the potential exploitation of Western electoral systems by adversarial foreign forces, particularly in orchestrating the "color revolutions."

Against this background, on the one hand, elections are employed as a means rather than an end. The monopoly exerted by grassroots government, particularly at the town(ship) level about village-level elections, personnel appointments, political leadership, and financial budgets, continues to solidify. On the other hand, grassroots consultative governance—characterized by "developing grassroots consultations, facilitating democratic channels, enhancing mechanisms for grassroots elections,

[17] In 1982, Deng Xiaoping abrogated the lifelong leadership system instituted during Mao Zedong's era, as an integral component of the Reform and Opening Up policy. This strategic maneuver, beyond attenuating the political sway of the elderly and ensuring a seamless transition of the CCP top leaders, was designed to facilitate efficacious succession within the party leadership. Subsequently, in 2018, Xi Jinping annulled the constitutional constraint on the number of terms permissible for Chinese president, thereby consolidating executive authority. Furthermore, the CCP constitution did not impose limitations on the number of terms applicable to the positions of general secretary and chairman of the Central Military Commission. Consequently, post-constitutional amendment, Xi Jinping acquired the prerogative to perpetuate his incumbency in the highest echelons of both the party and the nation without encumbrances.

consultations, transparency, accountability, and engaging in diverse forms of grassroots democratic consultations, promoting the institutionalization of grassroots consultations"—has emerged as a significant facet of grassroots democracy. To note, consultation is seemingly gaining traction on the functionalist front, being instrumentalized as a path to address practical conflicts and uphold stability at the grassroots level.[18]

Grassroots Democracy and Chinese Democratization

In around 1990s, various spheres within China, including officialdom, academia, Western political circles, and many Chinese observers, all perceived grassroots democracy that driven by grassroots elections, as a pivotal catalyst for China's bottom-up democratization. This perspective regarded it as a distinct manifestation of democracy in China. Such characterization stemmed not only from the prevalence of election-based democratic practices during this historical epoch, exemplified by grassroots activities like village self-governance and cadre elections, including the direct elections of township cadres, but also found validation in Deng's proclamations on political reform in China, particularly following the Thirteenth National Congress in the 1990s. Deng unequivocally stated, "...political report of the Thirteenth National Congress was approved by the Party's representative assembly, and not a single word can be altered."[19]

In contrast to the recurrent discourse on political reform themes such as the "separation of Party and government," the "establishment of the socialist consultative dialogue system," and other *sensitive* subjects consistently addressed in preceding Party congresses, like the intraparty democracy and checks on power, grassroots democracy is often upheld as an exemplar for political reform and democratization in China. "The Western interest in elections and the perceived existence of grassroots democracy in China are considered advantageous for enhancing China's

[18] This pragmatic-oriented consultation and sometimes deliberation is often referred to as "functionalist interaction." See, He (2011).

[19] *Deng Xiaoping Wenxuan [Selected Works of Deng Xiaoping]*, Vol. 3. Renmin Chubanshe, People's Publishing House, 1993. p. 296.

international image."[20] Nevertheless, given that over four decades have elapsed since the inception of the Reform and Opening Up, it thus becomes imperative to examine how the relationship between grassroots democracy and Chinese democratization has evolved. How to examine the entangled relationships between the two that necessitate a comprehensive analysis. This entails scrutinizing four pivotal aspects: direct elections at the township level,[21] grassroots oligarchic politics, upper governmental intervention, and the roleplay of grassroots democracy within the framework of China's political reform.

In 1998, the Shizhong District (市中区) of Buyun Township in Suining City, Sichuan Province, conducted China's inaugural experimental direct election of the township head.[22] Simultaneously, under the CCP's auspices Organization Department, Nancheng Township (南城乡) in Qing Shen County, Meishan City, Sichuan Province, initiated a trial of direct elections for township heads. Subsequent exploratory endeavors in analogous direct elections for township heads unfolded in various provinces and cities, including Jiangsu, Guangxi, Henan, and Guangdong. Nevertheless, these endeavors encountered challenges due to direct conflicts with the Chinese Constitution and laws. Additionally, skepticism and outright opposition from local official towards political

[20] Allen C. Choate: Local Governance in China, http://www.dfzlw.org/bencandy.php?fid=31&id=1181.

[21] Grassroots democracy, or elections conducted at the grassroots level, typically pertains to the election of officials at the village level. However, direct elections conducted at the town(ship) level present more formidable challenges and, in a more nuanced fashion, exemplify the advancement of Chinese democracy at the grassroots level. This progression is discernible both in terms of methodological approach and fundamental essence.

[22] The process of directly electing the township head in Buyun Township is delineated through a systematic procedure. Initially, prospective candidates for the position are discerned via a comprehensive threefold method, encompassing recommendations from the entire electorate, self-nominations, and organizational endorsements. Subsequently, these identified candidates undergo scrutiny in a joint meeting comprised of village committee members, village leaders, and village representatives. This assembly collectively engages in a voting process to designate two official candidates. They in conjunction with a nominee endorsed by the local party committee, engage in a general election that involves the entire township resident populace. Ultimately, one township head is elected through this democratic process. The selected candidate, being the exclusive nominee for the position, undergoes a formal approval process during the immediately convened Township People's Congress. In this assembly, the decision-making is subjected to a vote by all representatives, ensuring adherence to legal procedures. See, Huang (2019).

reforms centered around township head direct elections led to inconclusive outcomes for most attempts. Despite being regarded as the "second wave of China's grassroots election democracy" (He & Lang, 2001) following direct elections at the village committee level, the resistance to expanding electoral democracy from grassroots organizations to local political power structures has steadily intensified.

In a meticulous examination, the elective process for township heads necessitates its occurrence within the confines of the township People's Congress, wherein the designation of the township head transpires through the assembly's electoral proceedings rather than through a direct mandate from the villagers. Consequently, the direct elections of the township heads in Buyun Township, encompassing subsequent instances in Pingba of Chongqing and Shiping County (石屏县) of Yunnan's Honghe Prefecture, were considered as political reforms contravening Chinese laws and were even deemed unconstitutional. This unequivocally dissuaded subsequent endeavors aimed at mitigating conflicts between grassroots and town(ship) levels or exploiting grassroots elections to foster grassroots democracy, thereby propelling democratic ideals in China. Moreover, within the framework of the CCP's "Party control of cadres" system, township heads, occupying roles as grassroots administrative officials, are designated and commissioned top-down by higher-level party organizations, in stark contrast to a bottom-up electoral process by villagers.[23] Even if the authentic implementation of direct elections for township heads were to materialize, it would unavoidably engage in the

[23] According to research conducted by Central China Normal University on cases pertaining to grassroots democracy, challenges are not only evident in township head direct elections, but also manifest in the turnover elections of village committees, where higher-level governmental interventions and manipulations are prevalent. The underlying causes of these challenges can be attributed to three primary concerns: firstly, apprehensions arise from the fear that elected village committees may deviate from compliance, leading to the potential failure in the implementation of superior policies and the unfulfillment of assigned tasks. Secondly, there is a worry about the interference in elections by clan and family influences, which may result in the appointment of faction or family leaders as "village officials," thereby posing threats to rural social stability. Thirdly, concerns persist regarding the significant representation of the village committee directors who are also representatives of the township party or People's Congress, as their potential lack of qualifications may influence elections during township turnovers. See Cunmin Zizhi de Chenggong Zhilu: Chengxu Guifan yu Sida Minzhu de Youji Jiehe [The Successful Path of Villager Autonomy: Organic Integration of Procedural Norms and Four Major Democracies]. Available at http://ccrs.ccnu.edu.cn/List/Details.aspx?tid=4567.

foundational discourse within Chinese politics pertaining to the intricate dynamics and conflicts between centralized authority and local autonomy. "Following the direct election of township heads, the political legitimacy of township party secretaries appointed from higher-ups would undoubtedly encounter challenges."[24] Consequently, since 2004, the momentum behind reforms in the direct election of township leaders has gradually come to a standstill.[25]

The grassroots oligarchy refers to the "elite rule in villages," encompassing a model of governance dominated by affluent villagers. Since 1993, in some grassroots electoral processes of provinces such as Zhejiang, Chongqing, Jilin, Shanxi, etc., previously prosperous private business owners, individual entrepreneurs, and large-scale livestock farmers actively participated in elections. They were elected based on their more abundant material conditions, social, and political resources. Since 2005, the signs of "the rich" entering politics have become more pronounced, with the emerging rural nouveau riche class taking center stage in village politics. However, accompanying this trend is the "entrenchment of the power of the riche class and the political silence of the vast majority of the villagers, signifying the gradual decline of grassroots democracy in China and the emergence of oligarchic politics."[26]

Academic research and practical investigations into the elite-dominated village governance model, where the rich or capable individuals play a central role, abound.[27] On the one hand, these studies point towards elite village governance as an irreversible trend in grassroots politics that aligns with central policies. This involves cultivating economic talents and wealth creators as village cadres to lead the villagers in achieving prosperity, therefore realizing the goal of enriching all the villagers *through* the initial wealth of a few. Simultaneously, the control of political power by elites, especially economic elites, can indeed stimulate and spur the development of grassroots economies. Leveraging their own political, economic, and

[24] Huang and Chen (2009, pp. 67–68).

[25] Following township direct elections, advancements persist via alternative mechanisms, including indirect elections and public nomination direct elections. This signifies a pioneering exploration of grassroots democratic experiments.

[26] Lin (2011).

[27] See, for example, Li et al. (2021), Wei and Wang (2021), Qi (2020), Qiu (2017), He (2011), and Ouyang (2011).

social resources, they can secure more material benefits for villagers. This underscores the objective benefits of elite village governance.

On the other hand, grassroots elite, endowed with more economic and social capital in the political power struggle, transforms grassroots elections into a crucible for the arena of the pecuniary politics. Bribery in grassroots election not only inherently instigates clan conflicts and economic polarization within grassroots politics but also consigns the villagers—the bedrock of grassroots democracy—to a subordinate position.[28] Elite village governance, sanctioned by national policies, converges with macroeconomic strategies, therefore sanctioning the pursuit of personal wealth and economic interests with the imprimatur and backing of the state and government. Concurrently, as the state progressively withdraws from grassroots via the implementation of tax reforms and diverse welfare policies, elite village governance becomes an inexorable choice amid resource governance gaps and the evolution of governance responsibilities. Solely elites, particularly economic elites, possess the ability to transmute economic advantages into governance resources and to amplify and fortify these network relationships utilizing their social advantages. Consequently, elite village governance emerges as a grassroots governance paradigm amalgamating interpersonal resources, economic criteria, moral thresholds, authority, and authoritarianism. So, it prevails not only in economically developed east coastal regions but is also pervasive in economically backward central and western regions. While elite governance may instigate an oligarchic trajectory in the grassroots governance, characterized by the increasing (re)consolidation of elite power and the concomitant restriction of villagers' participation in politics and collective affairs, it does not inherently imply insignificance for grassroots. Amid the continued primacy of material interests in grassroots politics, elite village governance persists, albeit with a discernibly escalating tendency towards oligarchization.

Examining grassroots democracy in China from the perspective of elite governance does not entail disparaging the paradigm of elites engaging in grassroots politics and gradually monopolizing the grassroots political power. It neither repudiates grassroots democracy oriented towards

[28] Takeuchi (2013).

economic or economic democracy, nor dismisses the "grassroots election of cadres (基层选主 *Jiceng Xuanzhu*)" grassroots election.[29] Instead, it contemplates the resolution of two issues within the framework of elite governance in villages. Firstly, it addresses the challenge of ensuring that elites, despite being elected/selected due to political, economic, and social advantages, also uphold equal opportunities for villagers to engage in village politics through democratic means—thus genuinely safeguarding the villagers' right to self-governance. In this process, the imperative lies in restricting the exchange of economic resources for political power, as economic democracy cannot, especially in the long run, overshadow or constitute the primary focus of grassroots democracy. Secondly, confronted with established facts, rectifying the trajectory of grassroots democracy necessitates commencing from the verifiable realities and constructing a grassroots deliberative system. Utilizing interaction to reintegrate marginalized or excluded villagers into the grassroots politics, thereby ensuring their substantive status, becomes indispensable in reflecting the essence of grassroots democracy.

At the grassroots level of governmental agencies and autonomous organizations established by the CCP, party organizations primarily function in providing political leadership, especially over village committees (administrative functions). According to the *Constitution of the Communist Party of China* and the *Interim Regulations on the Election of Grassroots Organizations of the Communist Party of China*, leaders of grassroots party organizations are elected differentially by the party member assembly or representative assembly. The candidate nominations are the responsibility of the previous party committee and require scrutiny and approval by the higher-level party organization or discussion and confirmation by the presidium of the assembly. However, in practices, they are often directly nominated and appointed by higher-level party organizations, lacking the participation of ordinary party members and even non-party villagers, and of course lacking the functionality of

[29] See Wang (2011).

competitive elections.[30] Much evidence demonstrates widespread intervention, interference, and even control by higher-level governments in rural elections and autonomy.

This is not only due to the fundamental provisions of the CCP in politics and institutions, but also stems from various motives, with varying outcomes resulting from these interventions. It can be affirmed that government intervention is not always negative; the government can play an actively supportive, organizational, and guiding role in grassroots autonomy. "Village self-governance can achieve unexpected accomplishments in economically and socially underdeveloped rural regions, closely related to the proactive roles played by the CCP and the government."[31] This government-/governance-driven democratization conspicuous in some developing countries is accentuated via the imprimatur of authoritarianism.[32] Higher-level governments can intervene administratively in village collective matters and mediate conflicts between the village and third parties.[33] In the late twentieth century to the early twenty-first century, when the overall democratic consciousness of peasants was relatively backward, this orchestration of top-down mobilization, propaganda, and organization by higher-level governments emerged as a constructive force, steering the political engagement of villagers and effectively establishing avenues for their participation.

Since the 18th National Congress, particularly in alignment with the stipulations delineated in the *Rural Revitalization Strategic Plan*, the articulated goal for the year 2022 is the assumption of "one shoulder

[30] The election of leaders within grassroots party organizations does not consistently fall prey to the intervention and interference of higher-level governments, as evidenced by the third session of village committee elections convened in Henan Province in 1998. During this electoral process, it became imperative that formal candidates for the village committee secured their positions via the electoral endorsement of representatives chosen by the villagers, thereby obviating the previously permissible deliberations facilitated under the auspices of party branches. Concurrently, the practice of electing village committee members through the representative assembly or household representatives was unequivocally proscribed, supplanted by the introduction of a direct voting system encompassing all the villagers. The voting mechanism transpired exclusively within confidential ballot booths, eschewing the antecedent practice of raising hands to signify decision-making. see China Youth Daily, November 13, 1998.

[31] Xu (1997).

[32] Similar analysis, see, for example, Warren (2009).

[33] Li and Yang (2023).

carry" by 50% of party secretary and head in village. In 2023, the Central No.1 Document expressly underscores the augmentation of the political and organizational functions of grassroots party organizations. While these measures fortify the CCP's political ascendancy at the grassroots level, especially town(ship) party committees, they concurrently precipitate instances of intrusion by them into grassroots autonomy. Setting aside the merits and drawbacks associated with higher-level intervention in grassroots autonomy and democracy, the more pivotal inquiry pertains to the nature of grassroots democracy deemed requisite, and how the relationships between the CCP and grassroots democracy necessitate adjustment. In a factual context, grassroots democracy in China is inherently interlinked to the extent and orientation of state intervention, whether constructive or detrimental, embodying attributes of "autonomy under rule of man."[34] Fundamentally, it persists as a state-provided construct, with its actual operation representing a confluence of spontaneously articulated democratic aspirations among villagers and purposeful promotion and intervention by the state.

In conclusion, after over four decades of development after the Reform and Opening Up, can grassroots democracy continue to shoulder the pivotal responsibility of propelling democratization in China from the grassroots level? Grassroots democracy, characterized by village elections and self-governance, stands as a living fossil in the realm of political reform since 1978.[35] This contrasts with more structured democratic modalities, such as urban community self-governance and direct township-level elections, wherein political parties and the government

[34] Hu (2000).

[35] Political reform after 1978 can be delineated across three distinct phases. The inaugural phase, spanning from 1978 to 1985, was characterized by the eradication of lifelong tenure, the advancement of the "Four Modernizations (四个现代化 *Sige Xiandaihua*)" among cadres, the decentralization of power, the promotion of direct democracy, and the cultivation of social autonomy. The subsequent phase, spanning from 1986 to 1991, aimed at the segregation of party and government functions, the demarcation of the boundaries between the political and economic domains, the rationalization of institutions towards the establishment of a "small government," the implementation of a civil service system, and the introduction of mechanisms facilitating social consultation and dialogue. The final phase, post-1992, articulates a comprehensive objective centered on the mutual reinforcement of marketization and democratization. This involves the establishment of a constitutional democratic system and a rule of law state aligned with both the principles of a market economy and the pursuit of social justice. See also Shen (2003).

play central roles in steering and guiding the process. Grounded in extensive villagers' participation and a profound historical and cultural backdrop, grassroots democracy exhibits stronger spontaneous and indigenous traits. Therefore, grassroots democracy emerges as a defining feature and integral element of/in Chinese democracy. Moreover, critique of prevailing issues within grassroots democracy does not negate the value of this democratic form itself, nor does it position political parties and the government in opposition to grassroots democracy on a "nationalistic" basis. Finally, even in the West, a wholly independent "mass autonomy and organization" divorced from political parties and governments is nonexistent; hence, the guidance, regulation, and support of the latter remain imperative for the former.

The contention that "grassroots democracy propels bottom-up democratization in China" fosters unrealistic expectations, overestimating the distinct boundaries among the party, state, and society. Despite an optimistic belief in the potential for the CCP's authoritarianism to allow some spaces for grassroots democracy, disillusionment inevitably arises when democratic outcomes fall short. A critical reflection on the prospective trajectory of grassroots democracy in China is imperative within these acknowledged parameters. This requires a nuanced re-consideration of the interplay among the party, government, and grassroots democracy, guiding popular demands into normative and institutionalized pathways. Simultaneously, caution must be then exercised to prevent societal instability and the threat to the CCP's authority arising from excessive and widespread political participation. Striking a delicate balance is paramount: mobilizing elite participation, particularly economic elites, in grassroots governance for local economic development while preventing the monopolization of political power that may undermine grassroots autonomy. This however entails harnessing the influential role of party organizations and members in further advancing grassroots democracy, guarding against excessive reliance on the personal wills and preferences of grassroots cadres in the governance process. Only through the integration of macro-background and micro-practices can we thoroughly explore the future prospects of grassroots democracy in China.

References

Allen C. Choate. "Local Governance in China." Available at http://www.dfzlw.org/bencandy.php?fid=31&id=1181 (Accessed October 07, 2023).

Avenarius, Christine B., and Xudong Zhao. "To Bribe or Not to Bribe: Comparing Perceptions About Justice, Morality, and Inequality Among Rural and Urban Chinese." *Urban Anthropology and Studies of Cultural Systems and World Economic Development* (2012): 247–291.

Bai, Shazhou. "Chongjin Shenshi Zhongguo Nongcun de Juicing Xuanju he Cumin Zizhi [Reexamining grassroots elections and villager autonomy in rural China]." Shiji Zhongguo, Century China, 2001. Available at http://www.chinaaffairs.org/gb/detail.asp?id=473 (Accessed October 07, 2023).

Chen, Xiwen. Laolao Bawo Shiwujie Sanzhong Quanhui de QuanjuYiyi [Thoroughly Grasping the Overall Significance of the Third Plenary Session of the Fifteenth Central Committee]. *Liaowang, Outlook* October 19, (42) 1998.

"Cunmin Zizhi de Chenggong Zhilu: Chengxu Guifan yu Sida Minzhu de Youji Jiehe [The Successful Path of Villager Autonomy: Organic Integration of Procedural Norms and Four Major Democracies]." Available at http://ccrs.ccnu.edu.cn/List/Details.aspx?tid=4567 (Accessed October 07, 2023).

He, Baogang, and Youxing Lang. "China's First Direct Election of the Township Head: A Case Study of Buyun." *Japanese Journal of Political Science* 2.1 (2001): 1–22.

He, Xuefeng. "Sun Furen zhicun-Yi Zhengjiang Fenghua Diaocha Wei Talon Jichu [On Rich People Governing Villages - Based on the Survey in Fenghua, Zhejiang]." *Shehui Kexue Yanjiu, Social Science Research* (2) 2011: 111–119.

Hu Yongjia. "CunminZizhi, Nongcun Minzhu yu Zhongguo Zhengzhi Fazhan [Village Autonomy, Rural Democracy and China's Political Development], 2020. Available at https://www.modernchinastudies.org/cn/issues/past-issues/71-mcs-2000-issue-4/554-2012-01-03-12-11-40.html (Accessed October 07, 2023).

Huang, Weiping, and Jiaxi Chen. *Zhongguo Xiangcun Xuanju Gaige Yanjiu [Research on China's Township Electoral Reform]*. Renmin Chubanshe, People's Publishing House, 2009. pp. 67–68.

Huang, Weiping. *Zhongguo Juicing Minzhu Fazhan 40 Nian [40 Years of Development of Grassroots Democracy in China]*. 2019. Available at https://www.rccp.pku.edu.cn/mzyt/91578.htm (Accessed October 07, 2023).

Kelliher, Daniel. *Peasant Power in China: The Era of Rural Reform, 1979–1989*. Yale University Press, 1992.

Lang, Youxing. *Fazhan Zhong de Minzhu: Zhengzhi Jingling you Cumin Xuanju [Democracy in Development: Political Elites and Village Elections]*. Xebec Daxue Chubanshe, Northwest University Press, 2009.

Li, Fan. Zhongguo Jiceng Minzhu de Fazhan he Zhengzhi Gaige [The Development of Grassroots Democracy and Political Reform in China]. 2011. Available at https://www.aisixiang.com/data/4040.html (Accessed October 07, 2023).

Li, Rongxing, and Renhao Yang. "Revisiting Deliberative Governance: The Case of Land Transactions in Rural China." *China Perspectives* 133 (2023): 51–61.
Li, Zupei, Hu Chaoyang, and Ma Pingrui. "Zailun Furen Zhicun: Jiyu Difang Zhengfu Zizhuxing Shijiao de Jieshi [Rediscussing 'Rich Man Governing the Village'—An Explanation Based on the Perspective of Local Government Autonomy]." *Xinan Daxue Xuebao (Shehui Kexueban), Journal of Southwest University (Social Science Edition)* (5) 2021: 25–36+223.
Lin, Huihuang. "Guatou Zhengzhi yu Zhongguo Jiceng Minzhu [Oligarchy and Grassroots Democracy in China]." Available at https://www.aisixiang.com/data/40392.html (Accessed October 07, 2023).
Lin, Huihuang. "Guatou Zhengzhi yu Zhongguo Juicing Minzhu [Oligarchic Politics and Grassroots Democracy in China]." Available at https://www.aisixiang.com/data/40392.html, 2011 (Accessed October 07, 2023).
Liu, Qingfeng, and Xiaochun Guan, eds. *90 Niandai Zhongguo Nongcun Zhuangkuang: Jihui yu Kunjing [The Situation of Rural China in the 1990s: Opportunities and Dilemmas]*. Xianggang Zhongwen Daxue Chubanshe, Chinese University of Hong Kong Press, 1998.
Madsen, Richard. *Morality and Power in a Chinese Village*. University of California Press, 2022.
Oi, Jean C., and Daniel Little. "State and Peasant in Contemporary China: The Political Economy of Village Government." *Economic Development and Cultural Change* 42.3 (1994): 663–666.
Ouyang, Jing. "Furen Zhicun: Jizhi yu Jixiao Yanjiu [Rich Man Governing the Village: Research on Mechanism and Performance]." *Guangdong Shehui Kexue, Guangdong Social Sciences* 5 (2011): 197–202.
Peng, Zhen. "Tongue Juicing Zizhi Shixing Juicing Zhijie Minzhu [Implementing Direct Democracy at the Grassroots Level Through Mass Autonomy." In *Peng Zhen Wenxuan, Selected Works of Peng Zhen*. Renmin Chubanshe, People's Publishing House, 1991. p. 125.
Qi, Yan. "Cong 'Zili' Dao 'Fengxian Paichi': Zhengfu Shijiaoxia de Furen Zhicun [From 'Self-Interest' to 'Self-Interest': 'Risk Exclusion': Rich Governing Villages from the Government's Perspective]." *Lanzhou Xuekan, Lanzhou Academic Journal* (3) 2020: 131–141.
Qiu, Ye. "Furen Zhicun de Leixing yu Jiceng minzhu Shijian Jizhi Yanjiu [Research on the Types of Rich People Governing Villages and the Practical Mechanism of Grassroots Democracy]." *Zhongguo Nongcun Yanjiu, Rural China Observation* (1) 2017: 52–66+142.
Ren, Zhongping and Zhang, Lulu. "Xinshidai Juicing Minzhu Xuanju you Minzhu Zhili de Junking Fazhan-Yi Sichuan Sheng Juicing Minzhu Fazhan de Lujing Yanhua Weili [Balanced Development of Grassroots Democratic Elections and Democratic Governance in the New Era: A Case Study of

the Evolution of Grassroots Democracy Development in Sichuan Province]." *Tansuo, Exploration* 6 (2018): 72–79+2.

Shen Yansheng. "Guanyu Cumin Ziji ji Cumin Zizhi Yanjiu de Pings [Review on Villagers' Autonomy and Research on Villagers' Self-Government]." Available at https://www.modernchinastudies.org/cn/issues/past-issues/81-mcs-2003-issue-2/1292-2012-01-06-09-16-39.html (Accessed October 07, 2023).

Shue, Vivienne. *The Reach of the State: Sketches of the Chinese Body Politic*. Stanford University Press, 1990.

Takeuchi, Hiroki. "Vote Buying, Village Elections, and Authoritarian Rule in Rural China: A Game-Theoretic Analysis." *Journal of East Asian Studies* 13.1 (2013): 69–105.

Unger, Jonathan. "'Rich Man, Poor Man': The Making of New Classes in the Countryside." In*China's Quiet Revolution: New Interactions Between State and Society*, David Goodman and Beverley Hopper, eds., New York: St. Martin's Press, 1994. pp. 43–63.

Wan, Qian. *Patron Client Relationships and Co-operative Development in Rural China*. Diss. University of Saskatchewan, 2023.

Wang, Jingwen. Meiguo Fuanmotuan Yanzhong de Zhongguo Juicing Minzhu [China's Grassroots Democracy as Seen by an American Observation Team]. *Liaowang, Outlook* 14 (1998).

Wang, Shaoguang. Chaoyue Xuanzhu [Beyond "Choosing the Lord"], 2011. Available at https://www.aisixiang.com/data/38943.html (Accessed October 07, 2023).

Wang, Shuna, and Yang Yao. "Grassroots Democracy and Local Governance: Evidence from Rural China." *World Development* 35.10 (2007): 1635–1649.

Warren, Mark E. "Governance-Driven Democratization." *Critical policy studies* 3.1 (2009): 3–13.

Wei, Chenglin, and Mulin Wang. "Neiwai Youbie: Furen Zhicun Xingwei Chayi de Zhidu Luoji yu Qishi [Differences Between Inside and Outside: Institutional Logic and Enlightenment of Differences in Rich People's Village Governance Behavior]." *Huanan Nongye Daxue Xuebao (Shehui Kexueban), Journal of Huazhong Agricultural University (Social Science Edition)* 5 (2021): 110–119+196.

Weiping, Huang, and Jiaxi Chen. "China's Grassroots Democracy: Development and Assessment." *International Journal of China Studies* 2.2 (2011): 177.

Wu, Jing. "Zhongguo Cunguan Xuanju Zouxiang Changtaihua [China's Village Official Elections Are Moving towards 'Normalization']." *People's Daily* January 9, 2008.

Xu, Yong. "Minzhuhua Jinchengzhong Zhengfu de Zhudongxing-dui Sichuan Dachuan Cumin Zizhi Shifan Hoodong de Dacha he Simao [Government Initiative in the Process of Democracy—Investigation and Thoughts on

Villager Self-Government Demonstration Activities in Dachuan, Sichuan]." *Zhanlue yu Guanli, Strategy and Management* 3 (1997): 21–42.

Xu, Yong. "Shehui Dongguan, Zizhu Canyu you Zhengzhi Zhenghe-Zhongguo Jiceng Minzhu Fazhan 60 Nina Yanjiu [Social Mobilization, Autonomous Participation, and Political Integration: A 60-Year Study of Grassroots Democratic Political Development in China]." *Shehui Kexue Zhanxian, Social Science Front* 6 (2009): 19–26.

Yu, Keping. "Zengliang Minzhu, 'Sanlun Liangpiaozhi' Zhenzhang Xuanju de Zhengzhi Yiyi [Incremental Democracy-'Three Rounds, Two Votes' System in Town Mayor Elections]." *Makesi Zhuyi yu Xianshi, Marxism and Reality* 3 (2000): 27–28.

Yu, Keping. "Zhongguo Zhengzhi Fazhan 30 Nian [Thirty Years of Political Development in China]." *Hebei Xuekan, Hebei Academic Journal* 3 (2008): 1–6.

Zheng, Yongnian. *Zhongguo Hui Biande Minzhu Ma [Will China Become democratic?, Liang'an Jiceng Xuanju yu Zhengszhi Shehui Bianqian, Daxue Zhongxifang Xuezhe Duihua [In Cross-Strait Grassroots Elections and Political and Social Changes—Dialogue Between Eastern and Western Scholars at Harvard University].* Taiwan Taibei Yuedan ChubansheTaipei, Yuedan Publishing House, 1998. p. 448.

Zhong, Zuwen. Yushang Xintaijie, Sannian Nongcun Jiceng Zuzhi Zhengdun he Jianshe Zongsu [Leaping to a New Level: An Overview of the Three-Year Rural Grassroots Organization Restructuring and Construction]. *People's Daily*, July 1, 1998.

Consultative Democracy

The examination of consultative democracy[1] in China has experienced a discernible decline since the convening of the 18th National Congress of the CCP in 2012. This attenuation is evident in the convergence of the official discourse and academic perspectives, wherein the term "Xieshang Minzhu" has been embraced as a conceptual instrument accentuating the significance of soliciting public input, fostering consensus, and ultimately achieving a "consensus democracy." Although scholarly debates persist, the focal point of inquiry has shifted towards the formulation of a distinct Chinese paradigm of "deliberative democracy," and accentuating its merits within the broader context of Chinese democratic practices and in juxtaposition to Western liberal democratic models.

While intellectual discourses endure, the crux of the matter lies in the delineation and accentuation of the distinctive characteristics inherent in "consultative democracy" in China, particularly in its reconciliation with the country's political and social milieu, and the wider democratic discourse. Diverging from the Western path, where research on deliberative democracy frequently endeavors to (re)address the challenges within

[1] In this monograph, I consistently employ the term "consultative democracy" as the counterpart to China's concept of "协商民主 (*Xieshang Minzhu*)." This choice transcends mere translational tactic and preference; rather, it encapsulates the centrality and role of consultation within the realms of Chinese politics, particularly in ideology, governance, and political culture. See Li (2022).

R. Li, *Democratizing China's Political Imaginaries*,
https://doi.org/10.1007/978-981-97-3670-6_6

representative democracy grounded in electoral processes, the inception and application of consultative democracy in China are intricately interwoven with its tradition and political cultures, encompassing paternalistic and patriarchal governance, centralized authority, an emphasis on good governance, and the pursuit of a harmonious and stable societal order. Consequently, Chinese scholarship on consultative democracy propounds an original and thought-provoking proposition within the framework of comparative politics—an unparalleled manifestation of consultative democracy that intricately enmeshed with traditional values, cultural nuances, authoritarianism, consultation, deliberation, and democracy.

Cartography of Consultation and Deliberation in China

The development of the methods, ideas, and theories of consultation and deliberation in China has undergone a nuanced historical process. Although there are parallels with the modern Western concept of "deliberative democracy," Chinese ideas possess a unique developmental path. Notably, during the New Democratic Revolution, the CCP, in collaboration with other political entities and non-party individuals, laid the foundation for a United Front and methods of a quasi-deliberative democracy. This was particularly evident during the establishment and construction of the "Three-Three System (三三制 *Sansan Zhi*)" democratic political power in Yan'an,[2] marking the germination and embryonic stage of "deliberative democracy."

From the issuance of the "May Day Manifesto (五一口号 *Wuyi Kouhao*)" by the Central Committee of the Communist Party of China in

[2] The "Three-Three System," implemented during the CCP's revolutionary era, was a socio-political organizational structure aimed at fostering collective unity and discipline among party members. This system divided party members into three groups: the first consisting of those who were regarded as models of revolutionary commitment and dedication, the second comprising those with average revolutionary fervor who required encouragement and guidance, and the third comprising those who were deemed to be in need of remedial ideological education and political rectification. Through this system, party leadership could effectively allocate resources, provide targeted support and education, and ensure ideological cohesion among members. It served as a mechanism for maintaining discipline and fostering ideological alignment within the party ranks, contributing to the consolidation of party authority and the success of the Communist revolution.

1948 to the preparations for the New Political Consultative Conference, Mao Zedong and the Central Committee transitioned from informal to organized institutionalized forms of consultative democracy. This ideological development underscored the importance of political and social organizations with different class foundations that engaging in dialogue and negotiation to achieve "as much consensus as possible." The convening of the First Plenary Session of the Chinese People's Political Consultative Conference and the founding of the People's Republic of China marked the establishment of the multi-party cooperation and political consultation system led by the CCP, heralding the nationwide implementation of consultative democracy as a new democratic form. In this period, consultative democracy was overshadowed and traced its trajectory within the context of the New Democratic Revolution (新民主主义革命 *Xinminzhu Zhuyi Geming*), precisely designated as "New Democratic Consultative Democracy."

In 1954, with the convening of the National People's Congress, the National Committee of the Chinese People's Political Consultative Conference concluded its functions as the state's political authority, marking a significant transformation. Specifically, the CPPCC transitioned from a dual structure encompassing both political consultation and state power attributes to serving solely as a consultative democracy agency. Simultaneously, the shift from the New Democratic Consultative Democracy to Socialist Consultative Democracy commenced within the broader shift from a New Democracy to Socialism. Nevertheless, various political and mass movements, such as the Great Leap Forward, anti-rightist campaigns, and the Cultural Revolution, rendered this shift vulnerable. After the Third Plenary Session of the Eleventh Central Committee, especially the rectification movements and comprehensive reforms, notably the Reform and Opening Up initiative in 1978, the political consultative system was institutionalized within the framework of the "Two Sessions"—the National People's Congress and the CPPCC. Consultation subsequently became entrenched within specific institutionalized political structures.

Subsequently, consultation gradually acquired democratic connotations, particularly as reconciled within Deng Xiaoping's discourse on socialist democracy with *Chinese characteristics*. In 1991, Jiang Zemin, during the "Party Member Leaders Meeting of the Two Sessions," first proposed the important idea that socialist democracy in China takes two forms: "The people exercising their rights through elections and voting, and comprehensive consultations amongst various sectors of the populace before elections and voting to reach consensus on common issues as much as possible, are two important forms of socialist democracy in our country."[3] In the 2006 document issued by the Central Committee of the Communist Party of China, the very idea of two forms of democracy within the socialist framework was articulated for the first time,

> Within the expansive territory and populous confines of our country, critical matters pertaining to the national economy and the welfare of the populace undergo extensive consultation under the auspices of the Chinese Communist Party, epitomizing the harmonization of democratic principles with centralized governance. Through mechanisms such as elections and voting, the populace exercises their rights, while diverse segments of society engage in comprehensive consultations preceding pivotal decisions, endeavoring to foster consensus on matters of collective import. These mechanisms delineate two pivotal manifestations of socialist democracy within our nation.[4]

On November 5, 2007, the State Council Information Office of China promulgated the White Paper entitled "China's Political Party System: Cooperation and Consultation (中国的政党制度 *Zhongguo de Zhengdang Zhidu*)," which marked the inaugural acknowledgment of the combination of "electoral democracy" and "consultative democracy." This Paper underscored the amalgamation of the two as a pivotal characteristic of socialist democratic principles in China. It delineated that:

> Within China, the framework of People's Congresses and the multi-party cooperation and political consultation system orchestrated by the Chinese Communist Party are mutually reinforcing. Citizens exercise their political rights through electoral processes and voting mechanisms, while substantive consultations are undertaken amongst diverse societal factions prior to significant decision-making endeavors, endeavoring to garner

[3] General Office of the National Committee of the Chinese People's Political Consultative Conference, and Documentation Research Office of the Central Committee of the Communist Party of China, eds. *Selections of Important Documents of the People's Political Consultative Conference (Part 2)*. Zhonggong Zhongyang Wenxian Chubanshe, Zhongguo Wenshi Chubanshe, Central Literature Publishing House, China Literature and History Publishing House, 2009. p. 506.

[4] Ibid. (part 3), p. 793.

consensus to the fullest extent possible. These modalities represent two vital manifestations of socialist democracy.[5]

This Paper also posited that:

The fusion of electoral democracy and consultative democracy augments the depth and scope of socialist democratic practices. By means of extensive political consultations, predominant deference is accorded to the will of the majority, alongside due consideration of the reasonable aspirations of minority groups. This approach ensures the optimal realization of democratic principles amid the populace and facilitates the fostering of societal harmony and development.[6]

In the Report on *Implementation of the Central Committee of the Chinese Communist Party on Strengthening the Work of the People's Political Consultative Conference*, issued by the General Office of the Central Committee of the Communist Party of China in 2011, the idea of "consultative democracy" was formally incorporated into the CCP's central document, thereby affirming the CPPCC as a crucial manifestation of "consultative democracy" in China. Subsequently, the 18th National Congress of the Communist Party of China, convened in 2012, underscored that "the system of People's Congresses is the fundamental political system to safeguard that the people are the masters of the country," while explicitly stating that "socialist consultative democracy is an important form of people's democracy in our country." The Congress called for the "enhancement of the socialist consultative democratic system," the "promotion of extensive, multi-tiered, and institutionalized development of consultative democracy," and the "full realization of the important role of the People's Political Consultative Conference as a conduit for consultative democracy."[7] Therefore, through the authoritative medium of reports and resolutions adopted by the Party Congress, both the electoral democracy and consultative democracy systems have been politically and theoretically established.

[5] The "China's Political Party System: Cooperation and Consultation," available at: https://www.gov.cn/zhengce/20%202106/25/content_5620794.htm (Accessed April 1, 2024).

[6] Ibid.

[7] Hu (2012, pp. 26–27).

The historical delineation of consultative democracy in China underscores three pivotal aspects: (1) Consultative democracy emerges within the Chinese context through three distinct modalities: methodological, theoretical, and institutional. (2) Its trajectory from New Democratic consultative democracy to Socialist consultative democracy is discernible through revolutionary, developmental, and reformative endeavors, with the latter persisting in a continuum of progressive refinement. (3) Consultative democracy synergizes with and intersects electoral democracy, thereby constituting a salient hallmark of socialist democracy imbued with *Chinese characteristic.*

The era of Xi Jinping has further imbued China with a distinct shade of consultative democracy. "Consultative democracy is not solely the prerogative of Western capitalist countries. Our socialist consultative democracy is not a mere transplant of Western "deliberative democracy," but rather cultivated within the rich soil of socialism in our country. It is firmly rooted, sourced, and possesses robust vitality within our context. It embodies a unique, distinctive, and insightful democratic framework within our socialist democratic polity."[8] Consultative democracy is delineated as "under the leadership of the Communist Party of China, various parties within the populace engage in extensive consultation prior to and during the decision-making process on major issues concerning reform, development, stability, and practical matters that involving the immediate interests of the masses, endeavoring to forge consensus, which constitutes a vital democratic form."[9]

In addition to perpetuating the nexus between consultative democracy and the United Front, and serving as a consensus democracy, Xi integrates

[8] Xi (2014).

[9] "The Central Committee of the Communist Party of China. Guanyu Jiaqiang Shehui Zhuyi Xieshang Minzhu de Yijian [Opinions on Strengthening the Construction of Socialist Consultative Democracy]." *Renmin Ribao, People's Daily*, 2015-02-10(1).

consultative democracy into a broader narrative, such as people's democracy[10] and the WPPD, reframed by Xi, perceives and interlinks consultative democracy as a prior form in achieving the people's sovereignty. Simultaneously, Xi's advocacy for socialist consultative democracy implies a call for a "broad, multi-layered, and institutionalized" development. This signals a departure from a mere consultative democracy towards a governance paradigm centered on consultation, amalgamating democratic decision-making with democratic governance. This paradigm shift aims to reestablish a "cooperative" state-society relationship.

The CCP, being a Leninist party characterized by highly centralized power, maintains a cautious stance towards democracy. Nevertheless, what underlies its very inclination towards consultative democracy? Primarily, this inclination can be traced back to the CCP's historical evolution from a politically feeble entity, initially forsaking liberalism in favor of Marxism, albeit in a distorted form. This trajectory towards embracing democratic norms is intricately intertwined with China's unique contextual factors, notably through the United Front strategy. It can be contended that the nascent concept of consultative democracy in China emanated from this very strategic idea. It is pertinent to note that the CCP attributes the initial dearth of consultative democratic initiatives following the setbacks of the First and Second United Fronts to its perceived lack of unequivocal leadership. However, subsequent to the promulgation of the "May Day Manifesto," the CCP's capacity to engage in equitable consultations with other democratic parties burgeoned under its leadership and aegis. Consequently, consultations led by the CCP emerged as the distinguishing characteristics of consultative democracy in China, thereby distinguishing it from Western counterparts.

Consultative democracy, grounded in the United Front, evolves from a conventional approach of making friends, marshaling and mobilizing

[10] The conceptualization of socialist consultative democracy as the quintessence of people's democracy is acknowledged as Xi Jinping's distinctive contribution to democratic theory within China among Chinese academia. Simultaneously, the reframing of the CPPCC as "the specialized consultative body for consultative democracy" represents a significant shift. Originally perceived as merely an "important channel" following the 18th National Congress, it has progressively been elevated to "the sole," then "the primary," and subsequently designated as "important," further accentuated by the qualifying term "specialized." This nuanced progression not only precisely delineates the CPPCC's role but also facilitates the indigenization of consultative democracy in Chinese practices. See Chen (2022).

intermediate forces, and ostracizing enemies,[11] towards a consensus democracy that prioritizes unanimity through extensive consultations and dialogues. This paradigmatical shift not only accommodates the progressively diverse interest groups in China post-market economic reforms but also underscores China's good governance while accentuating consultation while downplay the significance of electoral processes.

Secondly, establishing a "democracy" that is distinct from liberal democracy in the West inherently necessitates the further incorporation of resources from Chinese tradition and culture. Throughout Chinese history, many mechanisms such as examinations, imperial recruitment, recommendations, and selections have been observed, notably lacking the practice of elections. In China, the process of conferring power differs significantly from Western norms. For instance, documented in the *Book of Documents: Canon of Yao* (尚书·尧典 *Shangshu Yaodian*) and the *Book of Documents: Canon of Shun* (尚书·舜典 *Shangshu Shundian*), crucial national matters necessitated Yao and Shun to convene meetings with the "Four Peaks (四岳 *Si Yue*)" or the "Twelve Governors (十二有牧 *Shier Youmu*)" and "Four Peaks Group of Governors (四岳群牧 *Siyue Qunmu*)," they are essentially tribal chieftain assemblies. Major decisions were reached through consultations between tribal leaders like Yao and Shun and the chieftains, reflecting a form of "consultative democracy" rather than "electoral democracy." The term "selection (选/择 *Xuan/Ze*)" is evident in ancient Chinese classics, such as "selecting the virtuous and capable," yet this "selection" does not denote electoral processes; rather, it denotes recommendation. Shun's appointment as a tribal leader resulted from consultation and recommendation during the "Four Peaks" meeting, as documented in the *Book of Documents: Canon of Yao*. This method of leadership selection was referred to as "abdication (禅让 *Shanrang*)." Hence, in China, "selection" distinguishes between "election" and "recommendations," with "election" and "selection" being their respective English counterparts.

While elections involve voting, selections entail consultation. Both methodologies are democratic but quite differ in approach. China's tradition of consultative democracy gradually evolved into authoritarianism after the era of Yu and Xia. Although "consultation" persisted to a certain

[11] Van Slyke (1964).

extent within limits, veering away from the democratic essence of consultation that diverges from what is understood as "consultative democracy." Due to China's esteemed tradition of abdication-style consultative democracy, coupled with its millennia-long pursuit of the philosophical concept of "harmony in diversity," Chinese society however is more inclined towards a harmonious form of consultative democracy rather than the competitive democratic structures. Therefore, consultative democracy not only resonates with the realities of Chinese society but also possesses deep cultural foundations.

Thirdly, western scholarship on participatory democracy experienced a significant growth in the mid-twentieth century,[12] while around the 1970s, there was a notable surge in studies that pertaining to deliberative democracy.[13] Such alike democratic endeavors prompt introspection and scholarly discourse on democratic norms within the leadership and academia of China. Over the past three decades of Reform and Opening Up in 1978, China has witnessed a prolific period of research in the field of democratic politics. From the late 1970s to the early 1980s, there was a focus on studies concerning the institutionalization and legalization of democratic processes. In the mid-1980s, focus shifted towards studies examining reforms within the CCP and state leadership structures, as well as the dynamics between the CCP and governments. Subsequently, during the late 1980s to the very early 1990s, research extended to encompass analyses of party systems and proposals for alternative democratic frameworks. By the mid-1990s, there was an emergence of studies that centered on the fundamental strategy of governing in accordance with legal principles. In the twenty-first century, scholarly inquiries delved into the CCP's leadership styles and governance methodologies, encompassing concepts such as scientific governance, democratic governance, and governance under the rule of law.

Since the dawn of the twenty-first century, there has been a burgeoning interest in further exploring the development trajectory of socialist politics with *Chinese characteristics*, alongside investigations into consultative democracy and related themes in the intellectual purview. In 2001, during

[12] See for example, Verba (1967), Bachrach and Botwinick (1992), and Barber (2014).

[13] See for example, Miller (1992), Young (1996), Bohman and Rehg (Eds.) (1997), Bohman (1998), and Elster (Ed.) (1998).

his visit to China, Jürgen Habermas introduced the concept of deliberative democracy to Chinese audiences.[14] Subsequently, in 2003, Yu Keping's work, "Hot Issues in Contemporary Western Political Theory," provided an introduction to deliberative democracy theory in the West.[15] In 2004, Chen Jiagang's translated anthology, *Consultative Democracy*, further disseminated foreign scholarship in this domain. Concurrently, the "International Academic Symposium on Deliberative Democracy" held at Zhejiang University in Hangzhou in the same year garnered considerable attention within society. In 2005, the National Social Science Fund initiated the research topic "Consultative Democracy and Contemporary Chinese Political Practice." It was against this backdrop that the Western term "deliberative democracy" and its Chinese counterpart of "consultative democracy" began to be utilized as a conceptual framework for studying China's democratic politics.

Consultation in Chinese Ideology, Democracy, and Governance

If we regard the decision-making process as being refined by the "raw" public opinion through representatives, after full consideration of all contrasting views, they are empowered to make the final decision and then implement it.[16] To note, there remains a dichotomy. Deliberative democrats advocate that the deliberative processes have to be reconciled in all modes of decision-making processes, as only in this way could decisions be more democratic and legitimate. This can be true in mini-publics where on-the-spot decisions could be made after deliberation (or a simple voting) in mass democracy. This ideal nevertheless takes the realistic complexity for granted by ignoring the scale of the problem, limitations of time, expression ability, geography, professions, division of labor, enthusiasm, coercion, and so on. Even the more faddish "systemic turn" of

[14] In 2001, Jürgen Habermas delivered a seminal lecture in China, where he expounded upon "The Three Paradigms of Democracy." Available at https://www.aisixiang.com/data/113287.html (Accessed April 7, 2024).

[15] Available at https://www.aisixiang.com/data/6114.html (Accessed April 7, 2024).

[16] Fishkin (2009).

deliberative democracy is also to disassemble the large-scale deliberation into phased, small-scale processes for processing.[17]

Then, consulting the public on such a background is more valuable and favorable to the actual (other synonyms like raw, primitive, direct, unfiltered, etc.) options rather than the representative ones as described in the input democracy, for example, a process of "sounding out" and in which the public themselves feel each other out; they tentatively float trial balloons[18]; and they adjust their own positions in light of what they anticipate the reaction of others will be. Through the successive mutual adjustments of that sort, people converge: not so much on common preferences as on the common perceptions of the feasible set. When the feasible set has become sufficiently small, the choice largely tends to make itself.[19] Hence, when the representative closed-door meetings or some large-scale activities fail to deliver a fair and just deliberation, a broader consultation then can safeguard that the public voice to be heard and their voice could be more representative.

True and important though all that is, mainstream examination of Chinese "deliberative democracy" likely seeks resources and inspiration from Chinese traditional culture. For example, when ancient emperors sympathized with their people, they were obliged to consult the ministers before making decisions, which became a rather favorable way to check against tyrants, avoid mistaken political decisions, and developing policies that were in favor of people's interest in Chinese dynasties. These dialogues between emperors and ministers are being regarded as early *deliberations* in modern Chinese political discourses. But this (re)interpretation of deliberation and deliberative democracy involves a misconception and ambiguity, leading to a blurred distinction between deliberation and consultation. Take Confucianism, for instance, which espouses hierarchical feudalism, champions authority, and unduly emphasizes the role of the elite. Dialogues within this framework transpire amid a backdrop of inequality. Emperors partake in such dialogues, as conceptualized in China's people-centered democracy (民本 *Minben*), to underscore their obligations in governing the nation and advancing public welfare, rather than pursuing personal interests. This conceptualization

[17] Parkinson and Mansbridge (2012).

[18] Olsen (1972).

[19] Elster (1986).

has been subsequently reinterpreted in the sphere of meritocratic politics and effective governance within contemporary Chinese political discourse.

Describing a crucial aspect of Chinese politics as ***deliberation***, as many authors have done,[20] stems from the traditional belief that deliberation inherently fosters democracy. However, the "Chinese deliberation" is fundamentally consultative. Beyond its cultural heritage, owing to its Leninist Party nature, the CCP always maintains an air of opacity and secrecy in its democratic centralist doctrine. So, instead of a loose defining of deliberation, consultation aligns more accurately with the dynamics of Chinese politics. Given its immense significance as an ideological cornerstone, pivotal to the Chinese Communist Party's (CCP) leadership survival and governance from Mao to Xi in contemporary China (for a similar interpretation, see Tsang's 'consultative Leninist' in 2015). This legacy is entrenched in the CCP's rule through the tenet of "CCP leadership"—a fundamental yet distinct feature of Chinese politics. Mao's mass line, "from the masses, to the masses (群众路线 *Quanzhong Luxian*)," as described by Wang Shaoguang as "quanticipation," exemplifies this form of consultation where officials at every level are encouraged to listen to and gather public inputs to facilitate decision-making and policy implementation.

The link between the CCP and the public is further underscored during Xi's era. This hierarchical form of consultation is presented as the embodiment of people's democracy, encompassing two key aspects that, firstly, gathering public input to reflect the people's subjectivity, as highlighted in the official rhetoric, "the people are the masters of the country"; secondly, the CCP's benevolent leadership ensures the welfare of the people. Nevertheless, the CCP not only needs to persist in its paternalistic approach of making decisions *for* the people rather than *by/of* the people, but it also needs to strengthen the reconsolidation of power through ideological democratic centralization, thereby firmly anchoring decision-making authority. While this principle of consulting

[20] Most Chinese authors predominately utilize a "methodological nationalism" to elaborate on the historical roots and importance of "deliberation" in Chinese politics. Especially in the last two decades, there has been a strong consensus emphasizing the superiority of a distinctly Chinese approach to "deliberation," in contrast to Western frameworks that are grounded in individualism. Many China observers, like He Baogang, have attempted to reconcile the China's authoritarianism with deliberation. Nevertheless, the perplex understandings of deliberation in these conversations have resulted in a significant dearth of dialogue among these viewpoints.

the people may exhibit nuances in different leaders from Mao to Xi, its essence remains unaltered. In essence, all effective policies, governance strategies, and even the concept of Chinese democracy itself stem from this consultative paradigm.

To note, this consultative ideology is persistently coherent and functions respectively to "broaden its membership base, promote a new generation of leaders, reformulate its ideological content, appeal to nationalist impulses in society,"[21] and further to strengthen its organizational apparatus throughout the country, open the channels of discourse within the party and between the party-state and society. It is institutionalized in various forms like the more typical Chinese People's Political Consultative Conference (CPPCC), the United Front Work, as well as other consultative designs in hierarchies. Though they have introduced some changes which are commonly seen in democracies, especially in Chinese localities (e.g., villages and urban communities) where the public participation and "deliberation" are expanding in a monitored yet orderly way, the CCP seems to accept a pluralistic "deliberation" through a gradual empowerment, as indicated in "authoritarian deliberation," a concept coined by He Baogang and Mark Warren.[22] Local deliberations (limited deliberative empowerment) coexist in the absence of the regime democratization. Always note that these rare cases cannot change the consultative nature in ideology under the CCP's one-party rule and its pre-empting of democratization.

Besides, magnanimity and mercy on the part of the emperor towards the people form a very weak check and balance of power in Chinese tradition and the Confucianism. China's contemporary consultative politics, as per the CCP's ideology, adheres to the type of "authoritarian democracy," wherein the sovereignty and well-being of the people could only be realized through a robust and centralized state. Up to the present, the discourse encompassing neo-authoritarianism, the New Left, and liberalism in the 1990s—where a transitional phase of the authoritative and centralized governance aimed at incremental promotion of Chinese democracy—persists, but the CCP has continued its authoritarian rule in the new era and shows no sign of democratization. This ideology underpins the belief that sound decisions can best emerge through the very

[21] Shambaugh (2008, p. 89).

[22] See also Mei (2020).

top-down hierarchical consultation, akin to the mass line, than through participatory input from the grassroots. Under this "representational" system, according to Wang Shaoguang, the mess brought by social status, money, enthusiasm, and ability in political participation in liberalism can be avoided, and it avoids simple conflicts among Western competitive parties in votes. Therefore, in Wang's words, the CCP's representational democracy based on consultation—a mass line type—represents the genuine need of the people.

Consulting and listening to the people and building connections with them so as to provide better governance is deeply endorsed by and in the CCP's ideology, and Chinese people also regard a strong and centralized government as the safeguard of their well-beings. The consultative politics therefore highlights the CCP as the counterpart to Western liberalism, with the former not only achieving good decision-making and social order by further soliciting inputs while not resorting to the Western multi-party system and competitive election.

As articulated in Chinese official discourse and propaganda, "Chinese democracy is a combination of consultative democracy and electoral democracy."[23] This juxtaposition of the consultation with democracy might initially appear paradoxical, while it is important to highlight that consultations lack the distinct and applicable political contexts within well-established democracies, like in Lowi's "interest group pluralism" in America, Schmitter's "corporatist intermediation," Beer's Britain "in the collectivist age," and Lijphart's "consociational democracy."[24] In some non-democratic settings, such as China, for example, it too lays claim to a consultative democracy, albeit with nuanced distinctions.

An exemplar of consultative democracy refers to the Scandinavian model, wherein the political landscape thrives on the compromise, accommodation, and inclusivity, rather than adopting an adversarial and exclusionary stance, as observed in the Anglo-Saxon and Continental European counterparts.[25] Consultation per se involves the bargaining

[23] To avoid any potential ambiguity in the conceptual utilization, I differentiate between the academic use of deliberative democracy and the employment of consultative democracy within official contexts. This division serves as an analytical aid, preventing the blurring of the concept of deliberation and its synonyms.

[24] Cited from Goodin (2004, p. 90).

[25] Indicating a Scandinavian consultative democracy does not imply homogenizing the subtleties amid different Nordic countries. For instance, Norway emphasizes more

of policies, and the pathway through which these voices and consultations flow to decision-makers span communities, organizations, groups, and those representatives. This concept intertwines with participatory democracy, where individuals engage directly in politics to assert their sovereignty; deliberative democracy, where rational discourse and the pursuit of common good are pivotal to decision-making; and a voting-oriented electoral democracy which aims to gain the vote and press matters towards a prompt solution. While the consultative democracy values both the raw opinions and mutually justified consultations and consensus, it does not exclude the negotiations between the political parties and interest groups. The closer the relationship between consultation and decision-making and the broader the consultation, the more democratic it is.

The intricacies of consultative democracy, both in general and of the Chinese variant, remain of utmost importance. The former is commonly referred as the aforementioned "Nordic democracy," wherein "the government has over the years built up a large network of consultative boards and councils for the representation of all the relevant interests."[26] This pathway indicates more how more democratic and legitimate decision-makings are occurring before/during voting. More time is invested in understanding (counter-) views and justifications. This process in a way facilitates a final vote. Consultation can therefore be conducted individually mostly in communities and groups, mirroring practices in countries like Norway and Sweden. Similar modes of consultation can also be observed in Belgium through initiatives like G1000, which entails multi-stage deliberations and consultations to be divided into some online public consultations, citizen summits (mini-public deliberations), and in-depth citizen panels. Comparable efforts, such as G400 in France, have also been orchestrated.[27] For consultative democracy to thrive, it necessitates not only a representative government but also an open, pluralistic, and inclusive civil society.

community-based participation in politics, whereas in Sweden, diverse organizations facilitate consultations with the government.

[26] Rokkan (1966).

[27] The G1000 and G400 are designed to randomly select 1000 and 400 participants, respectively, for engagement in round-table public policy consultation. They function as the primary resources of information for hierarchical decision-making. See Caluwaerts and Reuchamps (2018) and Buge and Morio (2019).

In this context, the existing research on the Chinese "deliberative democracy (*xieshang minzhu* 协商民主)" displays variation in nomenclature. All these descriptive terminologies such as "deliberative democracy" found within Chinese mainstream indigenized studies, "authoritarian deliberation" or "deliberative authoritarianism,"[28] "authoritarian consultation" or "consultative authoritarianism"[29] in Western Chinese studies, as well as the rhetorical propaganda of "consultative democracy" as depicted in the CCP's discourse, along with other terms,[30] all advocate for a more conservative and prudent approach to consultation in Chinese politics, than a democracy-facilitating approach to deliberation. Consequently, even though Chinese consultative democracy emphasizes hierarchical top-down information gathering to ensure policy flexibility and adjustment, interactions between higher and lower levels of governance remain rigid and feeble. This consultative process takes place without involving elections or representatives. It might yield outcomes akin to Scandinavian consultation, but it is less influenced both by the public and their representatives.

Critiques might argue that within such a remiss process, the public is passively treated as mere information collector, rendering it undemocratic in every sense. On the other hand, the Chinese consultative democracy introduces a very system of checks and balances, where consultation is intertwined with decision-making. The final authority, however, rests with the CCP. Instead of wresting decision-making power from governing bodies and entrusting it to the public, this approach strengthens policy adaptability, responsiveness, and accountability. This consultation bears similarities to an overarching paternalistic "authoritarian democracy"—one that asserts "I understand what is in your best interest," as well as to participatory and deliberative democracy in liberal tradition. A crisis of legitimacy, arising from insufficient participation and deliberation, finds partial resolution via this consultative input and the improved governance it fosters. Intriguingly, the consultative methodology serves to fortify a tenacious authoritarianism in China.

[28] See, for example, He (2014).

[29] See, for example, Teets (2013) and Truex (2017).

[30] See, for example, Pan (2003) and Wang and Groot (2018).

Democratically desirable implies that people have the right to speak or not, to listen or not, to change or not. By analogy, the consultation may conditionally acknowledge the complexity of the reality and transfer the consultative inputs into a more democratized output (e.g., government performance). At its essence, if we temporarily separate the vital connection between input and output, between consultation and decision-making, a more normative perspective suggests that the more consultations, the more potential there is to enhance the representation and diversity of public opinions, and ultimately democratizing of the input processes. However, what truly enables consultative type of democracy possible, as proposed by Goodin, is that once the consultation is underway, a process of "mutual co-optation" might grant otherwise marginalized individuals some genuine influence over the decisions and outcomes that eventually materialize. Hence, fostering conversational dynamics in consultative scenarios can address shortcomings that "mere integration" fails to rectify, especially when deliberation is too crucial and naïve in promoting a meta-consensus that is based on a benign interaction among the public.[31]

This is how the consultative democracy works, and how it distinguishes itself with a Schumpeterian democracy, which endorses a law that democracy can only be achieved through participation and deliberation that embodies the popular sovereignty: "Increasing opportunities for input in these ways does not necessarily produce any increase in democracy...democratising the process, even if that has not much systematic linkage to democratising the outputs, might in a pinch be sufficient to satisfy input-democratic ends."[32] Within the framework of consultative democracy, consultation and democracy are intertwined to some extent. But how does China's consultative democracy fare? It turns out to be quite a hybrid form. In reality, not all Chinese consultations are used to formulate policies (for some practical considerations) or to analyze public preferences for further solidifying Chinese authoritarianism.

Some genuine consultations can be observed among certain cadres who are willing to listen to and deliberate with the public. But these

[31] Discourse theorists and deliberative democrats want to dress this up as a higher-order tenet of communicative ethics.

[32] Goodin (2006).

consultations are uneven without the presence of national and local elections that safeguards a regular transition of leadership. They tend to rely on the personal preferences, which renders the rhetorically repackaged conception of "substantial democracy" in Chinese discourse vulnerable within this process. Another key point is that China's consultations occur in an environment lacking freedom of speech. The right to speak freely is democratically crucial in China, if not, consultation could be "window dressing" in hearing the people's voice. These make China's consultative democracy inherently contradictory.

This uncertain consultation is tactically designed to form a regime type described as "consultative authoritarianism," signifying the CCP's final say on political issues, policy implementation, public participation, and legislation. As delineated by He and Warren, "consultative authoritarianism" is,

> A form of rule in which power holders use communication to collect the preferences of those their decisions will affect and take those preferences into account as information relevant to their decision-making...Whereas "consultation" implies that decision-makers ask for and receive information from those their decisions will affect, and "deliberative" implies that decision-makers will do more than solicit input; they will enable (or permit) space for people to discuss issues and to engage in the give and take of reasons, to which decisions are then responsive.[33]

The link between input (consultation) and output (responsiveness and decision-making) in Chinese context appears weaker and uneven. This implies that if good policies and effective governance are tied to input derived from consultation, it is likely coming from a top-down analysis of the collective public preferences, with democratized consultation and its facilitation on decision-making are mere by-products. Demonstrable practices are widespread in both the political and social consultations. For instance, various input channels, such as public hearings and legislative consultations (立法协商*lifa xieshang*, it is rhetorically called "deliberation" in the Chinese language) exist within Chinese legislation. These

[33] He and Warren (2011). The concept of consultative authoritarianism was first proposed by Harry Harding, he argues that consultative authoritarianism "increasingly recognizes the need to obtain information, advice, and support from key sectors of the population, but insists on (...) maintaining ultimate political power in the hands of the Party" Harding (2010, p. 45).

avenues involve non-official participants, including legal experts, citizens, social organizations (e.g., the Women's Federation, Labor Union), and sometimes NGOs, and their unprecedented involvement is particularly evident that in the online consultations. However, this participation and consultation often amount to mere symbolic gestures like "flower vase,"[34] given that the bottom-up opinions cannot justify their pertinence to decision in rather opaque closed-door infighting. Political consultations, and even more so the special consultative body of the CPPCC, which is portrayed as a "rubber stamp" are designed and role-played under the CCP's one-party rule.[35]

In various polities, one could encounter formal and decorative consultative institutions similar to the CPPCC, for example, the Democratic Front of Reunification (조국통일민 주주의전선) in North Korea, the Fatherland Front in Vietnam (Mặt trận Tổ quốc Việt Nam), and other similar institutions in former Eastern European socialist countries, such as Hungary, the Czech Republic, and Bulgaria. Western democracies, like France, have also implemented akin the consultative bodies to gather information and public opinions for decision-making purposes, such as the Economic, Social and Environmental Council (Le Conseil économique, social et environnemental, SECE). While these institutions and their consultations serve as institutionalized safeguards to uphold the semblance of representation, they do not hold genuine decision-making authority. But they are integrated into the state apparatus and the realm of partisan coalitions. However, the extent of their influence on outcomes and the degree of power-sharing with the ruling party differ across these entities. If, as assumed in theory, the more independent, broader, and varied the consultation, the more of the consultation functions to generate inputs into the policy processes, like some showcases in the Commission Nationale du Débat Public (National Commission for Public Debate, CNDP) in France, which has conducted some nationwide yet influential consultations in the form of public debates.[36]

[34] Wang (2003).

[35] Saich (2015) and Cabestan (2015).

[36] The author conducted fieldwork in more than 20 public debates (both mini-publics and nationwide) organized by the CNDP from 2019 to 2021. The CNDP is an advisory and consultative body that is independent of the French government. While lacking the decision-making authority of others, it nonetheless serves to recalibrate the dynamics of consultation, mobilization, and deliberation in public engagement.

In this context, consultative authoritarianism emerges as a nuanced hybrid model. It can display rigidity akin to "command authoritarianism" during some mass mobilizations. Take, for instance, the measures implemented in response to the Covid-19, where the CCP takes public concerns and interests into account while excessively prioritizing collective interests "at any cost" and taking consultation for granted through a mere top-down command. It can also be seen as "deliberative authoritarianism" on some other occasions, where genuine deliberative processes are observable in Chinese villages and communities.[37] These potentials, however, coexist in one toolbox. So, broadly speaking, the public participation and consultations in contemporary China do not really bind the regime to heeding or even responding to citizen demands in any way.

Consultative democracy highlighted in Chinese official discourse asserts that "people" exercise their rights through elections and voting, and all parties conduct full consultations before election and voting to reach consensus on common issues as much as possible, are two important forms of the "socialist democracy" (proposed by former president Jiang Zemin in 1991).[38] One has to stress that in the official framing, consultative democracy has two dimensions: firstly, political consultation and the multi-party cooperation and political consultation system under the CCP's leadership; and secondly, the social consultation and dialogue system. On the one hand, the CCP emphasizes the necessity for political consultation among the elites, especially but not exclusively with some other officially recognized parties; on the other hand, it expands the political and social consultation to the ordinary citizens. This consultative democracy tends to replace (and is sometimes conflated with) the Maoist

[37] Nearly all (particularly empirical) studies that investigating China's "deliberative democracy" that centers on Chinese localities, especially in the southeastern regions. A few cases of mini-public deliberations and participatory budgets may be authentically carried out in an interactive manner. Some observers feature this juxtaposition as deliberation thriving in Chinese local settings even as the CCP's regime maintains its undemocratic nature.

[38] The WPPD, as delineated in the authoritative White Paper titled "China: Democracy that Works," published by the State Council Information Office of China in 2021 and introduced under the auspices of Xi Jinping, aims to advance the integration of consultative democracy. This concept once again pushes the boundaries of consultative democracy across diverse domains. Consultative democracy, therefore, is aimed at better reaching out not so much to a party member but to society at large, particularly its co-opted elites. Available at: http://www.scio.gov.cn/ztk/dtzt/44689/47513/index.htm (Accessed June 6, 2023).

conception of the mass line: the Party and governments at national and local levels should have close contact and develop a direct dialogue with the masses constantly.[39]

Indeed, Chinese consultative democracy could only genuinely exhibit democratic traits under the condition that officials are willing to engage in equitable interactions with the public, assuming responsibility and responsiveness throughout the whole process and decision-making. Absent such conditions, it transforms into consultative authoritarianism, where consultation is adopted, whether rhetorically or tangibly, to either facilitate effective governance or reaffirm the CCP's legitimacy and Chinese authoritarianism. So, from Mao to Xi, utilizing consultation as a framework to characterize Chinese democracy and its functioning primarily serves to ensure the CCP's exclusive leadership. If we are still willing, to some extent, to categorize consultation in China as democratic, a crucial query arises regarding the interplay between one-party rule and the consultative process. In simpler terms, how can we ensure that consultative inputs and their transformations are maximized in the output while simultaneously expanding consultation to encompass greater diversity, representation, and authenticity? By re-addressing this challenge, the CCP could assert its democratic stance in representing the public needs.

When Stoker provided the classical definition of government as "the ability to make decisions and then the capacity to enforce them,"[40] he likely could not have foreseen that this framework would eventually encounter a rift that is between the government and the public. Kooiman and Van Vliet subsequently articulated that "the governance concept implies the establishment of a structure or order that cannot be imposed externally but arises from the intricate interactions that among

[39] The mass line is Mao's main theoretical contribution to the populist emphasis. Encouraging political mobilization, this discourse is conducted under the umbrella of the centralized party leadership. It was less institutionalized than the more recent discourse of "consultative democracy". Townsend underscored that, "the mass campaign indicates Mao's rejection to the routine administration- with its implied mistrust of bureaucracy- and its arousal of popular emotions and interests." The more endorsed and equipped discourse of consultative democracy is designed in a more general sense as the main democratic form in contemporary China with various policy supports and empirical evidence. See Townsend (1977).

[40] Stoker (1998, p. 46).

a multitude of governing and mutually influencing actors."[41] Deliberative democrats encapsulate this evolving trajectory. For instance, Dryzek, however, describes a deliberative turn "to address both its conceptual underpinnings and fundamental challenges arise in its application to an increasingly diverse array of problems and issues."[42] The dialogue-centered governance underscores the process of democratizing input, and this democratic prosperity values the cultivation of civil society, and in turn citizens actively deliberating and participating in politics could enhance a solid democracy. Such a normative paradigm finds its elucidation.

While it may be problematic to utilize this "deliberative turn" to describe the political changes in China, some qualified deliberative practices truly exist, as some optimists have assumed, but they are rare and uneven in hierarchies (at regime and local levels), power relations (with political and apolitical concerns), and geography (in the developed east coastal regions, like in Zhejiang and Jiangsu provinces, and the underdeveloped Midwest regions). It is likely a consultative governance adopted by the powerful state, and the latter authorities fixed such political consultations through laws and regulations and established institutions and infiltrated their influences within, therefore, effectively transforming consultations into legal forms. At some point, the CCP maintained control through the rather small local work units, which were tightly controlled and were far from forums of deliberative freedom as it considered ways to devolve power away from a centralized state party and created sites of quasi-deliberative freedom.[43] In this context, consultation proves advantageous for both officials and the public. It serves to accrue credibility and bolster the CCP's legitimacy, simultaneously granting people a voice in the process.

The impressive performance of the Chinese state can effectively promote consultative governance, which primarily pertains to the state's capacity to expand the franchise and scope of consultations. This notion finds support in Warren's argument that "democracy should not be limited to its state-centric manifestations… the state may have some new

[41] Kooiman (1993, p. 42); see also Kooiman and Van Vliet (2000).

[42] Dryzek (2012, p. 32).

[43] Leib (2006).

functions in generating, supporting, and organizing democracy."[44] To fully recognize the "deliberative politics" in China might be somewhat hesitant. For instance, some state-sponsored deliberative processes are predominantly employed to reinforce authoritarian rule. Most "deliberative" forms within the Chinese context are linked to government officials than being entrusted to an independent body external to Chinese political institutions. Nevertheless, consultative approaches are pervasive.

Suggesting that the CCP is compelled to engage in consultations to avoid elections, which could jeopardize its one-party rule, therefore underestimates the vital role of consultative governance in safeguarding the CCP's survival. This analysis is twofold: firstly, consultative governance not only integrates the elite coalition and fosters corporatist governance, it nevertheless fosters extensive public consultation that enhances the good governance and policy formulation. Secondly, though political consultation amid CCP-led elites lack binding force, the CCP is (un)willing to incorporate the social elites into its decision-making structure, thereby establishing a form of coalition or what could be termed as "co-governance." While this integration does not entail sharing substantive political power with the CCP, collaboration with elites and provision of specific privileges renders dissenting voices external to the system powerless. These consulted elites or groups are governed by various consultative bodies such as the CPPCC. They do not possess veto authority, yet they contribute to a delicate equilibrium within the CCP's rule.

While the public consultations are susceptible to interference, they commonly adopt a *functionalist* approach to address the practical issues, alleviate public grievances, and manage social resistance within governance. So, applying the conventional concept of legitimacy in deliberation to China's consultative politics proves challenging due to various conceptual and methodological pitfalls.[45] Consultative governance in China adheres to a rather pragmatism tradition, it exercises caution in promoting public empowerment and cultivating civil society, which could lead to some democratic consequences. As a matter of fact, it prioritizes the

[44] Warren (2004).

[45] Schubert (2008).

top-down good governance through limited participation and consultation as a strategy to mitigate the prospect of rapid democratization.[46] As Schubert and Sandby-Thomas would argue, this consultative governance serves as the primary foundation for the CCP's legitimacy. It identifies the actual contested processes that stimulate, shape, and sustain social support.[47]

Some authors have aptly pointed out how the CCP employs consultation, which they refer to as "administrative absorption," in governance to safeguard its monopoly while strategically appeasing, aligning with, and leveraging social elites and the public to garner their support.[48] Despite holding superior positions in terms of power, wealth, knowledge, prestige, and social status, elites retain stronger influence and lobbying capability and augmented by institutionalized consultations within the party, the government, the People's Congress, and the (C)PPCC. While they may have been divested of political power, as vested interests, they still stand to benefit from policy adjustments and compromises with the CCP. But in lacking mobilizational and organizational capability of the public, their dissatisfactions are transferred upward through resistance or mass incident, as both mass line and consultative politics are designed to dispel public grievances and maintain social stability.

The consultative methodology within Chinese governance summarizes various mass lines from Mao's era. These include the United Front (with the centrists), administrative absorption, Jiang's "Three Represents," and more. All of these strategies were devised to reestablish alliances and cooperation with both elites and the public, all while ensuring the CCP's continued and unshakable leadership. While this approach might have brought administrative efficiency and responsiveness, Hong Kong offers a heuristic case examination. Here, the rule of law, an effective and transparent technocratic system, social freedoms (such as speech, press, publication, and association), along with a robust social welfare system safeguard the interests of both the elite and the public. However, it is

[46] This term "good governance" was first used in 1989 by the World Bank. It aims to "ensure respect for human rights and the rule of law; strengthen democracy; promote transparency and capacity in public administration." This definition was made by UN Secretary-General Kofi Annan. Available at http://www.soc.titech.acjp/uem/governance.html (Accessed December 12, 2023).

[47] Ibid, see also Sandby-Thomas (2014).

[48] For example, Jin (1997), Kang (2002), and Kang and Han (2008).

important to note that Hong Kong remains somewhat authoritarian when compared to Taiwan, despite sharing a similar cultural background. In a nutshell, the consultative governance in China underscores the CCP and a robust government as the safeguards of public welfare. Yet, it seldom explores the very origins of government power and the potential for bottom-up decision-making through empowering and encouraging public participation and deliberation.

Interconnecting consultation with good governance in China has become the prevailing analytical paradigm for elucidating the responsiveness,[49] accountability,[50] and adaptability[51] of the CCP and the Chinese government. Consultation should not be narrowly understood as a very unidirectional information collection in Chinese authoritarianism, nor should it be stretched to imply deliberation. Drawing from my interviews with staffs in the Internal Reference Departments under the State Council (though it is worth noting that public opinion collection could manifest in various ways), these departments circulate not only positive and cheerleading information but also both domestic and foreign, critical, and moderate perspectives to the higher-level authorities. It is important to emphasize that in Xi's era with rising authoritarianism, critical, and negative information is frequently encapsulated in quotation marks to signify a particular stance. This leads us to pose an open-ended question: Could a gradual shift towards consultation in politics, say, in the long run, eventually steer China towards democratization without altering its current political framework?

We could certainly use the term "deliberation" to describe Chinese politics in rhetoric, this is precisely what Chinese officials and academia are currently engaged in. As Yu Keping, a prestigious political scientist has elucidated, when the Western conception of "deliberative democracy" was introduced and translated into Chinese at the beginning of this century, the Central Compilation and Translation Bureau prepared two variations, both "deliberative democracy" and "consultative democracy." The former aligns more closely with China's political consultation system (政治协商制度*Zhengzhi Xieshang Zhidu*), while the latter is more encapsulated China's political reality. Previous examinations of "consultative Leninism" and

[49] See, for example, Chen et al. (2016) and Qiaoan and Teets (2020).

[50] See, for example, Tsai (2007) and Kung et al. (2009).

[51] See, for example, Dickson (2000), Oi (2003), and Shambaugh (2008).

"consultative authoritarianism" have predominantly concentrated on how the way of consultation in Chinese politics contributes to the durability and resilience of Chinese authoritarianism. Nevertheless, they overlook the critical aspect of how the consultation is conducted. Particularly when viewed through an indigenous lens, its significance within Chinese politics extends to ideological, democratic, and governmental aspects.

In conclusion, disentangling the diversity of consultation within Chinese ideology, democracy, and governance serves to legitimize a potential participatory democracy grounded in a broader, more diverse, and judicious approach to soliciting input encompassing both raw data and representative ideas. This, in turn, aims to counterbalance the prevailing democratic perspective centered around the mere "aggregation of vote" by emphasizing participation and deliberation, as per the liberal tradition. An exemplary model of such consultation might draw parallels with the Scandinavian paradigm, albeit not a flawless match, while the Chinese approach to consultation denotes a form that bears analogical qualities. While we chart a course towards democratic governance through consultation, China's manifestation vacillates between authoritarianism and democracy.

On the one hand, the CCP aligns its ideology with consultative methodologies, spanning from the mass line and the United Front strategies to administrative assimilation, even culminating in a renewed focus on nurturing close connections with the populace under successive leaders in the new millennium. The CCP has neatly repackaged this as China's new democratic discourse and governance model, touting heightened responsiveness and adaptability. In addition to what some have observed in the last two decades, some deliberative practices at the grassroots level in China—particularly within villages and communities in select developed southeastern coastal regions—underscore the efficiency, responsiveness, and adaptability of the Chinese politics through the integration of both elites and the public, achieved by means of attentive listening and robust consultation.

On the other hand, the CCP's Leninist authoritarianism prioritizes centralization over democracy, serving various objectives such as securing the CCP's exclusive hold on political power, ensuring good governance, and achieving societal stability and order, among many others. This concept of "enlightened autocracy" or "resilient authoritarianism," however, lacks a foundation in, or at least the CCP demonstrates no indication of, the democratization process characterized by active popular participation and thoughtful deliberation. Consequently, a more closer examination of Chinese consultation reveals potential pathways: it could steer China towards a technocracy akin to that of Singapore or Hong Kong, emphasizing adaptability to societal shifts; it might reinforce a Leninist and patriarchal model, wherein the CCP monopolizes political authority and continually suppresses the participation and deliberation arenas of the social elites and the general public; or it could lead to a consensus-based democracy resembling the Scandinavian model, grounded in consultation. The ultimate trajectory in Chinese politics remains an unanswered question.

References

Bachrach, Peter, and Aryeh Botwinick. *Power and Empowerment: A Radical Theory of Participatory Democracy*. Temple University Press, 1992.

Barber, Benjamin R. "Participatory Democracy." *The Encyclopedia of Political Thought* (2014): 2650–2654.

Beer, Samuel H. "Group Representation in Britain and the United States." *The Annals of the American Academy of Political and Social Science* 319.1 (1958): 130–140.

Bohman, James. "Survey Article: The Coming of Age of Deliberative Democracy." *Journal of Political Philosophy* 6.4 (1998): 400–425.

Bohman, James, and William Rehg, eds. *Deliberative Democracy: Essays on Reason and Politics*. MIT Press, 1997.

Buge, Éric, and Camille Morio. «Le Grand débat national, apports et limites pour la participation citoyenne.» *Revue du droit public et de la science politique en France et à l'étranger* 5 (2019): 1205.

Cabestan, Jean-Pierre. "The Chinese People's Political Consultative Conference (CPPCC): Its Role and its Future." *The EU-China Relationship: European Perspective: A Manual for Policy Makers* (2015): 51–62.

Caluwaerts, Didier, and Min Reuchamps. *The Legitimacy of Citizen-Led Deliberative Democracy: The G1000 in Belgium*. Routledge, 2018.

Chen, Fangnan. "Xi Jinping Guanyu Shehui Zhuyi Xieshang Minzhu de Yuanchuangxing Gongxian [Original Contribution of Xi Jinping's Important Exposition on Socialist Consultative Democracy]." *Lilun Tantao, Theoretical Discussion* 6 (2022): 44–51.

Chen, Jidong, Jennifer Pan, and Yiqing Xu. "Sources of Authoritarian Responsiveness: A Field Experiment in China." *American Journal of Political Science* 60.2 (2016): 383–400.

Dickson, Bruce J. "Cooptation and Corporatism in China: The Logic of Party Adaptation." *Political Science Quarterly* 115.4 (2000): 517–540.

Dryzek, John S. *Foundations and Frontiers of Deliberative Governance*. Oxford University Press, 2012.

Elster, Jon, ed. *Rational Choice*. New York: NYU Press, 1986.
Elster, Jon, ed. *Deliberative Democracy*. Vol. 1. Cambridge University Press, 1998.
Fishkin, James. *When the People Speak: Deliberative Democracy and Public Consultation*. Oup Oxford, 2009.
General Office of the National Committee of the Chinese People's Political Consultative Conference, and Documentation Research Office of the Central Committee of the Communist Party of China, eds. *Selections of Important Documents of the People's Political Consultative Conference (Part 2)*. Zhonggong Zhongyang Wenxian Chubanshe, Zhongguo Wenshi Chubanshe, Central Literature Publishing House, China Literature and History Publishing House, 2009.
Goodin, Robert E. "Input Democracy." In *Power and Democracy: Critical Interventions*. Fredrik Engelstad and Øyvind Østerud, eds. Farnham: Ashgate, 2004. pp. 79–100.
Goodin, Robert E. *What's wrong with terrorism?*. Polity, 2006.
Harding, Harry. *China's Second Revolution: Reform After Mao*. Brookings Institution Press, 2010.
He, Baogang. "Deliberative Culture and Politics: The Persistence of Authoritarian Deliberation in China." *Political Theory* 42.1 (2014): 58–81.
He, Baogang, and Mark E. Warren. "Authoritarian Deliberation: The Deliberative Turn in Chinese Political Development." *Perspectives on Politics* 9.2 (2011): 269–289.
He, Baogang, and Mark E. Warren. "Authoritarian Deliberation in China." *Daedalus* 146.3 (2017): 155–166.
Hu, Jintao. *Jianding Buyi Yanzhe Zhongguo Test Shehui Zhuyi Daolu Tianjin Wei Quanmian Jiancheng Xiaokang Shehui Er Fendou [Unswervingly Move Forward along the Road of Socialism with Chinese Characteristics and Strive to Build a Moderately Prosperous Society in an All-Round Way]*. Renmin Chubanshe, People's Publishing House, 2012.
Jin, Yaoji. *Chinese Politics and Culture*. Oxford University Press, 1997.
Kang, Xiaoguang. "China: Political Development and Political Stability in the Era of Reform." *Chinese Economy* 35.5 (2002): 6–92.
Kang, Xiaoguang and Han, Heng. "Graduated Controls: The State-Society Relationship in Contemporary China." *Modern China* 34.1 (2008): 36–55.
Kooiman, Jan, ed. *Modern Governance: New Government-Society Interactions*. Sage, 1993.
Kooiman, Jan, and Martijn Van Vliet. "Self-Governance as a Mode of Societal Governance." *Public Management an International Journal of Research and Theory* 2.3 (2000): 359–378.
Kung, James, Cai Yongshun, and Xiulin Sun. "Rural Cadres and Governance in China: Incentive, Institution and Accountability." *The China Journal* 62 (2009): 61–77.
Leib, Ethan J. "Pragmatism in Designing Popular Deliberative Institutions in the United States and China." In *The Search for Deliberative Democracy in China*, Leib, Ethan J., ed. New York: Palgrave Macmillan, 2006. pp. 113–131.

Lijphart, Arend. "Consociational Democracy." *World Politics* 21.2 (1969): 207–225.

Li, Rongxin. *Consultative Democracy Or Consultative Authoritarianism?: Understanding Chinese Consultative Politics.* Springer Nature, 2022.

Lowi, Theodore. "The Public Philosophy: Interest-Group Liberalism." *American Political Science Review* 61.1 (1967): 5–24.

Mei, Ciqi. "Policy Style, Consistency and the Effectiveness of the Policy Mix in China's Fight Against COVID-19." *Policy and Society* 39.3 (2020): 309–325.

Miller, David. "Deliberative Democracy and Social Choice." *Political Studies* 40 (1992): 54–67.

Oi, Jean. "Bending Without Breaking, The Adaptability of Chinese Political Institutions." *Working Paper, How Far Across the River* (2003): 450–468.

Olsen, Johan P. "Voting, Sounding Out, and the Governance of Modern Organizations." *Acta Sociologica* 15.3 (1972): 267–283.

Pan, Wei. "Toward a Consultative Rule of Law Regime in China." *Journal of Contemporary China* 12.34 (2003): 3–43.

Parkinson, John, and Jane Mansbridge, eds. *Deliberative Systems: Deliberative Democracy at the Large Scale.* Cambridge University Press, 2012.

Qiaoan, Runya, and Jessica C. Teets. "Responsive Authoritarianism in China—A Review of Responsiveness in Xi and Hu Administrations." *Journal of Chinese Political Science* 25.1 (2020): 139–153.

Rokkan, Stein. *Norway: Numerical Democracy and Corporate Pluralism.* Chr. Michelsens institutt, 1966.

Saich, Anthony. "The National People's Congress: Functions and Membership." *Ash Center Policy Briefs Series* (2015).

Sandby-Thomas, Peter. "How Do You Solve a Problem Like Legitimacy? Contributing to a New Research Agenda." *Journal of Contemporary China* 23.88 (2014): 575–592.

Schmitter, Philippe C. "Corporatism is Dead! Long Live Corporatism!" *Government and Opposition* 24.1 (1989): 54–73.

Schubert, Gunter. "One-Party Rule and the Question of Legitimacy in Contemporary China: Preliminary Thoughts on Setting Up a New Research Agenda." *Journal of Contemporary China* 17.54 (2008): 191–204.

Shambaugh, David L. *China's Communist Party: Atrophy and Adaptation.* University of California Press, 2008.

Stoker, Gerry. "Governance as Theory: Five Propositions." *International Social Science Journal* 50.155 (1998): 17–28.

Teets, Jessica C. "Let Many Civil Societies Bloom: The Rise of Consultative Authoritarianism in China." *The China Quarterly* 213 (2013): 19–38.

The "China's Political Party System: Cooperation and Consultation." Available at: https://www.gov.cn/zhengce/20%202106/25/content_5620794.htm (Accessed April 1, 2024).

The Central Committee of the Communist Party of China. "Guanyu Jiaqiang Shehui Zhuyi Xieshang Minzhu de Yijian [Opinions on Strengthening the Construction of Socialist Consultative Democracy]." *Renmin Ribao, People's Daily* 2015-02-10(1).

Townsend, James R. "Chinese Populism and the Legacy of Mao Tse-Tung." *Asian Survey* 17.11 (1977): 1003–1015.

Truex, Rory. "Consultative Authoritarianism and Its Limits." *Comparative Political Studies* 50.3 (2017): 329–361.

Tsai, Lily L. *Accountability Without Democracy: Solidary Groups and Public Goods Provision in Rural China*. Cambridge University Press, 2007.

Tsang, Steve. "Contextualizing the China Dream: A Reinforced Consultative Leninist Approach to Government." In *China's Many Dreams: Comparative Perspectives on China's Search for National Rejuvenation*. Kerr, David, ed. London: Palgrave Macmillan UK, 2015. pp. 10–34.

Van Slyke, Lyman Page. *Friends and Enemies: The United Front and Its Place in Chinese Communist Story*. University of California, 1964.

Verba, Sidney. "Democratic Participation." *The Annals of the American Academy of Political and Social Science* 373.1 (1967): 53–78.

Wang, Xixin. "Public Participation and Its Limits: An Observation and Evaluation on Public Hearings as Experimented in China's Administrative Process." *Yale University China Law Center* (2003).

Wang, Shaoguang. "Changing Models of China's Policy Agenda Setting." *Modern China* 34.1 (2008): 56–87.

Wang, Shaoguang. "Representative Democracy and Representational Democracy (2014)." In *Voices from the Chinese Century: Public Intellectual Debate from Contemporary China*. Fogel, Joshua, Timothy Cheek, and David Ownby, eds. Columbia University Press, 2019. pp. 222–266.

Wang, Ray, and Gerry Groot. "Who Represents? Xi Jinping's Grand United Front Work, Legitimation, Participation and Consultative Democracy." *Journal of Contemporary China* 27.112 (2018): 569–583.

Warren, Mark E. "What Kind of Civil Society Is Best for Democracy?" *Portuguese Journal of Social Science* 3.1 (2004): 37–47.

Xi, Jinping. "Zai Qingzhu Zhongguo Renmin Zhengzhi Xieshang Huiyi Chengli 65 Zhounian Dahui Shang de Jianghua [In Celebration of the 65th Anniversary of the Founding of the Chinese People's Political Consultative Conference Speech at the Meeting]." *Renmin Ribao, People's Daily* 2014-09-22(2).

Young, Iris Marion. "Communication and the Other: Beyond Deliberative Democracy." In *Democracy and Difference: Contesting the Boundaries of the Political*, Benhabib, Seyla, ed. Princeton University Press, 1996. pp. 120–135.

Yu, Keping, ed. *Democracy and the Rule of Law in China*. Vol. 2. Brill, 2010.

Chinese Democracy

In the discourse surrounding the concept of Chinese democracy, there is a pervasive linguistic and rhetorical complexity marked by the use of terms such as "Chinese democracy (中国民主 *Zhongguo Minzhu*)," "Chinese-style democracy (中国式民主 *Zhongguo shi Minzhu*)," "socialist democracy with Chinese characteristics (社会主义民主/中国特色民主 *Shehui Zhuyi Minzhu/ Zhongguo Te'se Minzhu*)," and "people's democracy." Despite their distinct appellations, these terms collectively signify the unique manifestation of democracy in China, often juxtaposed and coexisted with democracy in the West. Employing the rhetoric of "Chinese democracy" for a comparative lens of its distinctive features can be accomplished without undue ambiguity. But if we position "Chinese democracy" as a pivotal concept in a hierarchical structure, necessitating consideration in relation to Chinese democracy, Western democracy, and any other forms of democracy, or even as a super-concept surpassing Western democracy, further scrutiny becomes imperative. To comprehend the concept of "Chinese democracy," several key issues necessitate clarification. First of all, a comprehensive understanding of the term "Chinese" (or Chinese style, Chinese model, Chinese characteristics, Chinese path, Chinese experience, Chineseness, etc.) is indispensable as it forms the foundational premise for comprehending any concept adorned with *this* prefix. Secondly, if "Chinese democracy" is deemed to exist, a meticulous

R. Li, *Democratizing China's Political Imaginaries*,
https://doi.org/10.1007/978-981-97-3670-6_7

consideration of its conceptualization in terms of paradigms and experiences becomes essential. Lastly, an inquiry into the evaluation of the statements "democracy is a good thing" and an alike metaphor of the "Chinese democracy is a good thing," along with an exploration of their relationships, requires careful re-examination.

Reconceptualization: Chinese Democracy

The "Chinese" or "Chinese style"[1] is firmly rooted in the distinctive dimensions of Chinese history, culture, society, politics, and economy, functioning as a comparative framework vis-à-vis the West. As China's comprehensive prowess burgeons, the Chinese style has assumed a prominent role in discussions surrounding a potentially "transcendent" political and economic paradigm, particularly concerning Western countries. What delineates this uniqueness? Uniqueness, inherently relative, manifests within universal dichotomies such as the capitalism and socialism, left and right, or the middle, as well as planned economies and market economies, centralization, and decentralization—features ubiquitous in any country or society. Emphasizing the abundance or scarcity of any factor proves inadequate in establishing uniqueness; it merely denotes *differentiation*. Typically, uniqueness manifests in the cultural or civilizational aspects, a concept elucidated by Huntington (1993) as the root of human conflicts. Thus, any country worldwide—be it the United States, France, Germany, India, Brazil, Japan, Egypt, etc.—harbors uniqueness akin to China. Striking a rebalance between generality and uniqueness involves recognizing a shared foundation of "human civilization" while preserving the continuity of distinct civilizations. Employing the sociological analytical framework of "big structures, long histories,"[2] premature assertions about the sustainability of the "Chinese style" in contemporary political and economic systems, and its potential to furnish valuable insights for other countries, particularly those developing ones, necessitate scrutiny over more protracted historical periods.

A possible "Chinese style" is inherently entwined with national emotions, nationalism, a sense of shame, and pride. It proves increasingly

[1] Lu and MacFarquhar (2016), Chen (2014), Zhang (2013), Xu (2011a), Yao (2010), Bell (2016), and Zhao (2010a).

[2] See Tilly (1984) and Skocpol (1984).

challenging to disentangle this notion from ideology and indigenization. Amid intense confrontations between China and the West, the attempts to either amalgamate with the West or wholly embrace the West are viewed as survival strategies. However, irrespective of the approach, Chinese style cannot be entirely discarded. In contemporary times, especially post-reform era, indigenization founded on national awareness progressively reshapes and integrates traditional Chinese culture into modern narratives. With China's rising, the Chinese style, enriched with practical experience and intuitive thinking, is confidently asserted. Over the past decade, this confidence has surged, signaling a trajectory towards transcending the East-West dichotomy. This trend is evident not only in practical domains like political systems and economic models but also in the realm of academic and disciplinary autonomy. Given the power asymmetry between the East and West, constructing a discourse system, paradigm, or practical model from China's perspective to interpret its situation is justifiable. However, these efforts should steer clear of pure idealism, necessitating that the Chinese style respects and adheres to the common values[3] of human society. Based on this foundation, it is imperative to showcase the diversity of human civilization.[4]

[3] In the CCP's discourse, universal values have been stigmatized due to their inherent contradiction with indigenization endeavors, and their perceived hindrance to the assertive advancement of CCP's authoritarian rule.

[4] Two cases may be heuristic on the reconceptualization of "Chinese-style." In 2012, the Journal of Chinese Political Science orchestrated a specialized discussion on the indigenization of Chinese social sciences, especially the political science. Advocates, typified by Zhang Weiwei, asserted the supremacy of the "Chinese style" that grounded in China's uniqueness and personal sentiments, extending this "Chinese characteristic" to encompass various domains, including history, culture, population, territory, civilization, and society. Conversely, scholars such as Yu Keping, Zhong Yang, He Baogang, Wu Guoguang, Jeffrey C. Isaac, Björn Alpermann, opposed the lens advocating complete indigenization of Chinese politics and political science. They contended that for a science to be deemed "scientific" in China, it must possess a degree of universality, incorporating concepts, methods, and principles acknowledged by political scientists globally. Notably, analyses emphasizing China's uniqueness by Zhang Weiwei, among others deviate from traditional examinations of Chinese civilization and culture, attributing China's economic growth and enhanced national strength solely to the superiority of Chinese culture, politics, economy, and society, resulting in potentially biased comparative analyses. See Zhang (2012), Gan (2011), and Yu (2011). In a 2009 seminar on "Chinese Democracy" at Wuhan University, authors including Yu Zhongsheng, Lin Shangli, Zheng Yongnian, and Wang Shaoguang equated Chinese democracy with a fusion of various democratic models. They underscored the CCP's pivotal role in promoting Chinese-style democracy and elucidated diverse modes of democratic models. Chinese democracy, as analyzed

In Western scholarly discourse about China, the construction of the Chinese image has endured a protracted process reshaped by the conceptualizations of Western authors across centuries. This image has functioned as a tool wielded in Western debates. Bell envisions a Confucian China, for example, to perpetuate debates in Western politics and traditions regarding the tensions between liberal democracy and communitarian/republican ideal.[5] Additionally, post-revolutionary China has been consistently framed within Western discourse as adhering to the paradigm of "Stalinist totalitarianism,"[6] thereby categorizing contemporary China as an authoritarian state,[7] among other classifications. The Western tendency to depict non-Western countries and politics beyond its own framework reflects an inherent infusion of the ideological nuances. Nevertheless, select strands of Western scholarship on China redirect their focus towards further understanding the "Chineseness" intrinsic to China, encompassing its cultural, political, economic, and social facets.[8] These analyses, while valuable in offering comparative perspectives for comprehending China, are often influenced by value judgments such as Orientalism, moral assessments, and distinctions between progress and backwardness, as well as rationality and sensibility.[9]

Considering this contextual background, rather than hastily delineating Chinese democracy as a surpassing model vis-à-vis Western liberal democracy, it proves more pertinent to accentuate the distinctive attributes and developmental path characterizing democracy in China. The multifaceted dimensions of analyzing Chinese democracy necessitate attention to three

by Wang Shaoguang, exhibits distinctive features, drawing upon Pitkin's representative theory and Western representative democracy. This involves introducing market competition, reforming the planned system, and assimilating sporadic experiments at the macro level to achieve policy flexibility. Local governments consistently reinforce government responsiveness in policy implementation to bolster the legitimacy of the CCP. Analyses of the CCP's learning, adaptability, accountability, and authoritarian resilience hinge on ensuring and consolidating the CCP's rule while developing Chinese-style democracy. See Chen et al. (2010), Ahlers et al. (2016), Tsai and Dean (2017), Shambaugh (2008), Gore (2019), Guo (2007), Nathan (2017), Fewsmith and Nathan (2019), Wright (2010), and Gilley (2009).

5 A response to Bell's ideas, see Nathan (2015).

6 See MacFarquhar (1958).

7 See Heurlin (2016) and Teets (2014).

8 See for example, Perdue (2004) and Ang (1994).

9 Abe (1998).

critical dimensions: the intricate interplay between the CCP and Chinese democracy, the nexus between Chinese traditional culture and democratic principles, and the distinctive implementation pathways guiding Chinese democratic processes.

Seeing the historical evolution of democracy in the contemporary world, Chinese democracy has charted a distinctive course, diverging from the grassroots individualistic democratic paradigm that arose in the Western context, particularly following the revolutions in England and France. During the New Culture Movement, intellectual elites briefly dominated discussions and exploration on democracy in China. Subsequently, officials, notably political parties, assumed a prominent and, at times, absolute role in steering democracy in Chinese context. Following the adoption of Marxist democratic ideologies by the CCP, the populace transitioned into subjects utilized, mobilized, and unified for active participation in revolution, reform, and socialist construction. This democratic model has notably shaped the implementation of Chinese-style democracy, characterized by top-down, inside-out mass lines, political consultation, and similar mechanisms. Post the era of Reform and Opening Up, deliberations on the rectifying injustices and cases related to truth criteria, both possessing democratic attributes, were instigated and propelled by those enlightened within the party and reformists. These discussions resonated with intellectuals and elites outside the party. In the 1990s, Deng Xiaoping's doctrine of "No Arguing" quelled debates on political system reform, redirecting attention towards the development path centered on "placing economic construction at the core" and "ensuring social stability."[10]

Jiang Zemin's "Three Represents" liberated itself from the CCP's ideological constraints, and incorporating emerging social constituencies into the construction of China's democratic discourse. During the era

[10] In the 1990s, liberals in China were largely expunged from the politics, resulting in their marginalization. Despite persisting as an undercurrent among Chinese intellectuals post the late 1980s, and retaining some international sway, their function within the sanctioned political domain was eradicated. The political sidelining of liberals evolved into an incontrovertible objective reality. Confronted with the waning influence of them, Deng Xiaoping's Southern Tour and the political reports of the 15th National Congress of the Communist Party of China primarily sought to dismantle the prevailing discourse hegemony of the leftists and forestall China from retracing the pitfalls of the leftist trajectory. See also Li (1998) and Hu (1999).

of Hu Jintao and Wen Jiabao, a more pragmatic and utilitarian democratic approach was implemented, enhancing people's living standards through benevolent policies. Post the 18th Party Congress, building upon the synthesis of democratic theories and practices from ancient and contemporary global sources, Xi Jinping introduced the concept of the WPPD, thereby elevating and endeavoring to redirect a more discreet yet ambiguous manifestation of Chinese democracy.

In evaluating the foundational distinctions between Western and Chinese democratic paradigms, the concept of "constructive democracy" emerges as a central tenet within the ambit of Chinese democracy, orchestrated under the CCP's aegis and leadership. This construct does not conflate Chinese-style democracy with the CCP's democracy but accentuates the pivotal role the CCP plays in configuring the democratic design in China. Despite this design as patriarchal and paternalistic, this *democracy*, notwithstanding its undemocratic attributes, adeptly negotiates the dilemmas faced by other developing and post-colonial countries in their democratization. It is conceivable that this preemptive design could mitigate Huntington's "explosive participation" in societies characterized by inadequate institutional and economic development, averting the collapse witnessed in socialist regimes in the Soviet Union and Eastern Europe due to imbalances between social stability, state capacity, and democratization.[11] Nevertheless, it is imperative to acknowledge and rectify myriad challenges within the party-led democracy in China. Constitutionalizing and institutionalizing the people's rights within the democratic framework is essential to forestall undue encroachments and interventions by governmental entities.

Chinese-style democracy aptly designates the amalgamation and evolution of numerous elements from traditional Chinese culture within China's democratic framework. This influence is deeply rooted in the enduring consistency and robustness of the Chinese political system throughout the history, forming the basis for the claim that it can "maintain longevity without deterioration."[12] "If rejuvenation can be achieved within established institutions, guided by contemporary currents and

[11] While the failure of the Soviet and Eastern European socialist regimes is rather complex, it primarily attributable to the pervasive concentration of power within the elite and the autocrat systems precluded the genuine empowerment of the people. See Kotz and Weir (2013).

[12] Qian (1998c, pp. 19–20).

infused with the spirit of the present age, it offers a plausible trajectory for China's current political landscape."[13] Indeed, the modern Chinese political milieu maintains intricate and unbroken ties with traditional Chinese values, transcending simplistic interpretations of "cultural determinism." The traditional idea of *Minben* has engendered modern democratic thought in China, accentuating a people-centric approach. While traditional China lacked the Western concept of the "rule of law," the Confucian "*lifa*" (ritual and law 礼法) served as an ideological foundation shared between rulers and the people, legitimizing rulers while also imposing some constraints on imperial authority—an association pertinent to the moral and ethical facets of contemporary Chinese democracy and the early concept of "consultative democracy." As a representative "ethical" culture, traditional Chinese culture integrates notions of hierarchy and order from traditional family and bureaucratic systems into the modern democratic framework, emphasizing the importance of individuals and the societal ideal of "ultimate goodness (至善 *Zhishan*)."

When juxtaposing contemporary Chinese-style democracy with traditional Chinese governance, discernible parallels manifest. It is posited that the enduring reservoir of cultural inspiration and sanctuary for "Chinese-style democracy: emanates from the traditional political structures." As Qian Mu (钱穆) asserted:

> In the feudal epoch, emblematic of China's erstwhile unified societal structure, the embryonic phase of Chinese democracy and spirit materialized. Conversely, the epoch characterized by contemporary administrative consolidation at the county level denotes the culmination of Chinese democratic thought and spirit. The traditional Chinese political framework eschewed absolute monarchy, aristocratic dominion, military governance, and hierarchy-based (whether bourgeois or proletarian) dictatorship. Further exploration into nuanced intricacies appears superfluous. Nevertheless, the traditional Chinese political system unquestionably aligns with a variant of democratic governance. Prudent selection of term allows us to appropriately label it as "Chinese-style democratic politics".[14]

Simultaneously, the non-democratic aspects in the Chinese-style democracy also stem from the influence of the "despotism" aspects

[13] Qian (1998b, p. 12).

[14] Qian (1998a, pp. 107–108).

ingrained in traditional Chinese culture,[15] as articulated by Liang Qichao in his work *On Enlightened Despotism:*

> In a despotic state prioritizing individual interests over the collective well-being of the state, governance is inherently detrimental. Conversely, a virtuous system often emerges when governance aligns with the interests of the state as a very legal entity. Despots prioritizing the people they govern are condemned for practicing the barbaric despotism, whereas those prioritizing the people under their rule are hailed as enlightened despots. The enlightened despotism often arises due to external competitive pressures essential for self-preservation. In Chinese history, such enlightened despotism prevails during periods of those coexisting nations, contrasting with centralized rule eras where its manifestation is scarce. Some challenges in governing a large nation were formidable in ancient times due to inadequate communication infrastructure. In epochs of coexisting nations within a confined space, despotic rule was more effectively enforced. Conversely, during times of imperial unity, authority spanned thin, resulting in governance described as permissive than despotic. This is exemplified by figures like Emperor Wen of Han and Emperor Taizong of Tang, who, despite possessing enlightened spirits, operated within a political context characterized more as laissez-faire due to geographical constraints.[16]

Traditional culture has, of course, shaped the contemporary style of Chinese democracy. Diverging from "Western democracy" in both theoretical underpinnings and value orientation, Chinese-style democracy takes on unique characteristics as it charts its course for the future. The central inquiry around pivotal theoretical debates. These deliberations encompass the incremental implementation of comprehensive

[15] In contemporary discourse, the concept of "Chinese despotism" finds its roots in Montesquieu's seminal work, *The Spirit of Laws*. Within this treatise, Montesquieu characterizes several Asian countries, notably China, as the "despotic states," embodying a political framework lacking in legal structures, regulations, centralized authority, characterized by coercive governance, terror, human subjugation, and a dearth of individual freedoms. Cohler et al. (1989). Modern Chinese intellectuals such as Yan Fu and Liang Qichao adopt the concept of "Chinese despotism" not merely as a derivative of Western influence, but as a profound critique of the inherent foundations of Chinese monarchical despotism. Their goal is to scrutinize the despotic system critically and to actively engage in transformative endeavors within the Chinese socio-political landscape. See also Liang (2003), Hou (2008), and Zhang (1986).

[16] Liang (2003, pp. 20–22).

political reforms as a means to advance democratic evolution in China. Alternatively, they consider navigating a transitional phase aimed at sustaining neo-authoritarianism or exploring the pathway towards democratization in China. However, these discussions risk succumbing to the dichotomy surrounding Chinese-style democracy, and radical political reforms portraying modern China as an authoritarian regime, and are deemed unacceptable by the CCP. Consequently, an empirical analysis directs attention to the possibility of achieving political reforms and democratic progression while upholding the CCP's predominant ruling. This inherently underscores the distinctive approach to realizing Chinese-style democracy, which involves advancing the people's democracy via intraparty democracy, fostering electoral democracy through consultative democracy, and promoting upper-level democracy through grassroots democracy.

If, in any way, the CCP shows signs to democracy, then intraparty democracy is crucial for realizing people's democracy and a uniquely Chinese democratic style. Achieving intraparty democracy not only aims at reforming the CCP's institutional framework, including the People's Congress system and the multi-party cooperation and political consultation system. Additionally, addressing how to implement self-supervision and check-and-balances on power in the Party is also a crucial aspect of intraparty democracy. Initiatives, for example, building a clean and honest political environment, combating corruption, and constraining the exercise of power are powerful measures to strengthen the Party's internal construction. As early as the early 1990s, Jiang Zemin proposed the democratic model of "election democracy" combined with "consultative democracy" in China. Xi Jinping also highlights a consultive methodology may play in Chinese politics and envisioning a more compelling form of Chinese democracy that extends beyond mere reliance on elections. Its extensive, multi-level, and institutionalized development in China has also made consultation not only an important form of democracy but also a crucial mode of governance, in which safeguards the right of the public to participate in politics and ensures the formulation of sound policy. Grassroots democracy symbolized by village and urban community self-governance has been widely recognized by both domestically and internationally as the most plausible path for bottom-up democratization in China. Nevertheless, grassroots autonomy is diminishing in the face of the CCP's assertive centralization at the grassroots level.

It seems, empirically, Chinese democracy is a grand yet ambiguous concept encompassing various democratic forms in China that intricately interconnect and operate cohesively in support of this overarching term. If we baselessly regard Chinese democracy as a very confluence of these concrete democratic forms, although it extends far beyond them, we will find that, while not unique to China, it is indeed imbued with Chinese characteristics. If we use the term "style" to equalize these features, we can refer to Herder's (2006) understanding of "democratic models" as a theoretical framework. Which aims to display and explain basic elements and relationships of a specific democratic form, forming a complex "network structure." Chinese-style democracy is a relative and dynamic concept, holding significance in China studies. However, caution is needed to prevent it from becoming a one-sided propaganda tool, shielding against acknowledging shortcomings in Chinese democratic practice. Genuine progress in constructing Chinese democracy requires a dialectical perspective on the relations between Chinese-style democracy and the general theory and practice of democracy.

"Democracy Is a Good Thing" or "Chinese Democracy Is a Good Thing"

The assertion that "democracy is a good thing"[17] does not inherently endorse the conclusion that "Chinese democracy is a good thing." The assessment of Chinese democracy should not negate the inherent merit of democracy itself, whether considered as a value orientation, ideology, or mode of governance. Regardless of its utilization as a rhetorical device, politically correct stance, or a façade for authoritarianism, democracy is progressively recognized and embraced by a majority of Chinese people and the CCP. Despite diverse interpretations of democracy, as the adage goes, "a thousand readers have a thousand Hamlets." In contrast to the extensive intellectual, theoretical, and practical exploration of democracy rooted in ancient Greek democracy (demo-kratia) in the West, particularly in Western and Southern Europe, China's genuine pursuit of democracy spans less than two hundred years. Modern Chinese history, from the Opium War onward, has witnessed recurrent interaction between China and the West, with almost all pre-1978 attempts at democratic

[17] See Yu (2009).

thought and practices in China culminating in failure. The pre-reform period was characterized by tumultuous democratic explorations, while the following era, encompassing the CCP's exploration of democracy and the broader intellectual elite's engagement, especially among the intellectuals, gradually molded the phenomenon of "Chinese democracy."

The discourse on Chinese democracy, spanning diverse temporal and cultural contexts, grapples with two inextricable paradoxes. The first is the conundrum of constructing democracy in China, with the term "construct" signaling experiential and constructivist methodologies as opposed to liberal approaches. While liberalism often endeavors to establish the "superiority" of a particular system through the construction of an idealized structure, this tends to sideline individualism in methodology, neglecting or sacrificing individual choices. Hoppe (2006) and Rothbard (1970, 1978), for example, asserting the "natural superiority of private property rights" unwittingly fall into the trap of "institutional superiority," akin to experiential approaches such as "planned economy" and "Keynesianism." The distinction between Western democracy as products of experientialism or individual choices within liberalism is not the focus here. To liberate discourse from "institutional fetishism" towards the West, it is therefore imperative to fully harness individual rational choices in the exploration of democracy. This necessitates affording individuals the capacity for rational "trial and error" and the ability to resist the imposition of a "pre-established system" characteristic of experientialism—a notion fundamentally incongruent with China's party-led democratic model dominated by elites.

The paradox under consideration pertains to the amalgamation of traditional Chinese culture with contemporary democratic ideals. While deconstructing Western democratic discourse, authors—particularly Western experts in Chinese studies—endeavor to extract spiritual, moral, and cultural foundations from traditional Chinese doctrines like the Confucianism, Daoism, and Legalism to showcase the cultural underpinnings and distinctiveness supporting Chinese democracy. Relations between *Minben* and democracy,[18] the exploration of pre-capitalist Chinese cultural uniqueness,[19] the Confucianism (Chinese version of

[18] See, for example, Wang and Titunik (2014) and Murthy (2000).

[19] See, for example, Wang (2004/2008).

communitarianism) versus liberalism debate,[20] the quest for a new world order (天下 *Tianxia*) to replace Western global power structures,[21] and attempts to utilize the Confucian moral and political education system of the "Three Institutes (三院制 *Sanyuan Zhi*)" instead of the Western "bicameral system,"[22] all seek to formulate a democratic model emancipated from Western influence. For many non-Western countries, including developing and post-colonial ones, this process involves classic debates in democratic studies, addressing themes like the balance between the indigenization and Westernization, uniqueness and universalness, and regionalism and totality. Failure to strike a rebalance may result in extremes of complete Westernization or closed rigidity, for example, the Sinocentrism, as demonstrated by numerous examples. It is crucial to recognize that democracy extends beyond mere Western liberal democracy, and severing China's uniqueness from democratic principles risks succumbing to the peril of "excessive indigenization." Consequently, scrutinizing key concepts and discourses of Chinese democracy, evaluating the traits of contemporary Chinese democracy, and determining the extent to which it circumvents the aforementioned paradox constitute the foundational inquiry in assessing Chinese democracy.

Conceptions, for example, the meritocratic/elite democracy,[23] patriarchal/patricentric democracy,[24] empowerment democracy,[25] and Confucian democracy[26] are intricately interwoven with traditional Chinese discourses, Confucianism, in particular. Simultaneously, Western democracy has exerted a profound influence on the very trajectory of Chinese democracy. Spanning from the intellectual contributions of Kang Youwei

[20] See, for example, Bell (2017). However, Bell's portrayal of the "Chinese model" does not accurately depict a real China. Throughout centuries, Western observers have consistently attempted to construct an image of China or rhetorical objects to serve as weapons and counterparts in their debates, particularly perpetuating the longstanding debate within Western political thought—the debate between liberal democracy and socialism. Similar discourses also encompass "Eastern authoritarianism." see also Wittfogel (1957).

[21] See Zhao (2011).

[22] See Xiao (2017).

[23] Bell (2012), He and Warren (2020), Bell and Li (2013), Gilley (2004), and Lu (2011).

[24] Kandiyoti (1988), Hamilton (1990), and Stacey (1983).

[25] Wang (1997) and Li (2003).

[26] Hall and Ames (1999), Fukuyama (1995), Li (1997), and Elstein (2014).

and Liang Qichao to the transformative era of Sun Yat-sen, and from the Republic of China to the People's Republic of China, the evolution of Chinese democracy reflects a continuum from the imitation to critical reflection, differentiation, and indigenization. Modern Chinese history is entwined with dynamic interactions with the West, notably Europe and America. Studies on Chinese democracy have burgeoned in last three decades, with both Western and Chinese scholars conducting diverse analyses on the prospect of a "Chinese-style democracy." They however reveal three core characteristics of Chinese democracy—performance democracy, nationalism democracy, and Confucianism—with the goal of assessing the conceptual framework of Chinese-style democracy from an alternative perspective.

The Cultural Revolution and the Tiananmen Square incident constitute pivotal events that critically examined the legitimacy of the CCP's governance post the establishment of the People's Republic of China. These occurrences however triggered two significant reflections: firstly, a scrutiny of the underlying causes of political unrest in China, exemplified by the Cultural Revolution, and secondly, an investigation into whether China's economic progress could be sustained without the presence of democracy. Consequently, in the post-1990s era, the CCP strategically shifted its focus towards the path of "Development is the hard truth (发展才是硬道理 *Fazhan Caishi Yingdaoli*)." Embracing market-oriented reforms despite encountering impediments, this shift was notably influenced by the collapse of former socialist regimes, led by the Soviet Union. Simultaneously, the governance challenges faced by developing countries due to internal disorder solidified the CCP's development model, emphasizing "prioritizing economic development to maintain social stability and order." This paradigm shift shattered the misconception in modernization theory suggesting that "without democracy, there is no development." Following this altered perspective, economic development emerged as the primary source of legitimacy for the CCP. It subsequently became the principal means to actualize democracy in China—enhancing the populace's well-being through economic progress, and in turn, satisfying their demands for political reforms, particularly democratization.

In the 1980s and 1990s, the phenomenon of "economic growth with low democratic demands" manifested in China, characterized by a notably modest starting point for the Chinese economy. The equilibrium between the economic benefits derived from development and the constraint on political reforms imposed by the CCP was sustained, striking a rebalance between economic and politics. The governance of Hu Jintao and Wen Jiabao witnessed enhancements in the urban–rural social security system and healthcare, consolidating the CCP's legitimacy through a "performance" paradigm and contributing to the discourse on Chinese democracy. The "low democratic demands" should not be misconstrued as an absence of democratic aspirations; some prevalent issues such as corruption, polarization, and environmental pollution resulting from rapid economic growth fueled widespread discontent among the populace. In response, the CCP implemented a series of measures aimed at safeguarding individual rights and curtailing governmental powers. Notably, the 1989 *Administrative Procedure Law of the People's Republic of China* granted ordinary citizens the right to legally challenge the government for improper conduct. The 2007 *Regulations on Open Government Information of the People's Republic of China* mandated the disclosure of non-classified information, including financial budgets. Concurrently, the enactment of the *Property Law of the People's Republic of China* in the same year provided a legal framework for citizens to protect their private property. These reforms, while upholding the CCP's monopoly, concurrently assuaged public dissatisfaction and addressed certain democratic demands.

Despite criticisms directed at Lipset's (1959) conclusion that concerning the interplay of economic development, legitimacy, and democratization,[27] it is evident that economic development, income augmentation, and enhanced welfare collectively exert a constructive and propelling influence on the people's endeavors on political reform and democratization. Such pursuits align harmoniously with both liberal traditions and contemporary political emphases on the state capacity and political order. The dual determinants accounting for the disparate economic and political development in China are discernible. Firstly, the considerable enhancement in the quality of life over the past four decades has somewhat mitigated the populace's clamor for political reform, notwithstanding extant social issues such as uneven wealth distribution and polarization. Secondly, while China upholds a highly centralized authoritarian system, the government's circumscribed intervention in personal affairs, regulation of speech and the internet, constraints on

[27] A transition in research emphasis towards political order and national capabilities in the latter half of the preceding century. See Huntington (1965, 2006), Huntington and Jervis (1997), and Huntington and Dunn (2004) and Fukuyama (2006).

public participation, and control over the private economy operate within acceptable bounds. This constrained "empowerment of the people" coexists with a resilient top-down authoritarian control, resulting in a relatively modest demand for political reform and democratic pursuits from the grassroots. Thirdly, the molding of China's political culture by CCP's traditional values and the ideological influence has engendered distinctive characteristics of Chinese democracy, divergent from Western liberal democracy. These characteristics encompass a proclivity for pragmatism or economic interests and an emphasis on harmonious values, thereby influencing public support for the government and reshaping the populace's comprehension of democracy to a certain extent.

The extension of "performance" transcends the economic domain. In the first two decades of the twenty-first century, good governance (善治 *Shanzhi*), characterized as "a management process maximizes public interest, encompassing legitimacy, transparency, accountability, rule of law, responsiveness, effectiveness, and stability,"[28] stands as an exemplar that fortifying the preeminence of Chinese democracy. While good governance can augment the legitimacy of the CCP by refining governance and advancing public interests, the query persists as to whether it invariably fosters democracy. Good governance primarily concentrates on optimizing the governing capabilities of rulers, but accords less consideration to the foundational issue of the origin of rulers' authority—the inquiry of "who should govern." Diverging from approaches advocated by scholars like Yu Keping, who advocate leveraging good governance for political reform, the good governance and Chinese democracy formulated by authors such as Wang Shaoguang in the new left mirrors a variant of "good governance" grounded in the central authority[29]—akin to the "enlightened despotism," "soft authoritarianism," or "responsive authoritarianism." This "responsibility-centric" manifestation of democracy perpetuates the Confucian stress on the "people-oriented" governance (as opposed to democracy) and the Mao era's mass line (an amalgamation of central authority and mass democracy), wherein rulers wield substantial authority, shoulder boundless responsibility, and deviate from the Western "power-centric" democratic paradigm.

[28] See also Yu (2018) and Li (2020).

[29] Wang (2008), see also Zhao (2010b).

Further expanding the connotations of performance encompasses not only tangible dimensions like economic development and good governance but also extends to the intangible dimensions of national pride and confidence. These sentiments, whether disseminated through the overarching narrative of the CCP or propelled by grassroots populism and patriotism, intricately intertwine with the CCP's governance. Particularly in the last decade, marked by a gradual deceleration in material growth, this "spiritual performance" gains heightened significance that compared to its "material performance" counterpart. Notably, it serves as a potent means to legitimize the rule of the CCP. Concurrently, it fortifies the public alignment with the "Chinese model," inherently encompassing the concept of Chinese-style democracy.

In conclusion, the combination of performance democracy with economic development and good governance encounters dual primary challenges. Firstly, a performance-centric democracy hinges upon a robust state and government apparatus to propel economic growth, furnish welfare, and enact policies. This aligns with the accentuation of centralized authority in CCP's the "democratic centralism" and the nationalist pursuit of a potent state. However, the tangible benefits associated with this approach necessitate uninterrupted delivery and productivity from political entities or the government. To note, any disjunction between supply and demand may precipitate societal unrest. Conversely, performance democracy, beyond relying on the authoritative might of the government, necessitates "mass (direct) democracy" to further bestow legitimacy upon political authority. This manifestation of mass democracy, while aspiring to coexist with authoritarianism supported by a robust state or political faction, gradually transforms into populist authoritarianism. This essentially entails the devolution of broad public will to individuals or select political entities, denoted as "authoritarian democracy." Secondly, there exists a sustainability predicament with performance democracy. The rendition of it undertaken by the CCP in the four decades after 1978 fails to obfuscate increasingly acute societal issues such as polarization and corruption. While Western societies typically redress these incongruities through elite consensus, electoral politics, and interest group dynamics, the reliance of the CCP on an all-encompassing state to propel performance lacks the impetus for internal democratic reforms, rendering it unsustainable without reform.

Nationalism, patriotism, and statism collectively delineate the public distinctive affinity towards a particular ethnicity, nation, or country. This sentiment originates from the expansion of individual sovereignty to the collective identity of the nation,[30] intertwining the nationalism, patriotism, and populism as pivotal elements of Chinese democracy. These are closely associated with the unique "party-state" system prevailing under the governance of the CCP. In the context of socialist regime, the relationship between the party and the state often remains nebulous, yet the former undeniably wields absolute control over the state machinery. The robustness of this control however enables the classification of nations based on the configuration of decision-making powers, including the interplay between the party and the government, as well as the varying degrees of local autonomy in policy implementation. Xu Chengang therefore characterizes China's "party-state system" as "authoritarianism with decentralized authority (地方分权威权主义 *Difang Fenquan Weiquan Zhuyi*)."[31] Consequently, within this authoritarian framework, nationalism assumes paramount significance as a means to address the legitimacy crisis stemming from the party's limited public participation. Chinese nationalism is influenced by two opposing forces: the top-down pressure exerted by the CCP and the state, and the bottom-up impact emanating from social populists.

The nationalism propagated by the CCP, specifically characterized as state nationalism, intricately binds the Chinese nation to the CCP regime. It asserts that the people's affection and endorsement of the Chinese nation and the country are inseparable from their support for the CCP regime. This manifestation of patriotism or nationalism mandates individuals to subordinate personal interests to national concerns, showcasing allegiance to the country, with the CCP serving as the sole entity tasked with realizing national interests, distinct from regime interests. The welfare and future of the people are intimately interlinked to both the nation and the party. On the one hand, state strength enhances people's identification with the nation, thus fostering heightened pride in the "Chinese narrative" and the "Chinese model." On the other hand, the CCP can exploit this nationalistic sentiment to bolster its own legitimacy

[30] In the late medieval period, Jean Bodin first introduced the concept of "sovereignty." By the nineteenth century, sovereignty underwent a transformation from the absolute power of monarchs to the sovereignty of the people. See Bodin (1992), edited by Julian and Franklin.

[31] See Xu (2011a), see also Przeworski (2016).

while managing and directing nationalist sentiments and discourse.[32] The grassroots nationalism often encompasses populist elements, which can be more fervent than government stances, particularly amid the disparities between China's burgeoning comprehensive power and its position in the world. Populist nationalists may articulate heightened expectations of the government. In an authoritarian system buttressed by legitimacy derived from performance, a reciprocal tension emerges between citizen demands and governmental responses, posing a grassroots challenge to national authority. And consequently, nationalism, functioning as a dual-edged instrument, possesses the capacity to fortify "Chinese-style democracy" grounded in "Chinese characteristics" while simultaneously posing a threat to this democracy due to inherent populist elements.

In comparison with conventional analyses that posit Confucianism as the predominant traditional foundation for contemporary Chinese democratic politics, this part diverges from an exploration of the intrinsic nature of Confucianism, its modernization, and its interaction with the modern democratic principles. Instead, the focus is redirected towards two discernible facets of Chinese democracy influenced by Confucianism, namely, communitarianism and an elite/merit-based democratic framework.[33] In response to Bell's critique of John Rawls' theory of the "new social contract,"[34] which challenges the notion of a universally applicable

[32] Zhao (2005). In contrast to conventional analyses attributing the CCP's legitimacy primarily to "nationalism," a shift from nationalism to an intensified form termed "statism" is observed. Statism, characterized by an accentuated and politicized emphasis on the paramount role of the state across societal realms, functions as a populist strategy seeking to mask authoritarian tendencies through democratic semblance. This transition aligns more cohesively with the twenty-first-century representation of China, illustrating the incremental ascendancy of national power via top-down fortification and the mutually reinforcing dynamic between the ambitions of a potent state and the aspirations of the populace from the grassroots. See also Xu (2011a).

[33] In contrast to conventional analyses that classify Confucianism under various labels such as a "doctrine" as articulated by Jensen Lionel M., a "religion" or "ritual" according to Max Weber, or a "philosophical school" as defined by Nivison, David S, and expounded as "ethics" by Ames, Roger T, its precise categorization remains elusive. However, Confucianism unequivocally manifests considerable adaptability, functioning not only as a spiritual emblem within the Confucian cultural sphere, spanning China and broader Asian regions, but also as an "Eastern counterpart" to liberal democracy grounded in Western individualistic principles. See Jensen (1997), Weber and Gerth (1953), Nivison (1996), and Ames (2011).

[34] In comparison with traditional analyses, the seminal work *A Theory of Justice* published by Rawls in 1971, along with his classic exposition of the "social contract

set of values and contends that an individualistic emphasis neglects the relational ties an individual has within society, the author aligns with Bell's doctoral advisor Miller. The argument posits that a singular standard of justice is non-existent, given diverse societies prioritize and arrange values differently.[35] These philosophical debates and theoretical constructs serve as the underpinnings for communitarianism. Within the context of the "Confucian Democracy" series, Confucianism is therefore portrayed as an evolved manifestation of "communitarianism" and "republicanism."[36] Notably, Chinese Confucianism is positioned as superior to the "Singaporean Confucianism," primarily due to the latter's excessive paternalism, which is seen as undermining intercommunal harmony.[37]

In the pursuit of reestablishing the nexus between individuals and the collective or society, the goal is to align the manifestation of individual values with societal values. By fostering interactions among individuals, the objective is to further instill the shared virtues. This endeavor transcends conventional paradigms such as socialism or republicanism, aspiring to emancipate individuals from the relentless pursuit of the self-interest and antagonistic market behaviors. It constitutes a foundational tenet within the framework of the communicative action and rationality theory.[38] This classical discourse on the interplay between individual and society finds resonance in Confucianism. As scrutinized by both socialist thinkers and Confucian scholars, the emphasis on the collective or community is not inherently anti-democratic[39]; rather, it seeks to anchor the realization of individual happiness within the overarching objectives of society as a whole. Therefore, the accentuation of either the individual

theory," is regarded as establishing the conceptual groundwork for twentieth-century liberal democracy. See Rawls (1971, 2001).

[35] Miller (2001).

[36] Bell (2000, 2009).

[37] Bell (1995).

[38] For classic discussions of republicanism, see, for example, Pettit (1997); for communicative action, see for example Habermas (1985).

[39] In contrast to the tenets of socialism, republicanism, collectivism, and Confucianism, which underscore the intimate interrelation between the individual and either the collective or the state, the Austrian School, epitomized by the intellectual contributions of Hayek, proffers a critical analysis of notions such as collectivism, hierarchical structures, centralized planning, and centralization. See Hayek (1967).

or the collective should not be employed as a criterion for (re)evaluating the efficacy of a political system founded upon this paradigm.

The discourse of the "elite/meritocratic politics" frequently characterizes the Chinese bureaucratic system. Since Weber, many analyses from diverse lens of China's bureaucracy have emphasized its effective functioning predicated on the selection of capable individuals. However, these analyses present certain limitations. Firstly, it is imperative to recognize that any political system, whether in China or the Western context, inherently possesses elements of elitism. Attributing the success of the "Chinese model" solely to elites is inherently biased, as it disregards other significant facets of Chinese politics, such as factional struggles and the centralized power structure that aimed at achieving monumental tasks within the system. Secondly, while a meticulous examination and selection process may foster a cadre of technically proficient bureaucrats, it concurrently engenders a consequential system of promotion and appointment grounded in political considerations and personal affiliations, commonly referred to as the "promotion of officials only from above."[40] Lastly, underscoring the role of elite and good governance in Chinese democracy inadvertently diminishes attention to two critical considerations: first of all, the inquiry into whether elites are engendered through democratic mechanisms (elections or appointments); and secondly, the establishment of mechanisms to constrain elite power, such as checks and balances and supervision. Both of these dimensions persist as unresolved challenges in the elite system operating under an authoritarian regime.

The critique of elite politics in the framework of liberal democracy is not solely rooted in Weber's theory of the social division of labor; it also assumes the character of sophistry, particularly in light of Bell's analyses in social psychology and behavioral economics regarding "irrational" voters. This perspective casts doubt on the public trust, especially in authoritarian systems that lack essential democratic procedures for selecting bureaucrats and instituting checks on power. The notion that elites could ensure good governance through their exceptional abilities and moral foundations, as scrutinized by Martin (2013) in comparison with authoritarian systems, is primarily contingent upon the personal conduct and the elites' magnanimity. However, in authoritarian regimes, the absence of democratic safeguards raises questions about the reliability of such governance. While

[40] Henry (2015).

defending elite politics in China, certain analyses simultaneously acknowledge the flaws of the existing elite system and strive to reconceptualize an idealized alternative to Western liberal democracy due to inherent imperfections in the latter's institutional design. However, Finley Moses I, in works such as *Democracy in Ancient Worlds* and *Ancient Democracy and Modern Democracy*, critiques Chinese elite politics. He argues that simplifying politics as a game for elites or a tool for elite political objectives is a degradation of popular subjectivity. In situations lacking democratic procedures for electing bureaucrats and implementing effective checks on power, such a system is prone to tilting towards dictatorship.[41]

In summary, Confucianism and liberalism reveal disparities in value orientations and institutional structures. De Bary (1998, 2009), for instance, extensively contrasts Confucian communitarianism with the individual-collective dynamics inherent in liberal democracy. Angle (2009, 2013) contends that Confucian thought is not inherently incompatible with popular democracy and human rights. Chan (2013), drawing upon traditional Confucian resources, rationalizes the legitimacy of limited government, individual moral autonomy, and women's rights. Jiang (2014) and Yan (2011) liken Confucianism to a "humane authority" and advocate its implementation in Chinese governance. Nevertheless, the prevailing viewpoint among contemporary Western and Chinese scholars tends to perceive Confucianism as a synthesis of collectivism, hierarchy, and authoritarianism. From a Western perspective, concepts like hierarchy and elitism are typically grounded in the conservative traditions. However, seeking analogous inspiration in Confucianism represents an effort to eschew essentialism and construct a distinctive analytical framework for comprehending Confucianism beyond the simplistic categorizations such as communitarianism or Burkeanism. From a Chinese standpoint, whether during the "neo-Confucianism" of the 1990s to the early twenty-first century, the "Confucian Revival" in the present century, or the CCP's promotion of "cultural confidence," Confucianism, as a resource in traditional Chinese culture, not only underscores the distinctiveness of Chinese civilization but also furnishes significant spiritual and moral underpinnings for Chinese democracy.

In contemporary China, particularly after 1978, the features that manifested in Chinese democratic discourse embody a fusion of enduring

[41] Finley (1983, 2018); see also Nathan (1973) and Nathan et al. (Eds.) (2013).

classical themes derived from centuries-long deliberations on Chinese democracy, alongside innovative features emblematic of the present era. Embracing a lens of cultural relativism, it becomes apparent that China's distinct culture has undeniably molded the unique configuration of its political terrain, a phenomenon not to be exclusively construed as the imposition of authoritarianism upon China. Despite China's millennial history, the evolution of an autonomous knowledge system and academic disciplines progressively disentangling from Western (especially Anglo-American) and Soviet influences constitutes a relatively recent endeavor. China's global rapport exists in a state of both coexistence and conflict. Against this backdrop, the proposal that "Chinese democracy is a good thing" not only necessitates empirical substantiation but also calls for further refinement within theoretical frameworks and paradigms.

References

Abe, Stanley K. "No Questions, No Answers: China and a Book from the Sky." *Boundary* 25.3 (1998): 169–192.

Ahlers, Anna L., Thomas Heberer, and Gunter Schubert. "Whither Local Governance in Contemporary China? Reconfiguration for More Effective Policy Implementation." *Journal of Chinese Governance* 1.1 (2016): 55–77.

Ames, Roger T. *Confucian Role Ethics: A Vocabulary*. The Chinese University of Hong Kong Press, 2011.

Ang, Ien. "The Differential Politics of Chineseness." *Southeast Asian Journal of Social Science* 22 (1994): 72–79.

Angle, Stephen C. *Sagehood: The Contemporary Significance of Neo-Confucian Philosophy*. Oxford University Press, 2009

Angle, Stephen C., and Michael A. Slote, eds. *Virtue Ethics and Confucianism*. New York: Routledge, 2013.

Bell, Daniel A. *East Meets West*. Princeton University Press, 2000.

Bell, Daniel A. *Beyond Liberal Democracy*. Princeton University Press, 2009.

Bell, Daniel A. "Meritocracy Is a Good Thing." *New Perspectives Quarterly* 29.4 (2012): 9–18.

Bell, Daniel A. *The China Model*. Princeton University Press, 2016.

Bell, Daniel A. *The China Model: Political Meritocracy and the Limits of Democracy*. Princeton University Press, 2017.

Bell, Daniel A., and Chenyang Li, eds. *The East Asian Challenge for Democracy: Political Meritocracy in Comparative Perspective*. Cambridge University Press, 2013.

Bell, Daniel A., et al. *Towards Illiberal Democracy in Pacific Asia*. Palgrave Macmillan UK, 1995.

Bodin, Jean, and Bodin Jean. *Bodin: On Sovereignty*. Cambridge University Press, 1992.

Chen, Gang, Zhu Haiying, Fu Xiaogang, et al. "Zhongguoshi Minzhu Guoji Yantaohui Zongshu [A Review of the International Symposium on Chinese-Style Democracy]." *Wuhan Daxue Xuebao (Renwen Shekeban), Journal of Wuhan University (Humanities Edition)* 1 (2010): 123–128.

Chan, Joseph. *Confucian Perfectionism: A Political Philosophy for Modern Times. Vol. 6*. Princeton University Press, 2013

Chen, Shuguang. "Lijie Zhongguo Moshi de Fangfalun Yuanze [Methodological Principles for Understanding the 'Chinese Model']." *Qiushi, Qiushi* 12 (2014): 49–51.

Cohler, Anne M., Basia Carolyn Miller, and Harold Samuel Stone. *Montesquieu: The Spirit of the Laws*. Cambridge University Press, 1989.

Elstein, David. *Democracy in Contemporary Confucian Philosophy*. Routledge, 2014.

De Bary, William Theodore, and William Theodore De Bary. *Asian Values and Human Rights: A Confucian Communitarian Perspective*. Harvard University Press, 1998.

De Bary, William Theodore, and William Theodore De Bary. *The Trouble with Confucianism*. Harvard University Press, 2009

Fewsmith, Joseph, and Andrew J. Nathan. "Authoritarian Resilience Revisited: Joseph Fewsmith with Response from Andrew J. Nathan." *Journal of Contemporary China* 28.116 (2019): 167–179.

Finley, Moses I. *Democracy Ancient and Modern*. Rutgers University Press, 2018.

Finley, Moses I., and Moses Immanuel Finley. *Politics in the Ancient World*. Cambridge University Press, 1983.

Fukuyama, Francis. "Confucianism and Democracy." *Journal of Democracy* 6.2 (1995): 20–33.

Fukuyama, Francis. *The End of History and the Last Man*. Simon and Schuster, 2006.

Gan, Yang. "Zhongguo Daolu Haishi Zhongguo Moshi [Chinese Road or Chinese Model?]." *Wenhua Zongheng, Culture Perspective* 5 (2011): 82–86.

Gilley, Bruce. *China's Democratic Future: How It Will Happen and Where It Will Lead*. Columbia University Press, 2004.

Gilley, Bruce. *The Right to Rule: How States Win and Lose Legitimacy*. Columbia University Press, 2009.

Gore, Lance LP. "The Communist Party-Dominated Governance Model of China: Legitimacy, Accountability, and Meritocracy." *Polity* 51.1 (2019): 161–194.

Guo, Gang. "Retrospective Economic Accountability Under Authoritarianism: Evidence from China." *Political Research Quarterly* 60.3 (2007): 378–390.

Habermas, Jürgen. *The Theory of Communicative Action: Volume 1: Reason and the Rationalization of Society*. Beacon Press, 1985.

Hall, David L., and Roger T. Ames. *The Democracy of the Dead: Dewey, Confucius, and the Hope for Democracy in China*. Open Court Publishing Company, 1999.

Hamilton, Gary G. "Patriarchy, Patrimonialism, and Filial Piety: A Comparison of China and Western Europe." *British Journal of Sociology* (1990): 77–104.

Hayek, Friedrich August. *Collectivist Economic Planning*. Ludwig von Mises Institute, 1967.

He, Baogang, and Mark E. Warren. "Can Meritocracy Replace Democracy? A Conceptual Framework." *Philosophy & Social Criticism* 46.9 (2020): 1093–1112.

Henry, Paulson. *Dealing with China: An Insider Unmasks the New Economic Superpower*. Grand Central Publishing, 2015.

Heurlin, Christopher. *Responsive Authoritarianism in China*. Cambridge University Press, 2016.

Hoppe, Hans-Hermann. *Economics and Ethics of Private Property*. Ludwig von Mises Institute, 2006.

Hou, Xudong. "Zhongguo Gudai Zhuanzhishuo de Zhishi Kaogu [Intellectual Archeology of Ancient Chinese Autocracy Theory]." *Jindaishi Yanjiu, Modern History Research* 4 (2008): 27.

Hu, Wei. "Dangnei Minzhu yu Zhengzhi Fazhan: Kaifa Zhongguo Minzhuhua de Tizhinei Ziyuan [Intraparty Democracy and Political Development: Developing Institutional Resources for China's Democracy]." *Fudan Xuebao (Shehui Kexueban), Journal of Fudan University (Social Science Edition)* 1 (1999): 1–11+141.

Huntington, Samuel P. "Political Development and Political Decay." *World Politics* 17.3 (1965): 386–430.

Huntington, Samuel P. "Te Clash of Civilizations." *Foreign Afairs* 72.3 (1993): 22–49.

Huntington, Samuel P. *Political Order in Changing Societies*. Yale University Press, 2006.

Huntington, Samuel P., and Robert Jervis. "The Clash of Civilizations and the Remaking of World Order." *Finance and Development-English Edition* 34.2 (1997): 51.

Huntington, Samuel P., and Steve Dunn. *Who Are We?: The Challenges to America's National Identity*. Simon and Schuster, 2004.

Jensen, Lionel M. *Manufacturing Confucianism: Chinese Traditions and Universal Civilization*. Duke University Press, 1997.

Jiang, Qing. "Rujia Xianzheng Zhixu: *Zhongguo de Guoqu Ruge Suzao Zhongguo de Zhengzhi Weilai* [Confucian Constitutional Order: How China's Past

Shapes Its Political Future].” *Hong Kong Chengshi Daxue Chubanshe*. University of Hong Kong Press, 2014.

Kandiyoti, Deniz. “Bargaining with Patriarchy.” *Gender & Society* 2.3 (1988): 274–290.

Karl, A. Wittfogel. *Oriental Despotism: A Comparative Study of Total Power*. Yale University Press and Oxford University Press, 1957.

Kotz, David, and Fred Weir. *Revolution from Above: The Demise of the Soviet System*. Routledge, 2013.

Li, Chenyang. “Confucian Value and Democratic Value.” *Journal of Value Inquiry* 31 (1997): 183.

Li, Rui. “Jieshou Lishi Jiaoxun, Jiaqiang Dangnei Minzhu-Guanyu Fang ‘Zuo’ de Ganxiang yu Yijian [Accept Historical Lessons and Strengthen Intra-party Democracy—Thoughts and Opinions on Preventing ‘Leftism’].” *Gaige, Reform* 1 (1998): 74–80.

Li, Lianjiang. “The Empowering Effect of Village Elections in China.” *Asian Survey* 43.4 (2003): 648–662.

Li, He. “The Chinese Discourse on Good Governance: Content and Implications.” *Journal of Contemporary China* 29.126 (2020): 824–837.

Liang, Qichao. “Caiman Zhuanzhilun [On Enlightened Despotism].” In *Yinbinshi Heji, Collected Works of Yinbingshi, Vol. 17*. Zhonghua Shuju, Zhonghua Book Company. pp. 20–22.

Liang, Qichao. “Zhongguo Zhuanzhi Zhengzhi Jinhua Shilun [On the Evolution of Chinese Autocratic Politics].” In *Yinbinshi Heji, Collected Works of Yinbingshi*, Vol. 9. Zhonghua Shuju, Zhonghua Book Company, 2003.

Lipset, Seymour Martin. “Some Social Requisites of Democracy: Economic Development and Political Legitimacy.” *American Political Science Review* 53.1 (1959): 69–105.

Lu, Rey-ching. *Chinese Democracy and Elite Thinking*. Springer, 2011.

Lu, Keli, and Roderick MacFarquhar. “Hawaii Xuezhe Shiyezhong de Zhongguo Moshi you Zhongguo Yanjiu: Duihua Roderick MacFarquhar [The Chinese Model and China Studies from the Perspectives of Overseas Scholars—A Dialogue with Roderick MacFarquhar].” *Guowai Lilun Dongtai, Foreign Theoretical Trends* 2 (2016): 1–8.

MacFarquhar, Roderick. “The Case of Communist China.” *Problems of Communism* 7 (1958): 1.

Martin, Brian. “Effective Crisis Governance.” *In State of the World 2013*. Island Press, 2013

Miller, David. *Principles of Social Justice*. Harvard University Press, 2001.

Murthy, Viren. “The Democratic Potential of Confucian *Minben* Thought.” *Asian Philosophy* 10.1 (2000): 33–47.

Nathan, Andrew J. “A Factionalism Model for CCP Politics.” *The China Quarterly* 53 (1973): 34–66.

Nathan, Andrew J. "The Problem with the China Model." *China File* (2015).
Nathan, Andrew J. "China's Changing of the Guard: Authoritarian Resilience." In *Critical Readings on the Communist Party of China (4 Vols. Set)*. Brill, 2017. pp. 86–99.
Nathan, Andrew J., Larry Diamond, and Marc F. Plattner, eds. *Will China Democratize?* JHU Press, 2013.
Nivison, David S. *The Ways of Confucianism: Investigations in Chinese Philosophy*. Open Court Publishing, 1996.
Perdue, Peter C. "A Frontier View of Chineseness." In *The Resurgence of East Asia*. Routledge, 2004. pp. 65–91.
Pettit, Philip. *Republicanism: A Theory of Freedom and Government*. Oxford University Press, 1997.
Przeworski, Adam. "Party-State?: Parties, States and Economic Reforms in the Soviet Union and China." In *Governance and Adaptability of the Chinese Communist Party: A Comparative Perspective*. Central Compilation & Translation Press, 2016.
Qian Mu. "Zhongguo Minzhu Jingshen [Chinese Democratic Spirit]." In *Wenhua yu Jiaoyu, Culture and Education, The Complete Works of Qian Binsi, Vol. 41*. Liaojing Cuban Shiye Gufen Youxian Gongsi, Lianjing Publishing Co., Ltd., 1998a. pp. 107–108.
Qian, Mu. "Zhongguo Chuantong Zhengzhi yu Wuquan Xianfa [Traditional Chinese Politics and the Five-Power Constitution]." In *Zhengxue Siyan, Private Words on Political Science, The Complete Works of Qian Binsi, Vol. 40*. Liaojing Cuban Shiye Gufen Youxian Gongsi, Lianjing Publishing Co., Ltd., 1998b. p. 12.
Qian, Mu. "Zhongguo Lishi Yanjiufa [Chinese History Research Methods]." In *Qian Binsi Xiansheng Quanji, The Complete Works of Qian Binsi, Vol. 31*. Liaojing Cuban Shiye Gufen Youxian Gongsi, Lianjing Publishing Co., Ltd., 1998c. pp. 19–20.
Rawls, John. *A Theory of Justice*. Cambridge University Press, 1971.
Rawls, John. *Justice as Fairness: A Restatement*. Harvard University Press, 2001.
Rothbard, Murray Newton. *Power and Market*. Ludwig von Mises Institute, 1970.
Rothbard, Murray Newton. *For a New Liberty: The Libertarian Manifesto*. Ludwig von Mises Institute, 1978.
Shambaugh, David L., and Joseph J. Brinley. *China's Communist Party: Atrophy and Adaptation*. University of California Press, 2008.
Skocpol, Theda. "Sociology's Historical Imagination." In *Vision and Method in Historical Sociology* 8 (1984): 1.
Stacey, Judith. *Patriarchy and Socialist Revolution in China*. University of California Press, 1983.

Teets, Jessica C. *Civil Society Under Authoritarianism: The China Model*. Cambridge University Press, 2014.
Tilly, Charles. *Big Structures, Large Processes, Huge Comparisons*. The Russell Sage Foundation, 1984.
Tsai, Wen-Hsuan, and Nicola Dean. "The CCP's Learning System: Thought Unification and Regime Adaptation." In *Critical Readings on the Communist Party of China (4 Vols. Set)*. Brill, 2017. pp. 1049–1071.
Wang, Xu. "Mutual Empowerment of State and Peasantry: Grassroots Democracy in Rural China." *World Development* 25.9 (1997): 1431–1442.
Wang, Hui. *Xiandai Zhongguo Sixiang de Xingqi [The Rise of Modern Chinese Thought] (Four Volumes)*. Beijing Salian Chubanshe, Beijing Sanlian Bookstore 2004 (updated edition 2008).
Wang, Shaoguang. *Minzhu Sijiang [Four Lectures on Democracy]*. Shenghuo, Dushu, Xinzhi Sanlian Shudian, Life·Reading·New Knowledge Sanlian Bookstore, 2008.
Wang, Enbao, and Regina F. Titunik. *Democracy in China: The Theory and Practice of Minben*. Routledge, 2014.
Weber, Max, and Hans H. Gerth. "The Religion of China, Confucianism and Taoism." *Philosophy* 28.105 (1953).
Wright, Teresa. *Accepting Authoritarianism: State-Society Relations in China's Reform Era*. Stanford University Press, 2010.
Xiao, Gongqin. "Gaige Yilai Zhongguo Zhengzhi de 'Qu Liangjihua Chongtu' Jiqi Yiyi [The 'De-Bipolarization' of Chinese Politics since Reform and Its Historical Significance]." Available at https://m.aisixiang.com/data/18779-3.html (Accessed October 7, 2023).
Xiao, Qiang. "Dangdai Dalu Xinrujia Pipan: YI Jiang Qing, King Xiaoguang, You Hailing, Chen Ming, Liu Feng Weili [Criticism of Contemporary Mainland New Confucianism—Taking Jiang Qing, Kang Xiaoguang, Yu Donghai, Chen Ming, and Qiu Feng as Examples]." *Wenshizhe, Literature, History and Philosophy* 1 (2017): 11–21.
Xu, Chenggang. "The Fundamental Institutions of China's Reforms and Development." *Journal of Economic Literature* 49.4 (2011a): 1076–1151.
Xu, Haoran. "Ruhe Gaikuo Zhongguo Fazhan Jingyan: Jiyu Zhongguo Moshi yu Zhongguo Te'se Shehui Zhuyi Daolu de Bijiao Fenxi [How to Summarize China's Development Experience—A Comparative Analysis Based on the Chinese Model and the Road of Socialism with Chinese Characteristics]." *Kexue Shehui Zhuyi, Scientific Socialism* 6 (2011b): 49–52.
Xu, Jilin. "Jinru 21 Shiji Yilai de Guojia Zhuyi Sichao [Nationalist Ideology Since the 21st Century]." In *Dangdai Zhongguo de Qimeng yu Fanqimeng [Enlightenment and Counter-Enlightenment in Contemporary China]* Shehui Kexue Wenxian Chubanshe, Social Sciences Literature Press, 2011c.

Yan, Xuetong., Daniel A. Bell., Sun, Zhe. *Ancient Chinese Thought, Modern Chinese Power*. Princeton University Press, 2011.

Yao, Yang. "Zhongguo Daolu de Shoji Yiyi [The World Significance of China's Road]." *Guoji Jingji Pinglun, International Economic Review* 1 (2010): 7–18.

Yu, Keping. *Democracy Is a Good Thing: Essays on Politics, Society, and Culture in Contemporary China*. Rowman & Littlefield, 2009.

Yu, Keping. *Democracy Is a Good Thing: Essays on Politics, Society, and Culture in Contemporary China*. Brookings Institution Press, 2011.

Yu, Keping. "Governance and Good Governance: A New Framework for Political Analysis." *Fudan Journal of the Humanities and Social Sciences* 11.1 (2018): 1–8.

Zhang, Junmai. *Zhongguo Zhuanzhi Junzhu Zhengzhi zhi Pingyi [Commentary on the Politics of Chinese Autocratic Monarchy]*. Hongwenguan Chubanshe, Hongwenguan Press, 1986.

Zhang, Weiwei. *Zhongguo Zhenhan: Yige 'Wenming Guojia' de Jueqi [China Shock: The Rise of a 'Civilized Country']*. Shanghai Renmin Chubanshe, Shanghai People's Publishing House, 2012.

Zhang, Weiwei. "Zhongguo Moshi Bupa yu Xifang Jingzheng [The Chinese Model is Not Afraid of Competing with the Western Model]." *Qiushi, Qiushi* 9 (2013): 62–63.

Zhao, Suisheng. "China's Pragmatic Nationalism: Is It Manageable?" *The Washington Quarterly* 29.1 (2005): 131–144.

Zhao, Dingxin. "Ping Wang Shaoguang 'Minzhu Sijiang' [Comment on Wang Shaoguang's 'Four Lectures on Democracy']." *Zhengzhi Sixiangshi, History of Political Thought* 21 (2010a): 182–186.

Zhao, Suisheng. "The China Model: Can It Replace the Western Model of Modernization?" *Journal of Contemporary China* 19.65 (2010b): 419–436.

Zhao, Tingyang. *Tianxia Tixi: Shijie Zhidu Zhexue Daolun [The System of the Tianxia: An Introduction to the Philosophy of World Institutions]*. Zhongguo Renmin Daxue Chubanshe, Renmin University of China Press, 2011.

Chinese Democracy Onward

Democracy and Democratic Discourses in China: A Reassessment

From Fukuyama's assertion of the "end of history" in 1989 to his latter acknowledgment of the significance of the non-Western "Chinese model" in his 2009 interview in the "Central Review" (themed "Japan Confronts the Chinese Century"),[1] a mere two decades have elapsed, witnessing a notable transformation in Fukuyama's perspectives. As a steadfast proponent of liberal democracy and market economy, why did Fukuyama, well-versed in and an advocate for liberal democracy and market economy, undergo such a paradigm shift? Those well acquainted with Fukuyama or his oeuvre comprehend that his utilization of the Chinese case—though he deeply values China's pivotal experiences since its Reform and Opening Up, the distinctiveness of China's authoritarian system, and China's impact on Asia, particularly East Asia—is essentially an endeavor to reaffirm that modernization models that beyond the liberal democratic framework will inevitably confront pressures for democratization and grapple with formidable challenges that are challenging to sustain in the future. In his 2007 essay, *The End of History Revisited*, presented at the invitation of the perpetual foundation, he therefore makes a compelling

[1] See also Fukuyama (1995, 2010, 2020).

R. Li, *Democratizing China's Political Imaginaries*,
https://doi.org/10.1007/978-981-97-3670-6_8

argument that England's successful modernization went through three stages: economic development produced societal development, which in turn led to political development, of the modernization process.[2]

For the interplay between factors of modernization and democratization, their correlation is not absolute; however, a logical nexus persists between the two. In contrast to Huntington, Fukuyama asserts that modernization itself wields a cultural influence, giving rise to a shared political cultural dimension—the liberal democratic system—amid diverse cultural particularities. Despite the existence of contemporary phenomena such as the "East Asian model" or the "Chinese model," which deviate from the liberal democratic system, Fukuyama argues that they ultimately converge, with human aspirations gravitating towards liberal democracy and a market economy. Hence, it is acknowledged that Fukuyama's perspective represents just one among numerous Western scholars, and his views may not universally persuade and reliable. Particularly in the latter half of the twentieth century, debates have intensified around concepts like the "state/political capacity," "social order," and "governance efficiency," intersecting with the inquiry into "political system type—democratic /non-democratic." Among these, "Chinese model" stands out as notably contentious, challenging the prevailing Western narrative of development. Within this expansive conceptual framework, Chinese democracy unmistakably emerges as highly emblematic.

The examination of the meaning of modernity/modernization and its linearity is not the primary focus of this book. Notably, since the latter of the twentieth century, a phenomenon termed "alternative modernity" has surfaced in non-Western regions (comprising developing nations,

[2] Any modernized development inevitably requires modern science and technology, serving as the fundamental driving force and common platform for the process of universalization. The maximization of the benefits from science and technology will lead to the universalization of economic structures, with a free-market economy being the most optimal system for benefit optimization. The development of a market economy and the increase in per capita income will result in a series of changes in social structures and cultural values, including urbanization, the expansion of the industrial working class, improved education accessibility, diverse channels of information dissemination, the rise of professional classes, accumulation of wealth, enhanced awareness of property rights, and the rich development of civil society. This will gradually alter traditional political culture, giving rise to increasingly strong demands for civic political participation, namely, the pressure for democratization. When this pressure surpasses a certain "threshold," it will ultimately lead to the universalization of political systems, transitioning towards a liberal democratic framework.

colonies, post-colonies, and third-world countries). This challenges, and at times contradicts, the predominant Western narrative on modernization. Prominent figures within this movement include, but are not restricted to, Yeats William Butler, Gökalp Ziya, Mariátegui José Carlos, Jamal-al-din Afghani, Savarkar Vinayak, Gandhi Mahatma, Kita Ikki, and Partha Chatterjee. In the context of China, Professor Wang Hui introduces the notion of "early modernity" in his three-volume work, *The Rise of Modern Chinese Thought*, challenging and even negating the mainstream Western narrative of modernization. This concept distinguishes itself from the static portrayal of the Chinese Empire presented by Hegel, Marx, and Weber. The recurring theme of it in Chinese history encompasses typical modern elements such as the evolution of commodity exchange, heightened social mobility and equality, and a deliberate awareness of historical disruptions. These persistent modern factors in China challenge the assertions of the Japanese Kyoto School, exemplified by Miyazaki Shigeharu and Naito Kanan, which contend that the Song Dynasty in China already manifested similar "early modernity" characteristics to the West.[3] Although China's early modernity trajectory paralleled that of the West, it ultimately deviated, leading to a missed opportunity for modernization. Regrettably, despite Wang Hui's significant efforts to readdress traditional theories in overseas Chinese studies, particularly within the Western paradigm, and to challenge the very dichotomy of empire/nation (national state), he falls short of providing a more refined conceptual framework for characterizing the political order in China.

In recent years, China's modernization process and its future trajectory have emerged as a significant focal point within both official and intellectual domains. This heightened attention is particularly discernible following the introduction of the paradigm of "Chinese-style modernization (中国式现代化 *Zhongguoshi Xiandaihua*)."[4] Within this framework,

[3] See Ichisada (1974) and Fogel (1984).

[4] The inception of "Chinese-style modernization" can be traced back to Deng Xiaoping's address during the Central Committee Political Bureau meeting on March 23, 1979. Deng, in introducing the term, articulated, "In discussions with foreign entities, I have employed a novel phrase: Chinese-style modernization. By the conclusion of this century, our attainment is likely to only approximate the developmental status of advanced nations in the 1970s, with per capita income remaining relatively modest." Deng Xiaoping correlated Chinese-style modernization with the realization of a moderately prosperous society, emphasizing economic development. In the subsequent century, Xi Jinping reiterated the

key tenets such as the CCP's stewardship, the socialist trajectory characterized by Chinese attributes, the WPPD, and the concept of a shared human destiny have all been intricately woven into the overarching narrative of Chinese-style modernization. From this vantage point, the recognition of modernization and its fundamental constituent, including economic development, societal diversity, and the safeguarding of individual freedoms and rights, is widespread. Nonetheless, the myriad pathways to achieving modernization introduce a complex challenge. Therefore, any evaluation of Chinese-style democracy necessitates a contextual grounding within the above macro-level framework and its intricate interconnections, all while acknowledging the evolving landscape of diverse democratic practices within the Chinese milieu.

In essence, the evaluation of the merit of Chinese democracy is contingent upon its alignment with universal democratic norms. This assessment, however, transcends mere rhetoric and ideological declarations, given the propensity of contemporary authoritarian or even totalitarian regimes to veil their repressive nature behind democratic semblances. Consequently, the array of values and institutional frameworks falling under the ambit of the universality does not represent a substantive divergence in the democratization process. In other words, the one-party rule, whether operating within a single-party or multi-party framework, does not intrinsically impede the realization of Chinese democracy. This is contingent upon the establishment of a delicate equilibrium of power, a system of accountability, and the creation of a political structure capable of accommodating representatives from diverse interest groups. Moreover, fostering an environment of open and rational peaceful competition amid these groups is essential, creating the prerequisites for sustained political stability at the institutional level, exemplified by intraparty democracy. While this may constitute an aspect of the "uniqueness" of Chinese democracy, it concurrently underscores the overarching significance of "divergent paths converging" within the democratic paradigm.

concept of Chinese-style modernization in the July 1 Speech, commemorating the centenary of the founding of the Communist Party in 2021. This conceptual framework was reaffirmed in the resolution of the Sixth Plenary Session of the 19th Central Committee, which assessed the Party's centennial struggle, acknowledging significant achievements and historical experiences. The political report presented at the 20th National Congress of the Communist Party in 2022 further expounded on Chinese-style modernization, offering a detailed elucidation of its principles and objectives by Xi Jinping.

In scrutinizing the sustainability of factors underpinning democratization, it is apparent that each democratization wave arises from a delicate equilibrium between democratic (re)consolidation and regression. For instance, Taiwan underwent a process of liberalization in the 1950s, notably accelerating during Chiang Ching-kuo's presidency; however, democratization only commenced in 1987. Similarly, South Korea experienced democratic politics in the 1950s under Lee Seung-man but later transitioned into a military authoritarian regime, and solidifying its democratic system only in the 1990s via political transformations. The economic ascendance and enhanced influence of authoritarian Chinese regime from the 1990s to the early 2000s posed a challenge to traditional democratic development theories, giving rise to the "China model." Nevertheless, sustainability is compromised when relying on non-democratic elements, such as suppressing public participation and utilizing economic development to secure popular support and trust. While not fully endorsing Fukuyama's claim of irresistible advantages for liberal democracy in the "long run," enduring democratic forces, including checks on power, the rule of law, and government accountability, are imperative to counter the "Chinese democratic" model.[5]

Therefore, the imperative lies in attaining an equilibrium and amalgamation of national capabilities, social order, political systems, and the democratization. In the third wave of the democratization, roughly one-fifth of countries regressed into authoritarianism or witnessed significant erosion of democratic institutions. The "Pendulum theory" heavily influences many Latin American countries, suggesting that economic downturns and societal instability within a democratic framework can precipitate a resurgence of authoritarianism. Conversely, authoritarian regimes, under pressure from Western democracies, may succumb to democratic systems. This cyclic oscillation between democracy and authoritarianism recurs approximately every two decades in many Latin American countries.[6] Also, post the early twenty-first-century Middle East conflicts,

[5] However, an indefinite reliance on the "long run" will perpetually exempt theory from validation. Despite Fukuyama later attempting to validate the appeal of liberal democratic systems by establishing a specific criterion of "achieving a certain per capita gross domestic product ($6,000/1992)" the analysis that directly correlates economic development or modernization with democratization still fails to escape the logic of the "Lipsetian argument."

[6] See Willis et al. (1999), Remmer (1992), and Brachet-Marquez (1997).

the United States' endeavor to "transplant" its democratic model in the region proved futile. Countries such as Afghanistan, Iraq, Somalia, Haiti, East Timor, and Papua New Guinea instituted a "democratic system" based on the party competition and democratic elections amid social disorder and inadequate national capacity. Nevertheless, these systems proved rather unsustainable, failing to safeguard democratic rights and propelling nations back into economic, political, and social regression. So, democracy should not be the exclusive yardstick for assessing political system superiority or inferiority; instead, the synchronization of state capabilities, political systems, and other multifaceted factors is imperative.

Recognition of Chinese-style democracy as a distinct form, with its unique characteristics, hinges on fulfilling three prerequisites: adherence to universal democratic values, a sustainable democratic impetus, and coordination among the state capabilities, social order, and political systems. This acknowledgment is pivotal for facilitating a meaningful discourse between the East and West on the subject of democracy. Social scientists, despite their inability to predict the future accurately, will continue to engage in ongoing debates regarding Chinese democracy. Nevertheless, what remains unequivocal, however, is that the trajectory towards democracy (or democratization) in China is arduous and protracted.

The Uncertain Future of Democracy in China

Whether the foundational tenets of "Chinese democracy," encompassing the people's democracy, WPPD, intraparty democracy, consultative democracy, grassroots democracy, and Chinese-style democracy, can be amalgamated to formulate a discourse on Chinese democracy, thus establishing it as a democratic paradigm coexistent with and parallel to Western liberal democracy, constitutes not only a pivotal matter within the context of Sino-Western democratic competition but also the fundamental query dictating how China will shape its democratic narrative in the future. In order to reconsider this paradox, a comprehensive comprehension of two imperative issues is imperative. Firstly, an elucidation of the rationale underpinning Chinese democracy, elucidating why it adopts a contemporary form and the reasons for its reemphasis or reconstruction of specific democratic discourses across diverse historical epochs. Secondly, an examination of the prospective challenges confronting Chinese democracy and the trajectory it is poised to traverse. These inquiries, one retrospective in nature and the other forward-looking, jointly comprise the overarching framework for the analysis of Chinese democracy.

Despite the inexorable course of history, a conjecture emerges: had China evaded the two Opium Wars and adhered steadfastly to an isolationist policy encapsulated by the concept of "all under heaven," its feudal structure, anchored in monarchical absolutism, would also exhibit resilience, continuity, and vitality. Consequently, the likelihood of modern democracy taking root in China may have been nullified.[7] This proposition establishes the initial logic for Chinese democracy—rooted in the logic of history. This logical construct finds expression in the exploration and pursuit of contemporary democracy in China. Prompted by the Western democratic ideals, there is a gradual assimilation of democratic principles and values, predominantly derived from Western democratic thought, practices, and institutional design. Simultaneously, it seeks inspiration from China's traditions to authenticate a democratic model characterized by distinct "Chinese characteristics." Notably, this progression is not marked by an innate drive for democracy within China, whether originating from the top-down or bottom-up; instead, it entails a deliberate emulation of the more advanced democratic ideals and institutions of the West. Furthermore, this logic dictates that the primary goal of modern Chinese democracy is the "preservation of the nation and assurance of survival."[8] Democracy, in this context, consistently intertwines with the concepts of nation and state.

[7] A more macroscopic conjecture see Needham (1964), see also Lin (1995).

[8] Lin Shangli, the former Secretary-General of the Central Policy Research Office in China, argues that China's pursuit of democracy was not driven by an inherent desire for democratic governance. Instead, the intention was to utilize democracy as a means to rescue the nation, achieve a revival of civilization, and enhance national strength. This emphasis on the self-generated nature of China's democracy is grounded in two primary reasons. Firstly, China's democratic ideals did not originate from external influences but rather stemmed from a historical consciousness aimed at safeguarding the nation. Secondly, Chinese democracy did not involve integration into pre-existing political structures but rather constituted a deliberate effort to establish new political frameworks. However, this interpretation and underlying logic present a seeming contradiction. If the emergence of modern democracy is solely attributed to the imperative of rescuing the nation, then the impact of Western civilization would only serve to expedite or solidify this cause-and-effect relationship. In reality, the spontaneous generation of modern democracy in China would have been considerably challenging without the influence and reference of Western democracy. The exploration of democracy in twentieth-century China and the subsequent evolution of "Chinese-style democracy" all unfold within this contextual framework. See Lin (2011).

In contemporary China, in contrast to the Western trajectory, it lacks a comprehensive democratic revolution or a historically autonomous pursuit of a democratic constitutional system. Also, there is a dearth of historical precedents dedicated to "democracy for the sake of democracy." The post-revolutionary period has witnessed limited endeavors aimed at fostering democratic literacy and values among the populace. Confronted with pressing historical and pragmatic imperatives at the onset of the globalization process, such as the imperative to "save the nation" and attain national modernization, nearly all factors contributing to these objectives—be they political, economic, or military—have displayed instrumental, tactical, and pragmatic characteristics. Democracy, in this context, is no exception. This historical trajectory has molded the fundamental features of Chinese democracy, marked by a "centralized democracy" and "dependent democracy."[9] While ancient Chinese political and bureaucratic systems inherently emphasized centralization, contemporary Chinese politics are the same, especially in the consolidation of power to achieve diverse objectives by integrating national resources. This inclination is validated in the modern context, as reflected in the assertion that "China has accomplished in a few decades what the West took centuries to achieve," rooted in this particular political framework.

The concept of "dependent democracy" posits that the outlook of Chinese democracy consistently relies upon specific attributes and spheres within the political domain. Notably, political dynamics lack autonomy from the forces of modernization, and reciprocally, democracy lacks autonomy from political influences. Politics functions as a subservient entity contingent upon modernization, while democracy in China functions as a tool subject to political dictates. This paradigm delineates democracy as an instrument wielded for the governance of politics. Within

[9] Chinese democracy is a hybrid form by learning from the Western political ideologies, structures, and procedures. This encompasses concepts inherent in constitutional principles, including popular sovereignty, freedom, democracy, equality, human rights, rule of law, citizenship, taxpayers' rights, and more. Furthermore, the foundational institutional frameworks of modern states, like democratic and republican systems, electoral and recall mechanisms, impeachment procedures, term limits, and political procedural methodologies like election, legislative, decision-making, and litigation procedures, as well as the fundamental organizational structure involving the equilibrium amid the executive, legislative, and judicial branches, are influenced by Marxist theory. This influence is particularly discernible in Sinicized Marxism, which assimilates elements like democratic centralism, proletarian dictatorship, proletarian leadership, Leninist party principles, and the amalgamation of traditional Chinese political concepts.

this logic, the intrinsic nature and efficacy of democracy to restrict and supervise the exercise of power from grassroots levels are frequently circumscribed. In essence, democracy assumes a role as a tool employed by the ruling elite to legitimize their authority, particularly in a context where conventional democratic processes, such as elections, power decentralization, and empowerment, are intimately entwined with political legitimacy. The fundamental tenets and mechanisms of democracy are harnessed not for the customary bottom-up democratic procedures but rather for top-down authorization and management. Conversely, democracy serves as a conduit for connectivity and interaction between rulers and the governed. Concepts such as the "mass line," "good governance," and "deliberative /consultative democracy" accentuate the symbiotic relationship between cadre and the masses, yet concurrently, they often undermine the spontaneous and proactive logic inherent in bottom-up democratic processes.

The historical logic has profoundly reshaped the contemporary form of democracy in China. Over the long term, entrenched ideas of traditional political culture, like personalized rule, bureaucratic centrism, hierarchy, and consolidated power, continue to wield the substantial sway over Chinese politics and democracy, evident in present-day manifestations. A closer examination of short-term dynamics reveals that China's modern history has more directly contributed to the establishment of key features characterizing Chinese democracy. In the aftermath of the collapse of the feudal system, the imperative of "saving the nation and ensuring survival" propelled initiatives aimed at post-war recovery, economic restoration, the establishment of a new social and political order, and addressing external threats during the pre- and post-foundation of China. Subsequent endeavors, particularly post the Reform and Opening Up era, focused on robust economic development and enhancing China's international standing. The confidence in a prospective "Chinese model" since the turn of the century has collectively reshaped a democratic model distinguished by centralized power. In this context, democracy is invariably intertwined with politics and lacks autonomous standing. This logic aligns with Fukuyama's three-stage reinterpretation of political development. Firstly, the construction of state capacity involves the establishment of legitimate coercion, defining sovereignty, shaping administrative capabilities, implementing policies and regulations, taxation, and providing public goods. Secondly, the emphasis is on safeguarding private property rights and upholding the rule of law. Only in the third stage does democracy come into play. For many post-colonial and late-developing countries, the primacy of state capacity building and the government's ability to ensure a stable political and social order, coupled with sustained economic development, appears more pivotal than prioritizing the rule of law and democracy. Nevertheless, as internal and external environments stabilize, and the economic development attains a certain threshold, democracy emerges as an inevitable political choice.

The second logic of Chinese democracy pertains to the Party (CCP) logic. Political parties, inherent products of modern Western politics,[10] often constitute integral components of democratic systems. In Western democracies, institutions, laws, and civil society collaboratively shape the foundational elements of democratic governance. However, within the context of "Chinese democracy," the predominant proponent and architect is the CCP. The CCP, by infusing its will and principles into the discourse surrounding Chinese democracy, effectively molds the fundamental structure of the modern Chinese democratic ideals.[11] The logic underpinning the CCP's modern revolution and its subsequent initiatives in socialist and modernization endeavors delineate the political institutional framework upon which Chinese democracy relies and operates. This framework serves as the very cornerstone of the contemporary political system in China, encompassing the CCP's leadership and governance system, the structure of the People's Congress, the multi-party cooperation and political consultation system orchestrated by the CCP, as well as the systems of ethnic regional autonomy and grassroots mass autonomy, among others. These fundamental political systems not only underscore the unwavering the CCP's huge influence in reshaping the

[10] Classic analysis on political parties see, Krehbiel (1993) and Sartori (2005).

[11] The Constitution of the Chinese Communist Party stipulates that the CCP assumes a guiding role in the development of socialist democratic politics. Emphasizing the integral fusion of Party leadership, popular empowerment, and lawful governance, it follows the trajectory of socialist political development and the establishment of a legal system imbued with *Chinese characteristics*. The objective is to enhance socialist democracy, construct a distinctive socialist rule of law framework, establish a socialist rule of law nation, fortify the democratic "dictatorship of the people," and foster the development of socialist political civilization. Article 36 of the 2018 constitutional amendment incorporated into the inaugural paragraph of the first article explicitly asserts that "the leadership of the Chinese Communist Party is the defining feature of socialism with Chinese characteristics." Both the Party Constitution and the national Constitution, as the preeminent legal instruments of the CCP and the nation, respectively, accord utmost significance to the CCP's leadership within the socialist endeavor.

discourse of Chinese democracy but also dictate that modern Chinese democratic discourses are functioning within the prescribed parameters and confines of these institutional toolkits. Consequently, contemporary Chinese democracy inherently relies on these foundational institutional spaces and their expansive scopes.

To note, the rationale underpinning Western political parties lies in the stratification of individuals or society as a whole into distinct factions. These factions engage in competition via the electoral process, wherein certain citizens coalesce based on shared emotions or interests, thereby opposing the interests of other citizens or the enduring and collective interests of society. This distinctive modus operandi sets Western political parties apart from and is frequently misconstrued vis-à-vis, the operational framework of the CCP. The emergence of the CCP coincided with a transformative historical epoch marked by formidable shifts and intricate transitions in China. Given this unique historical milieu, the prospect of transitioning from Chinese tradition to modernity or emulating the Western paradigm for modernization is deemed implausible.[12] This underscores why the CCP eschews the Western liberal democratic system and its party model, opting instead for Marxism and configuring itself as a Leninist party characterized by centralized authority. This differentiation is manifest in its departure from the technocratic bureaucratic system that adheres to instrumental rationality and governs through hierarchical structures. Crucially, the CCP refrains from reducing itself to a ruling party representing the interests of specific classes or groups, engaged in the pursuit of interests through exchange and competition. Instead, it transcends partial interests, embodying a comprehensive existence that represents the whole populace. This expansive representativeness is internalized within the governance of the "missionary party."

Nonetheless, the logic of the CCP-lead democracy is characterized by both distinctiveness and innovation. In practices, the CPC charts a singular course by synthesizing the universal tenets of Marxism with the

[12] The pronouncement also signifies that within this logic, the CCP is difficult (unwilling) to replicate the Western multi-party competitive paradigm. Instead, it necessitates attaining the amalgamation of societal resources, mobilization of the masses, and the establishment of a collective life form absent in traditional China via a robust, unified, and core party leadership methodology. Concurrently, in the construction of social democracy, the facilitation of democratic processes analogous to the Western concept of "spontaneous order" proves challenging to realize in China. Rather, it mandates the impetus of more organized entities such as political parties or the state. See also Bai (2021).

specific nuances of the Chinese revolutionary experience. This departure from conventional political developmental paradigms is noteworthy. Also, during the formative years of Marxist ideology, the absence of a proletarian party in governance posed a challenge, preventing the formulation of a comprehensive and actionable blueprint for the CCP's governance and the nuanced examination of the interplay between the party and state. In light of these circumstances, an examination of the political party dynamics within the framework of Chinese democracy should not be oversimplified by mere juxtaposition with analyses pertaining to one-party and multi-party systems. The numerical representation of political parties and their respective dominion does not inherently serve as a litmus test for discerning democratic and non-democratic systems. That said, the congruence between the CCP's single-party rule and the principles of Chinese democracy does not hinge solely on the quantity of political entities, but rather on the CCP's adept management of critical realms, including intraparty democracy, institutionalized supervision of power, intricacies arising from the symbiotic party-state relations, effective party construction, corruption mitigation, and the promotion of sound governance. In this context, the one-party rule of the CCP and the principles of Chinese democracy need not be construed as inherently contradictory.

Currently, discussions pertaining to China's democratic transition from the 1980s and 90 s until the first decade of this century are diminishing. Instead, there is an emerging discourse emphasizing the merits of "Chinese democracy." The term "transition" implies an imperfect state of democracy in China, as evidenced by phenomena such as the neo-authoritarianism and the New Left around the turn of the century. This imperfection is further elucidated by conceptual frameworks put forth by scholars, including Professor Yu Keping, introducing ideas such as "incremental democracy," "progressive democracy," and Western analyses, notably the "sequentialism" argument. The latter seeks to delineate the future of democracy in China by envisioning a transitional model—a shift from temporary and transitional authoritarianism to a refined democratic form.[13] Throughout this process, some intellectuals[14] retain a certain capacity to influence, and the general public could attain a degree of discursive power in political reform.[15] However, in the new century, the CCP has further fortified its comprehensive control over politics, encompassing democracy, by overseeing realms such as "the party, government, military, civilian, and academic (党政军民学 *Dang Zheng Jun Min Xue*)." Concurrently, a sense of confidence grounded in China's burgeoning national strength and nationalism has redirected debates from the earlier pluralistic discussions on democracy towards considerations of demonstrating the superiority of modern "Chinese democracy." Consequently, intellectuals and the general public are progressively marginalized and metamorphosed into the "silent majority."

If the discourse concerning the future of democracy in China is contextualized within the broader image of political reform, it may assume enhanced significance. Political reform in China, while adhering to the aforementioned foundational logics, also carries practical imperatives. Sole reliance on economic growth, good governance, nationalism, and patriotism cannot inherently propel the process of democratization in China. In the immediate term, the paramount concern confronting political reform in China is the intricate interplay between "centralization" and "democracy." The assertion that "excessive centralization leads to authoritarianism," as exemplified by the planned economies, underscores the critical need to address this relationship. While centralization remains

[13] In Asia, the "Four Asian Tigers," encompassing Taiwan, Hong Kong, South Korea, and Singapore, along with countries like Mexico and Thailand, have experienced a shift from neo/soft authoritarianism towards a trajectory of democraticization within capitalist regimes. See Brumberg (2003).

[14] The discourse surrounding the "neo-authoritarianism" during the late 1980s to the 1990s transpired within the established framework of high-level authorities. Internally, party stalwarts such as Wu Jiaxiang (吴稼祥) and Wang Huning (王沪宁) championed the advancement of Chinese democracy, emphasizing "political stability and order" as a foundational imperative. Externally, a cohort of intellectuals, among them Xiao Gongqin (萧功秦), Cai Dingjian (蔡定剑), and Wang Zhanyang (王占阳), echoed the sentiments espoused by the central leadership. See Wu (1989), Wang (1988), Xiao (2014), and Cai and Wang (2011).

[15] In the backdrop of grassroots democracy, predominantly characterized by village/resident elections in the preceding century, many grassroots initiatives undertaken by villagers/residents to independently engage in grassroot governance exemplify the initiative and agency of the general populace within the framework of grassroots democracy. See Xu (2009) and Yu (2008).

an undisputed fundamental tenet in Chinese politics, an excess thereof hinders the actualization of democracy. Centralization raises some pivotal issues within Chinese political dynamics, including the nexus between the party and the government, the party and the state, and the party and the legal framework.[16]

China does not lack instances of "democratic centralization" in institutional design, exemplified by the establishment of the NPC at all levels, with the Constitution unequivocally designating it as the highest organ of state power. Significant strides have also been made in the internal regulations of the CCP and the legal and rule-of-law framework over the past four decades. However, in practices, the CCP remains the unequivocal predominant force.[17] The exercise, concentration, and corruption of power are inextricably interlinked. While institutions and laws are indispensable mechanisms to curtail and supervise power, the democratization of power centralization assumes paramount importance in Chinese politics. This necessitates, foremost, the realization of intraparty democracy. Experiences gleaned from many countries undergoing democratic transitions globally indicate that political reform initiated by the ruling party, involving the decisive relinquishment of excessively centralized systems, could garner public support and achieve success. The successful democratic transformation in Taiwan during the 1980s and the political system

[16] The disadvantages of centralized power manifest across multiple dimensions, notably within the national framework where the functions of the party supersede those of the state apparatus. This phenomenon extends to economic and social administration, wherein party committees and grassroots party organizations assume the roles typically held by administrative leadership and accountability for chief executives and managers. For the cadre personnel management, the dominance of "party control over cadres (党管干部 *Dang Guan Fnabu*)" prevails over the specific management practices of employing units. Additionally, within the system of People's Congresses and legal construction, instances of direct intervention by party committees at various levels in the same-level People's Congress and judicial organs serve as indicative examples of these drawbacks.

[17] Deng Xiaoping provided a discerning evaluation of the deficiencies inherent in the Soviet political system and the issue of "excessive concentration" within the political framework of both pre- and post-reform China. He articulated, "Excessive concentration of power, in my perspective, undergoes transformation from "highly centralized." The political authority of the state ought to remain centralized, underpinned by democratic principles. I posit that the crux of democratic centralism lies in democratic governance, not in centralism, nor in the amalgamation of democratic and centralized systems. True democracy necessitates centralization, yet centralized control bereft of democratic elements does not constitute democracy." See also Gao (2010).

reform led by the ruling party in mainland China in the same era substantiate this assertion, providing valuable insights for proactive reform by the ruling party.

In the long term, though the realization of democracy in China emphasizes various democratic forms, the trajectory towards Chinese democracy does not lie in proposing an exclusive or entirely novel singular solution. Rather, it entails the integration of all forms and practices of democracy, achieving mutual inclusivity among diverse democratic ideologies and forces. This transformative process converts political system reform and democratization from the admirable aspirations of a select few intellectuals into a robust consensus embraced by the entire Chinese populace. Only through such concerted efforts can/may a breakthrough in democratization in China be achieved. Furthermore, the third wave of democratization implies that existing democratic achievements may either be consolidated or jeopardized, facing setbacks or reversals. Therefore, it is imperative to maintain vigilance against the risk of undermining the valuable outcomes of political reforms, including democratic construction, since the initiation of Reform and Opening Up in China. Only by doing so can we solidify and underscore the accomplishments and significance of Chinese democracy.

References

Bai, Gang. "Siweiyiti de Zhongguo you Zhongguo Gongchandang [The Four Combinations of China and the Communist Party of China]," 2021. Available at https://www.aisixiang.com/data/129328.html (Accessed January 4, 2024).

Brachet-Marquez, Viviane. "Democratic Transition and Consolidation in Latin America: Steps Toward a New Theory of Democratization." *Current Sociology* 45.1 (1997): 15–53.

Brumberg, Daniel. "Liberalization Versus Democracy: Understanding Arab Political Reform." *Carnegie Endowment for International Peace*, 2003.

Cai, Dingjian and Zhanyang Wang, eds. *Zouxiang Xianzheng [Toward Constitutional Government]*. Falv Chubanshe, Law Press, 2011.

Fogel, Joshua A. *Politics and Sinology: The Case of Naitō Konan (1866–1934)*. Harvard University Asia Center Publications Program, 1984.

Fukuyama, Francis. "The End of History?" *The National Interest* 16 (1989): 3–18.

Fukuyama, Francis. "Reflections on the End of History, Five Years Later." *History and Theory* (1995): 27–43.

Fukuyama, Francis. "The 'End of History' 20 Years Later." *New Perspectives Quarterly* 27.1 (2010): 7–10.

Fukuyama, Francis. "30 Years of World Politics: What Has Changed?" *Journal of Democracy* 31.1 (2020): 11–21.

Gao, Fang. "Gaige Kaifang Yilai Zhongguo Zhengzhi Tizhi Gaige de Huigu yu Zhanwang [Review and Prospects of China's Political System Reform since Reform and Opening Up]." *Lilun Tantao, Theoretical Discussion* (2010): 20–22.

Ichisada, Miyazaki. "The Civil Service Examination: China's Examination Hell." *Chinese Education* 7.3 (1974): 6–64.

Krehbiel, Keith. "Where's the Party?" *British Journal of Political Science* 23.2 (1993): 235–266.

Lin, Justin Yifu. "The Needham Puzzle: Why the Industrial Revolution Did Not Originate in China." *Economic Development and Cultural Change* 43.2 (1995): 269–292.

Lin, Shangli. "Renmin Minzhu, Zhongguo Gongchandang 90 Nian de Tansuo [People's Democracy: 90 Years of Exploration by the Communist Party of China]," 2011. Available at https://www.aisixiang.com/data/41874.html (Accessed January 4, 2024).

Needham, Joseph. "Science and Society in East and West." *Science & Society* 28.4 (1964): 385–408.

Remmer, Karen L. "The Process of Democratization in Latin America." *Studies in Comparative International Development* 27.4 (1992): 3–24.

Sartori, Giovanni. "Party Types, Organisation and Functions." *West European Politics* 28.1 (2005): 5–32.

Wang, Huning. "Shehui Zhuyi Minzhu Zhengzhi Fazhan de Shanghai Fenxi [Ecological Analysis of the Development of Socialist Democratic Politics]." *Tianjin Shehui Kexue, Tianjin Social Sciences* 3 (1988): 12–20.

Willis, Eliza, Christopher da CB Garman, and Stephan Haggard. "The Politics of Decentralization in Latin America." *Latin American Research Review* 34.1 (1999): 7–56.

Wu, Jiaxiang. "Xinquanwei Zhuyi Pingshu [Review of New Authoritarianism]." *Shijie Jingji Baodao, World Economic Herald*, January 16, 1989.

Xiao, Gongqin. "Xinquanwei Zhuyi Ruhe Zouxing Minzhu [New Authoritativeness, How Does Socialism Move to Democracy]." *Fenghuang Zhoukan, Phoenix Weekly* 4 (2014).

Xu, Yong. "Shehui Dongyuan yu Zhengzhi Zhenghe-Zhongguo Jiceng Minzhu Zhengzhi Fazhan 60 Nian Yanjiu [Social Mobilization, Independent Participation and Political Integration—60 Years of Research on the Development of Grassroots Democratic Politics in China]." *Shehui Kexue Zhanxian, Social Science Front* 6 (2009): 19–26.

Yu, Keping. "Zhongguo Zhengzhi Fazhan 30 Nian [Thirty Years of Chinese Political Development]." *Hebei Xuekan, Hebei Academic Journal* 5 (2008): 1–6.

Index

R. Li, *Democratizing China's Political Imaginaries*,
https://doi.org/10.1007/978-981-97-3670-6

D

SPRINGER NATURE

GPSR Compliance

The European Union's (EU) General Product Safety Regulation (GPSR) is a set of rules that requires consumer products to be safe and our obligations to ensure this.

If you have any concerns about our products, you can contact us on ProductSafety@springernature.com

In case Publisher is established outside the EU, the EU authorized representative is:

Springer Nature Customer Service Center GmbH
Europaplatz 3
69115 Heidelberg, Germany

The manufacturer's authorised representative in the EU is Springer Nature Customer Service Centre GmbH, Europaplatz 3, 69115 Heidelberg, Germany. If you have any concerns regarding our products, please contact ProductSafety@springernature.com

Printed and bound by CPI Group (UK) Ltd, Croydon, CR0 4YY
01/10/2026
02225854-0003